Journal of Pentecostal Theology
Supplement Series
15

School of the Word

Editors
John Christopher Thomas
Rickie D. Moore
Steven J. Land

Sheffield Academic Press
Sheffield

Pentecostals after

a Century

Global Perspectives on a Movement

in Transition

Edited by
Allan H. Anderson and
Walter J. Hollenweger

Sheffield Academic Press

Copyright © 1999 Sheffield Academic Press

Published by
Sheffield Academic Press Ltd
Mansion House
19 Kingfield Road
Sheffield S11 9AS
England

British Library Cataloguing in Publication Data

A catalogue record for this book is available
from the British Library

ISBN 1-84127-006-7

CONTENTS

FOREWORD

Harvey Cox

I am still trying to explain to polite but puzzled inquirers who identify
me with *The Secular City*, a book I wrote nearly 35 years ago, how and
why I became interested in Pentecostalism. Isn't this, they ask, a complete about-face, a sort of scholarly equivalent of eating crow? I do not
deny having changed my mind over three and a half decades. Only dead
people have not. But as I think about my own spiritual and intellectual
trajectory, my interest in the fastest growing Christian movement in the
world seems more like a natural development than a retraction. The
thesis of my earlier book was that God, despite the fears of many religious people, is also present in the 'secular', in those spheres of life that
are not usually thought of as 'religious'. Have not Pentecostals vigorously reclaimed many of these spheres as places where we are invited,
on a daily basis, to 'walk with God'? *The Secular City* was also, at
points, a severe criticism of the traditional churches for ignoring the
marginated populations of the world. Pentecostalism continues this vig-
orous critique, and appeals to millions of people the other churches
have consistently failed to reach. Finally, I argued in *The Secular City*
that there was a kernel of truth in the overblown claims of the so-called
(and now forgotten) 'death of God' theologians. They saw, in a
somewhat sensational way, that the abstract deity of western theologies
and philosophical systems had come to the end of its run. Their forecast
of what would come next was dramatically mistaken, but the volcanic
eruption of a Christian movement that relies on the direct experience of
the Divine Spirit rather than on archaic creeds and stately rituals seems
to corroborate their diagnosis while it completely undercuts their pre-
scription.

In a nutshell, my interest in Pentecostalism arises from my recognition that this powerful moving of the Spirit, so thoroughly documented
by this excellent book is responding to many of the conditions I wrote

about so many years ago. Neither as a Christian nor as a scholar can I
ignore what is going on before our eyes as the twentieth century draws
to a close. My response to people who are surprised at my interest in
(and affection for) Pentecostals is to express *my* surprise that they are
not interested. Even if they are non-believers, I point out to them that
there is much that Pentecostalism can teach us about our common future. I say this because I believe Pentecostalism represents a dramatic
example of a much larger development. After all, even sceptics simply
cannot ignore a religious movement that already encompasses 400
million people and is multiplying geometrically every day.

Indeed, by now, even the most casual observers of the world religious
scene have begun to suspect something of more than passing importance is going on. Maybe they have seen, or at least heard about, Robert
Duvall's brilliant film *The Apostle*, which portrays—honestly and not
dismissively—an American Pentecostal preacher. Or this suspicion
might dawn when they see the picture of a worried looking Pope John
Paul II with the caption 'Losing His Flock?' on the cover of a weekly
news magazine which reports that the pope is desperately worried about
the millions of Brazilians and other Latin Americans who are quitting
the Roman Catholic Church to join some other—usually a Pentecostal—church. Or they might discover the astonishing fact that the
largest single Christian congregation in the whole world—which I
visited a few years ago—is the Yoido Full Gospel (Pentecostal) Church
in Seoul, Korea. Or they might notice the sober projections by eminent
sociologists that—given current growth curves—by early in the next
century, Pentecostals in all their variegated manifestations may outnumber both Catholics and Protestants.

There is indeed something noteworthy going on, and it is not just
'religious'. No thoughtful person, believer or non-believer, can deny it.
Still, amazingly, many continue to do so. Why? As ebullient as they are
in their song and praise, Pentecostals still represent a quiet revolution.
They are not headline grabbers. They do not issue death decrees. They
are not allied to surging nationalist movements. They do not take credit
for kidnapping hostages or bombing airliners. Consequently, the spectacular growth of their churches does not often heave into public view.
Still, not only are they continuing to grow, I believe their growth holds
within it a host of significant clues to the meaning of the more general
global spiritual resurgence we are now witnessing.

Lots of people, of course, have tried to fathom the meaning of this revival, and some have even focused on the Pentecostal movement as a prime example. Earnest sociologists, puzzled psychologists, and diligent anthropologists have all taken their turns. But the picture they paint is often confused and contradictory. They point out that Pentecostalism seems to spread most quickly in the slums and shantytowns of the world's cities. Is it then a revival among the poor? Well, they concede, not exclusively. Its message also appeals to other classes and stations. Its promise of an unmediated experience of God, and of health and well being now, not just after death, attracts a wide variety of seekers.

But whom does it attract, and why? Again, as the contributors to this volume demonstrate, the picture is not uniform. Pentecostals vary in colour and gender and nationality. They may be teenagers or old folks, though young adults lead the way. They may be poverty stricken or perched somewhere in the lower ranges of the middle class: there are not many well-to-do. They are what one writer calls the 'discontents of modernity', not fully at home with today's reigning values and lifestyles. Another scholar even describes the movement as a 'symbolic rebellion' against the modern world. But that does not quite jibe either, for the people attracted to the Pentecostal message often seem even more dissatisfied with traditional religions than they are with the modern world that is subverting them. For this reason, another writer describes them as providing a 'different way of being modern'. Both may be right. Refugees from the multiple tyrannies of both tradition and modernity, Pentecostals are looking for what it takes to survive until a new day dawns. Is there anyone who does not find a little of this wistfulness within? I certainly do.

But how much does all this tell us? Are sociological or psychological analyses really enough to explain such a phenomenon? One historian has called the Pentecostal surge the most significant religious movement since the birth of Islam or the Protestant Reformation. But these previous historic upheavals have for centuries defied attempts to explain them in merely secular categories, however sophisticated. The present religious rebirth, for which Pentecostalism is such a dramatic example, also seems to slip through such conceptual grids. More and more, even the most sceptical observers are beginning to concede that—whether for weal or for woe—something more basic is underway.

One of the first things I learned when I was writing *Fire From Heaven* and managed to visit congregations on four continents, was that the movement looks and feels quite different to outsiders than it does to insiders. The many millions of people who are 'inside' see themselves as grateful beneficiaries of a wondrous stirring of the Spirit, an outpouring that has already radically transformed their own lives and is certain to change many more. They believe the message they bear is good news for a desperate age and that it marks a welcome new gift of grace and wholeness for the world. I cannot fully accept the totality of their interpretation of what their faith means, but that does not mean their interpretation is just to be seen as a curiosity. It is a key feature of the picture. This means that in trying to grasp the meaning of Pentecostalism as a suggestive clue to large religious and cultural changes, we must listen to both 'inside' and 'outside' voices. That is the great strength of the present volume.

The most important thing I learned as I came to know the worldwide Pentecostal movement is that it represents a clear signal that a big change is on the way for humankind. It is a change, furthermore, that will not be confined to some special religious or spiritual sphere. Granted, there are many reasons to doubt whether such a metamorphosis is actually at hand. It is true that in philosophy and literary criticism, something called 'postmodernism' is the rage. But intellectuals like to imagine themselves on the cutting edge, and post-modernism could be one more pedantic self-delusion. Gurus and crystal gazers talk about a 'New Age', but they sound suspiciously like the ageing hippies who, 30 years ago, were hailing the imminent dawning of the Age of Aquarius. The 'new world order' President Bush's 'Desert Storm' was supposed to introduce has turned out to be a mirage, and elsewhere in the international political arena we seem to be reeling backward to an era of ethnic and tribal blood letting, not moving into anything very new at all. There is every reason to share the scepticism of Ecclesiastes about whether there is ever any 'new thing under the sun'.

Still, despite the overheated atmosphere that will no doubt excite even more apocalyptic fantasies as 2000 CE arrives, the question stubbornly persists. Do the Pentecostal movement and the global religious stirring of which it is undoubtedly a part signal something larger and more significant that is underway?

I think so. As a life-long student of religions—Christian and non-Christian, historical and contemporary, seraphic and demonic—I have come to believe two things about them. The first conviction is widely shared among my colleagues today, namely that religious movements can never be understood apart from the cultural and political milieu in which they arise. I do not believe religious phenomena are 'caused' by other factors, economic or political ones for example. Still, they always come to life within a complex cluster of other cultural and social vectors. You have to look at the big picture.

I have also come to a second working premise, one that is not as widely shared among my colleagues. It is that although religion neither causes nor is caused by the other factors, it is often a very accurate barometer. It can provide the clearest and most graphically etched portrait, in miniature, of what is happening in the big picture. Freud once said that dreams are 'the royal road to the unconscious'. This may or may not be the case, but I am convinced that religion is the royal road to the heart of a civilization, the clearest indicator of its hopes and terrors, the surest indice of how it is changing.

The reason I believe religion is such an invaluable window into the larger whole is that human beings, so long as they are human, live according to patterns of value and meaning without which life would not make sense. These patterns may be coherent or confused, elegant or slap-dash, rooted in ancient traditions or pasted together in ad hoc ways. People may adhere to them tightly or loosely, consciously or unconsciously, studiously or unreflectively. But the patterns exist. They are encoded in gestures, idioms, recipes, rituals, seasonal festivals and family habits, doctrines, texts, liturgies and folk wisdom. They are constantly shifting, mixing with each other, declining into empty usages, bursting into new life. But they are always there. Without them human existence would be unliveable. And they constitute what, in the most inclusive use of the term, we mean by 'religion', that which binds life together. Even that most famous of atheists, Karl Marx, after all, once said that religion is 'the heart of a heartless world'.

Naturally, just as it takes practice and experience to 'decode' dreams, it also requires the combined efforts of many people—insiders and outsiders, observers and participants—to understand what the densely coded symbols and practices of a religion tell us about its environing culture. Religions always contain a mixture of emotional and rational elements, often fused into powerful compact bits of highly charged information. Understanding them requires a particular form of what the anthropologist Clifford Geertz calls 'close reading', one that brings his-

torical and comparative methods together with both intuitive and critical perspectives. But the result is worth the effort. Knowing the gods
and demons of a people and listening to their prayers and curses tell us
more about them than all the graphs and statistics one could assemble.

The present volume, therefore, should be viewed as something more
than a study of Pentecostalism, or even of religion. It is a concert of
mixed voices addressing a vast question: what is the meaning of the
massive transformation within which the current religious mutation is
an integral, perhaps even the most determinative, component?

Ultimately, of course, only the future itself can answer this question.
In the meantime, exploring the present, unanticipated worldwide explosion of Pentecostalism, decoding its hidden messages, and listening to
its inner voices, will give us some valuable hints. And that is all we ever
really have to go on. 'Come, Holy Spirit', the early Christian prayed,
'enliven Thy whole creation'.

ACKNOWLEDGMENTS

Pentecostals after a Century was my first writing project conceived outside South Africa, commenced less than a year after my arrival in England, but taking over two years to reach completion. It represents a very different type of study from what I have been used to. Walter Hollenweger in active retirement in Krattigen, Switzerland is the inspiration behind this publication, contributing much to it, and without whom the project would not have materialized. Colleagues at Selly Oak Colleges, particularly the Dean of the School of Mission and World Christianity, Andrew Kirk, entrusted me with the task of coordinating the consultation with Professor Hollenweger in June 1996. Out of this the idea of a publication was born, and I was given the space and time to complete it. Thanks are due to Lynne Price, who not only contributed an additional chapter but also did proof-reading at short notice, making invaluable suggestions for changes to improve the text. Chris Thomas of the *Journal of Pentecostal Theology* saw the potential in this book and made further important suggestions.

My special thanks to Harvey Cox for the stimulating Foreword; his *Fire from Heaven* is one of the most significant books on Pentecostalism I have read. My heartfelt thanks to the other main contributors to this volume: Robert Beckford in Birmingham, Roswith Gerloff in Leeds, Juan Sepúlveda in Santiago, Chile, Lee Hong Jung in Seoul, Korea, and Lynne Price in Birmingham each gave their full co-operation so that the script could be finalized. The respondents Joe Aldred, Bae Hyoen Sung, Patrick Kalilombe, Andrew Kirk, Richard Massey, Errol Oliver, Martin Robinson and all the participants in the consultation made valuable contributions to the debate. I thank my family Olwen, Matthew and Tami, for their love and patience, and above all, I give thanks to God, who by his creative Spirit has enabled me to complete a difficult assignment.

Allan H. Anderson
Centre for Missiology and World Christianity, University of
Birmingham, August 1999

LIST OF CONTRIBUTORS

ALLAN ANDERSON was formerly a Pentecostal minister, principal of Tshwane Theological College and researcher in the Research Institute for Theology and Religion at the University of South Africa (1989–1995). Since October 1995 he has directed the Research Unit for New Religions and Churches in the Centre for Missiology and World Christianity (formerly Selly Oak Colleges), and is Lecturer in the Department of Theology at the University of Birmingham. He has a DTh from the University of South Africa and has published three books on African initiated churches and pentecostals in South Africa.

ROBERT BECKFORD has a Black Pentecostal background and is a former tutor in Black Theology at Queens College, Birmingham. He has a PhD in Theology from the University of Birmingham, and has written his thesis on Black Pentecostal theology. He is author of *Jesus is Dread: Black Theology and Black Culture in Britain*.

HARVEY COX is one of the best known North American theologians. He is Victor Thomas Professor of Religion at Harvard University and author of many well-known books, including *The Secular City* and the recently published book on Pentecostalism, *Fire from Heaven: The Rise of Pentecostal Spirituality and the Reshaping of Religion in the Twenty-First Century*.

ROSWITH GERLOFF is a minister of the United Evangelical Church in Germany with many years' experience working among and researching Black Pentecostal and African Indigenous Churches in Britain. Founder and first Director of the Centre for Black and White Christian Partnership at Selly Oak Colleges, she studied under Walter Hollenweger and has a PhD from the University of Birmingham. She is presently senior research fellow at the University of Leeds and does research in the presence and significance of the African Christian diaspora in Europe. She is author of the two volumes in *A Plea for British Black Theologies*.

WALTER J. HOLLENWEGER lives in Switzerland, where he was a Pentecostal pastor, but later became a minister in the Swiss Reformed Church. After serving in the World Council of Churches in Geneva for six years as Secretary for Evangelism (1965–1971), he became the first Professor of Mission at the University of Birmingham and Selly Oak Colleges (1971–1989). He is well known for several publications, the foremost ones in English being *The Pentecostals* (1972), *Pentecost between Black and White* (1974), *Evangelism Today* (1976), *Conflict in Corinth* (1982) and a sequel to *The Pentecostals* entitled *Pentecostalism: Origins and Developments Worldwide* (1997). A Festschrift was published in his honour in 1992 entitled *Pentecost, Mission and Ecumenism*. In July 1996 he was made an Honorary Fellow of the Selly Oak Colleges.

LEE HONG JUNG, from South Korea, is former Director of the Centre for North East Asian Mission Studies in the School of Mission and World Christianity, Selly Oak Colleges and is currently ecumenical officer in the Presbyterian Church of Korea in Seoul, Korea. He has a PhD from the University of Birmingham.

LYNNE PRICE is a Methodist laywoman and freelance theologian. She is a former student of Walter Hollenweger and subsequently worked in the area of inter-faith relations. Her PhD from the University of Birmingham was published in 1996 as *Faithful Uncertainty: Leslie D. Weatherhead's Methodology of Creative Evangelism.*

JUAN SEPÚLVEDA, a minister of the Pentecostal Church Mission in Chile since 1981, is currently working in his home city of Santiago as a staff member of SEPADE (Evangelical Service for Development). He has published several articles both in Spanish and English, and completed a PhD at the University of Birmingham in 1996 with the thesis 'Gospel and Culture in Latin American Protestantism: Toward a New Theological Appreciation of Syncretism'.

Respondents

JOSEPH ALDRED is Director of the Centre for Black and White Christian Partnerships, Selly Oak Colleges and a bishop of the Church of God of Prophecy.

PATRICK KALILOMBE is a Roman Catholic bishop from Malawi and former Director of the Centre for Black and White Christian Partnerships, Selly Oak Colleges.

J. ANDREW KIRK is a former Anglican missionary in Argentina and now head of the Centre for Missiology and World Christianity (formerly Selly Oak Colleges), University of Birmingham.

RICHARD MASSEY is a PhD graduate of Walter Hollenweger at the University of Birmingham and is principal of Birmingham Bible Institute.

ERROL OLIVER is a doctoral candidate at the University of Birmingham and principal of Timothy School of Ministry in the Church of God of Prophecy.

MARTIN ROBINSON is a PhD graduate of Walter Hollenweger and Director of Mission and Theology at the Bible Society, Swindon.

BAE HYOEN SUNG has a PhD in theology from the University of Birmingham and is a pastor in the Yoido Full Gospel Church, Seoul, Korea.

INTRODUCTION:
WORLD PENTECOSTALISM AT A CROSSROADS

Allan Anderson

The Global Picture

Although there are inevitable uncertainties about the reliability of statistics of this magnitude, there can be no doubt that the Pentecostal movement has made an enormous impact on the shape of world Christianity at the close of the twentieth century and, as Harvey Cox's intriguing subtitle puts it, on the 'reshaping of religion in the twenty-first century'.[1] According to the well-known statistician of Christianity, David Barrett, there were an estimated 74 million 'Pentecostals/ Charismatics', or 6% of the world's Christian population in 1970.[2] In 1997 he estimated that this figure had reached 497 million or 27% of the Christian population, more than the total number of 'Protestants' and 'Anglicans' combined, and only 27 years later. Barrett projects that according to present trends the figure is likely to rise to 1,140 million or 44% of the total number of Christians by 2025.[3] Pentecostalism is therefore fast becoming the dominant expression of Christianity and one of the most extraordinary religious phenomena in the world of any time.

It is not always easy to define what is meant by 'pentecostal', as the term refers to a wide variety of movements scattered throughout the world, ranging from the fundamentalist and white middle class 'megachurches' to indigenous movements in the Third World that have adapted to their cultural and religious contexts to such an extent that many western pentecostals would probably doubt their qualifications as

1.   H. Cox, *Fire from Heaven: The Rise of Pentecostal Spirituality and the Reshaping of Religion in the Twenty-First Century* (London: Cassell, 1996).

2.   D.B. Barrett, 'Annual Statistical Table on Global Mission 1996', *International Bulletin of Missionary Research 20.1* (1996), pp. 24-25 (25).

3.   D.B. Barrett, 'Annual Statistical Table on Global Mission 1997', *International Bulletin of Missionary Research 21.1* (1997), pp. 24-25 (25).

'Christian' movements. Walter Hollenweger was one of the first to opt
for a more inclusive definition of 'pentecostal'.[4] Some North American
classical pentecostals do not approve of this broad delineation. Gary
McGee criticizes those whose 'classification garners together a bewildering array of indigenous churches reflecting varying degrees of syncretism along with classical Pentecostal and Charismatic constituencies'
and who are 'loading the terms ... with this much diversity'. He implies
that such groups as Zionists in Southern Africa, Kimbanguists in Central Africa and Spiritual Baptists in Trinidad should not be termed 'pentecostal' at all.[5] It is clear that McGee's reluctance to broaden the
definition stems from his identification of the classical Pentecostal
movement with North American conservative evangelicalism. Robert
Mapes Anderson has pointed out that whereas classical pentecostals in
North America usually define themselves in terms of the *doctrine* of
'initial evidence', the pentecostal movement is more correctly seen in a
much broader context as a movement concerned primarily with the
experience of the working of the Holy Spirit and the *practice* of spiritual gifts.[6] I have also argued elsewhere for the inclusion of African
pentecostal-type churches as genuinely pentecostal movements,[7] and
the same could be argued for many indigenous pentecostal churches all
over the world. In Third World Pentecostalism, experience and practice
are usually far more important than dogma. Pentecostalism today is in
any case both fundamentally and dominantly a *Third World* phenomenon. In spite of its significant growth in North America, less than
a quarter of its members in the world today are white, and this proportion continues to decrease.[8]

Hollenweger, the Pentecostal Scholar

At the risk of oversimplification, Walter Hollenweger's central thesis
seems to be that pentecostals have failed to understand themselves, their

---

4.   W.J. Hollenweger, *The Pentecostals* (London: SCM, 1972), p. 149.
5.   G. McGee, 'Pentecostal Missiology: Moving Beyond Triumphalism To
Face the Issues', *Pneuma* 16 (1994), pp. 275-81 (276-77).
6.   R.M. Anderson, *Vision of the Disinherited: The Making of American Pentecostalism* (Peabody, MA: Hendrickson, 1979), p. 4.
7.   A.H. Anderson, *Bazalwane: African Pentecostals in South Africa* (Pretoria:
University of South Africa Press, 1992), pp. 2-6.
8.   S.J. Land, *Pentecostal Spirituality: A Passion for the Kingdom* (JPTSup, 1;
Sheffield: Sheffield Academic Press, 1993), p. 21.

history and their experience. Hollenweger is himself a former Swiss Pentecostal pastor (until 1958), whose contributions in this book seem to demonstrate a sort of 'love-hate' relationship with the movement. He loves the Pentecostal experience but hates the materialistic ideology propagated by many pentecostals. He clearly and passionately loves what Pentecostalism has stood for in the *past*: its roots among the dispossessed, its radical freedom, its wide variety of expression, its original ecumenical vision and its non-racial character—but he hates what it often represents in the present in those places where it has *forgotten its roots*. This is the crux of Hollenweger's analysis of the pentecostal movement in this book, and that which inspired and impassioned many of his students while he was Professor of Mission at the University of Birmingham and at Selly Oak Colleges, a post he held for 18 years (1971–89). Out of this 'stable' emerged such unique pioneering research as Douglas Nelson's *For Such a Time as This: The Story of William J. Seymour and the Azusa Street Revival* (1981), Iain MacRobert's *The Black Roots and White Racism of Early Pentecostalism in the USA* (1988), Yoo Boo-Woong's *Korean Pentecostalism: Its History and Theology* (1988), Roswith Gerloff's *A Plea for British Black Theologies* (1992) and Hollenweger's own many writings, including *Pentecost between Black and White* (1974). Walter Hollenweger, as the only Professor of Mission at an English university during that time,[9] has done what no earlier scholar of Pentecostalism either inside or outside the movement had ever done: he has taught pentecostals to look at themselves both critically and with appreciation, ever mindful of the enormous contribution that this once despised 'sect' has made to world Christianity.

Pentecostalism: Promise and Problem

In June 1996 I facilitated a consultation on 'Pentecostalism: Promise and Problem' at the School of Mission and World Christianity, Selly Oak Colleges, in recognition of the work of this remarkable scholar. Walter Hollenweger was undoubtedly, and is still probably the foremost authority on Pentecostalism in the world. He has been the leading figure

---

9. J.A.B. Jongeneel *et al.* (eds.), *Pentecost, Mission and Ecumenism: Essays on Intercultural Theology. Festschrift in Honour of Professor Walter Hollenweger* (Frankfurt am Main: Peter Lang, 1992), p. 9 (contains a full bibliography of Hollenweger's works up to 1990).

in academic Pentecostal studies for three decades. Not only was he the keynote speaker at this consultation, but he had also come to receive an honorary fellowship of Selly Oak Colleges. The papers given at that consultation form the foundation of this book. Some 40 participants at the consultation from many different Christian denominations and from four continents—pentecostals, Charismatics, non-pentecostals, post-pentecostals and anti-pentecostals—all had come to sit at the feet of the expert and to interact with him. Hollenweger's dry and subtle humour permeated his spirited lectures. At times he was fired up with a passion that sometimes brought him close to tears. None was unaffected. From the outset there was animated discussion, both during the open discussions of the consultation and afterwards. The substance of Hollenweger's own lectures at this consultation has been greatly expanded in a new magisterial publication, *Pentecostalism: Origins and Development Worldwide*, the 1997 sequel to the pioneering 1972 English publication of *The Pentecostals*, and readers of this book may explore his analysis further in these two comprehensive volumes.

Pentecostalism in the Third World

Hollenweger points out that after almost a century since its emergence, Pentecostalism is at a crossroads. The way forward, he says, is to re-consider its roots and its spirituality in the light of the developments placing pentecostal churches in some parts of the world squarely in the 'religious right' and 'fundamentalist' camps. This too is the main theme of his new book, *Pentecostalism: Origins and Developments Worldwide*.[10] The consultation in Birmingham took the form of papers presented by invited specialists. After each paper, a respondent interacted directly with the content of the paper and was followed by an open discussion.

Eight of the ten articles of this book are a reworking of the papers given at this consultation, and the last two articles and this Introduction are new ones. The responses appear at the end of the first eight articles, occasionally reworked, and one is a new response. Hollenweger dedicated his 1972 English edition of *The Pentecostals* to his friends and teachers in the pentecostal movement whom he said taught him to love the Bible, while his teachers and friends in the Presbyterian Church

---

10. W.J. Hollenweger, *Pentecostalism: Origins and Development Worldwide* (Peabody, MA: Hendrickson, 1997), p.1.

taught him to understand it.[11] Hollenweger's substantial and incisive critical insights into Pentecostalism here and in his many books and articles reflect views shared by some scholars in the pentecostal churches themselves. There were very few pentecostal scholars about when he started research in the 1960s and published the first edition of *The Pentecostals* in German in 1969.

The contributors to this volume have divergent views on the subject of Pentecostalism, and are not responsible for each other's opinions. Although some may be considered 'outsiders' and some 'insiders', all share a common concern that as Pentecostalism reaches its first century, the movement must become relevant to the needs of the world of the next one. This book is essentially about Pentecostalism as a global phenomenon, with over half of its contents devoted to studies of pentecostal movements in the Third World. Four of the ten articles of the book are on Pentecostalism in the African Diaspora and in Africa itself, one article is on Korean Pentecostalism, and one on the phenomenon in Latin America. The contributors come from five continents and seven nations.

The African Connection

Hollenweger was one of the first to describe Pentecostalism in non-western categories, considering its growth in the Third World to have taken place not because of adherence to a particular pentecostal doctrine, but because of its roots in the spirituality of nineteenth-century African American slave religion. He outlined the main features of this spirituality to be an oral liturgy, a narrative theology and witness, the maximum participation of the whole community in worship and service, the inclusion of visions and dreams into public worship, and an understanding of the relationship between the body and the mind manifested by healing through prayer.[12] Hollenweger draws our attention to the significance of these features in 'The Black Roots of Pentecostalism', where his insights arising from many years of research experience are revealed. One of the most interesting illustrations of this phenomenon is demonstrated by Hollenweger's reconstruction of Dietrich Bonhoeffer's visit to a black pentecostal church in Harlem, New York,

---

11. Hollenweger, *Pentecostals*, p. vi.
12. W.J. Hollenweger, 'After Twenty Years' Research on Pentecostalism', *International Review of Mission* 75 (1985), pp. 3-12 (5-6).

in which the elements of pentecostal oral narrative are displayed. He goes on to consider the significance of the African American preacher William J. Seymour, and here he takes issue with James Goff's analysis of Charles Parham as founder of the movement. Hollenweger maintains that a serious consideration of the essence of Pentecostalism will locate the movement squarely in the black roots of the Azusa Street revival and that therefore William Seymour is the obvious choice for founder, as was apparently also recently acknowledged by the North American Assemblies of God.

Black Pentecostalism in Britain

The two following articles by Robert Beckford and Roswith Gerloff continue this theme by looking at the Black pentecostal movement in Britain, one of the largest expressions of Pentecostalism in this country. The two authors come from differing viewpoints. Beckford, whose doctoral research is on Black pentecostal theology, is the more critical, as Beckford belongs to a new generation of radical black pentecostals. He considers the role of 'Black pentecostals and Black politics' in his article. Beckford's penetrating critique of black pentecostals who are paralysed from effective social action through the underlying quietism of their type of Christianity, is described by him as manifested in 'spiritualization' and 'pacification'. The fundamental question to be asked is whether one can be both 'Black Pentecostal' and 'Black Conscious'. He examines the tension between certain forms of Black Pentecostalism and political mobilization and suggests ways in which this tension can be resolved, including the articulation of cultural resistance in black pentecostal churches and his interesting if controversial proposal of the embracing of a 'dread' Christ.

Gerloff, who studied for her doctorate under Hollenweger in the 1980s, appears as a more sympathetic outsider who has spent many years working with and observing the Black-led church movement in different parts of Europe. She draws from these considerable insights in her 'Pentecostals in the African Diaspora'. Gerloff sees the term 'African Diaspora' as an instrument for defining black international identity in the face of oppression and powerlessness, a reminder of the historical roots of the black people of Britain. She pleads for a British Black Pentecostal theology, describes the 'movement organization' of black majority churches and their community-oriented leadership, and the spirituality that makes mutual ecumenical sharing possible.

Pentecostals in the Southern Hemisphere

There are many other movements throughout the world, like most of the thousands of African initiated churches, which are phenomenologically 'pentecostal' movements, where the features outlined by Hollenweger have persisted, but which have developed a form of Christianity quite different from western Pentecostalism. Two of these are considered in the next two articles, both from the Southern Hemisphere. I elaborate on the growth, tensions and development of Pentecostalism in a racist South African society in 'Dangerous Memories'. There, like Azusa Street, Pentecostalism was born as a non-racial movement, but the truth about its origins and the many divisions that occurred soon after its commencement, and have continued to the present day, were indeed 'dangerous memories'.

In recent years, the greatest quantitative growth of Pentecostalism has been in sub-Saharan Africa, South East Asia, South Korea and especially in Latin America, where the growth has been so phenomenal that scholars are asking whether the whole continent is turning pentecostal. North American Methodist revivalist and missionary to Chile, Willis Hoover, was instrumental in the emergence of the Methodist Pentecostal Church in 1909, an indigenous church that has become the largest non-Catholic denomination in that country, where pentecostals now constitute 15% of the total population.[13] Juan Sepúlveda is a pentecostal pastor in Chile, whose doctoral research in Birmingham looked at the question of the indigenization of the vast pentecostal movement in Latin America, his main topic in his article, 'Indigenous Pentecostalism and the Chilean Experience'. In several parts of Latin America, pentecostals far outnumber all other Protestants and may soon be the majority.[14] In Brazil and Nicaragua they are 20% of the total population, and in Guatemala an astonishing 30%. Pentecostals are also growing rapidly in the Caribbean, particularly in Jamaica, Puerto Rico and Haiti.[15] Sepúlveda looks at Chilean Pentecostalism, one of the earliest expressions of the movement in the world that arose quite independently of Azusa Street and North American Pentecostalism, as an expression of

---

13. D. Martin, *Tongues of Fire: The Explosion of Protestantism in Latin America* (Oxford: Basil Blackwell, 1990), p. 29.
14. Cox, *Fire from Heaven*, p. 168.
15. Martin, *Tongues of Fire*, p. 51.

indigenous Christianity in Latin America. He says that its origins in and separation from Methodism were at least partly the result of a 'cultural clash' between an 'official' culture and a 'popular' culture, and that it was internal factors and not external social factors that resulted in its dynamic growth. In particular, it was Chilean Pentecostalism's ability to translate its message into the forms of popular Chilean culture and to spread among the poor masses that were its main strengths. Juan Sepúlveda's article has reinforced the contention that in Pentecostalism's ability to adapt to any cultural context lies its main strength.

The Korean Phenomenon

In some parts of Asia, Pentecostalism is growing rapidly. There are estimated to be almost six million pentecostals in Indonesia, and the Pentecostal Church of Indonesia numbered 1.3 million in 1990, the third largest Christian denomination in that predominantly Muslim country.[16] The rapidly growing house church movement in China seems to be mostly of an indigenous pentecostal type, and conservative estimates of this movement's numbers run into several millions. In South Korea, one of the most remarkable pentecostal movements exists, not only in the pentecostal denominations where the largest single congregation in the world is found, but in the majority of older Protestant churches themselves. The question to be asked in assessing Korean Pentecostalism is to what extent is this an indigenous Christianity or a foreign North American import. Some writers have suggested that Korean Pentecostalism has succeeded because it has combined Christianity with 'huge chunks of indigenous Korean shamanism',[17] but this is probably not so much a conscious syncretism as the 'aura' of shamanism and the joint acknowledgment of the world of spirits. Similarly, conservative Protestant Christianity with its strict moral law finds fertile ground in Korean Confucianism.[18] Pentecostal leaders unequivocally deny that there is any admixture of shamanism in their type of Pentecostalism, and like pentecostals all over the world they see divination as something to be rejected. Perhaps it is safer to consider that this is a culturally indigenous form of Korean Christianity that is *interacting* with

16. P. Johnstone, *Operation World* (Carlisle, UK: OM Publishing, 1993), p. 292.
17. Cox, *Fire from Heaven*, p. 222.
18. Martin, *Tongues of Fire*, pp. 140-41

shamanism. Harvey Cox sees this as 'helping people recover vital elements in their culture that are threatened by modernization'.[19]

Lee Hong Jung, in 1996 Sepúlveda's contemporary PhD candidate in Birmingham and director of the Centre for North East Asian Mission Studies at Selly Oak Colleges, takes up these issues and considers Pentecostalism in Korea from a 'minjung', non-pentecostal perspective in '*Minjung* and Pentecostal Movements in Korea'. His both passionate and sceptical critique applies to much of Protestant Christianity in Korea in general. He says that the pentecostal movement in Korea commenced as a people's movement, an expression of the *minjung*, the oppressed and exploited people of Korea, but it was soon fundamentalized and taken ideologically captive by North American missionaries. In his view, it became a syncretism of capitalism, shamanism and religious fundamentalism. Because the Protestant churches had made a 'religio-social myth' of the 'miraculous growth' of Pentecostalism, they had been 'pentecostalized' in the process. He analyses the different factors at work in this development and considers pentecostal preachers like Cho Yong-Gi (known to the West as Paul Yonggi Cho) to be fulfilling the role of a traditional shaman. Lee feels that although church growth in Korea may possibly be attributed to 'the moving force of the Spirit', his own conviction is that socio-historical factors are the probable root causes, such as the Korean churches' marriage to North American capitalism, thus rendering them 'centres of anti-communist agitation'. He suggests that for a true transformation to take place it is necessary for the Korean church to be 'reshamanized'.

The Prosperous Pentecostals

For many years now, the largest Christian congregation in the world with an estimated 800,000 members in 1995, has been a pentecostal one, the Yoido Full Gospel Church in Seoul, Korea.[20] Similar opulent buildings holding thousands of worshippers reflect the emerging pentecostal middle class in some parts of the Third World and in many cities in the West. There are several examples of this phenomenon in Korea and in South America, including the Jotabeche Cathedral in Santiago, Chile—in the late 1980s the second largest congregation in the world,

19. Cox, *Fire from Heaven*, pp. 224, 228.
20. Cox, *Fire from Heaven*, p. 221.

and the Temple of Brasil Para Cristo in São Paulo.[21] These megachurches notwithstanding, pentecostals in the Third World are usually
and predominantly a grassroots movement appealing especially to the
disadvantaged and underprivileged. Many, if not most, of the rapidly
growing Christian churches in the Third World are pentecostal, indigenous, and operate independently of western Pentecostalism. This phenomenon is so significant that the writer of the Foreword and author of
The Secular City, Harvey Cox, in his fascinating study entitled *Fire
from Heaven*, reverses his well known position on secularization and
speaks of Pentecostalism as a manifestation of the 'unanticipated reap-
pearance of primal spirituality in our time'.[22]

In North America[23] and in other parts of the world, large independent
pentecostal congregations have sprung up in the 1980s and 1990s, particularly in Africa and Latin America. Some of these churches form
loose associations or 'fellowships'. In several countries they are the
fastest growing section of Christianity, appealing especially to younger
people in the cities where there is an aspiring upward climbing and
formally educated clientele. The Deeper Life Church of William Ku-
muyi in Nigeria, and the Zimbabwe Assemblies of God Africa of
Ezekiel Guti have become denominations of national significance in a
short space of time. There are rapidly growing churches of this type
in Argentina, where Omar Cabrera's Vision del Futuro and Hector
Jimenez's Waves of Love and Peace in Buenos Aires are among the
largest Christian congregations in the world, with over 70,000 members
each.[24] After 1970 a new type of pentecostal movement also began in
Brazil, the most notorious being the Igreja Universal do Reino de Deus
(Universal Church of the Kingdom of God), a prosperity-oriented middle class movement founded in 1977 by Edir Macedo, which by 1990
had 700 churches and at least half a million members[25]—one estimate
made this the second largest Protestant denomination in Brazil (after the
Assemblies of God) with four million affiliates in 1990.[26] Some of these

21. Martin, *Tongues of Fire*, p. 142.

22. Cox, *Fire from Heaven*, p. 83.

23. Land, *Pentecostal Spirituality*, p. 22.

24. V. Synan, *The Spirit said 'Grow': The Astonishing Worldwide Expansion of
Pentecostal and Charismatic Churches* (Monrovia, CA: MARC, 1992), p. 16.

25. See P. Berryman, *Religion in the Megacity: Catholic and Protestant Por-
traits from Latin America* (New York: Orbis Books, 1996), p. 33.

26. Johnstone, *Operation World*, p. 128.

new churches have been criticized for propagating a 'prosperity gospel' after the pattern of their North American counterparts with which they sometimes identify, which seems to reproduce the worst forms of North American capitalism in Christian guise. There is a danger of generalization in making this assessment, especially when we fail to appreciate the reconstructions and innovations made by these new pentecostals in adapting to a radically different context.[27]

Only a few of these churches identify with the poor and the oppressed, although one of their African leaders, Mensa Otabil of Ghana, preaches a form of Black Consciousness which encourages pride in God-given blackness and is not too far removed from some forms of Black Theology. A similar trend is found in the preaching of African Caribbean charismatic Myles Monroe of the Bahamas, who has travelled extensively in Africa.[28] It would be simplistic to describe these new pentecostal movements as carbon copies of North American models, as such a view fails to appreciate their inner dynamics. As in many other forms of religious encounter, when one expression of Christianity interacts with another religio-cultural tradition, certain fundamental changes occur, and there emerges a new, constantly adapting renewal movement that is increasingly seeking to be relevant to the social context in which it is found. This is the promise of better things to come. Pentecostalism's inherent flexibility means that it is more easily able to adjust to any context, even when that context is a rapidly changing one, as is the case in many of the cities of the Third World. This also has bearing on the fact that many from the emerging middle class in many Third World cities are becoming pentecostals—God loves them too!

In his articles, Walter Hollenweger deliberates on some of these new developments, and returns to the subject of the origins of Pentecostalism and the Charismatic Movement. 'Rethinking Spirit Baptism: The Natural and the Supernatural' is about their 'Catholic roots'. After a brief discussion on the effects of Evangelicalism on the emergence of Pentecostalism, Hollenweger shows how Catholic elements were mediated to Pentecostalism through John Wesley, and in particular shows the influence of Catholicism on the teaching of 'Spirit baptism' that has become the hallmark of the movement. He discusses the doctrine of

27. P. Gifford, *New Dimensions in African Christianity* (Nairobi: All Africa Conference of Churches, 1992), p. 8.

28. From personal notes taken of his preaching in Pretoria, South Africa in 1994.

'initial evidence' (by no means a universal doctrine within Pentecostalism), and says that speaking in tongues and other gifts of the Holy Spirit are 'natural' phenomena, and that a dichotomy between 'natural' and 'supernatural' is a western invention that does not actually exist. He concludes the discussion of Spirit baptism by looking at a North American Presbyterian report on the Charismatic Movement.

Walter Hollenweger's last article in this publication is a rearrangement of a paper entitled 'Pentecostals and Crucial Issues for Mission' and two more informal sessions at the consultation, 'The Charismatic Renewal: A Theological Dilemma' (part of which is incorporated into this article), and 'The New Pentecostal Middle Class'. In this article, 'Crucial Issues for Pentecostals', Hollenweger tackles a number of topical issues which have relevance for pentecostals and for the mission of the church in the twenty-first century. He discusses the strategy of pioneer pentecostal missiologist Melvin Hodges, and says that western pentecostals have departed from this vision and have been insensitive to local cultures and Third World pentecostal theologies. He deals with specific instances where these issues are apparent: in the realms of 'signs and wonders', ecclesiology and hermeneutics. He says that pentecostals have lost their original ecumenical vision and have (in some places) embraced middle class values as they have become more visible as denominations. He challenges those who suppose that becoming a Christian solves all problems, a spiritual panacea for the woes of humankind, and says that instead of pentecostals in the West turning a blind eye to so many national and international evils (or worse, succumbing to their influence), the church should be developing an alternative system to capitalism. He concludes this article by describing the 'dialogical' process of evangelism, the outworking of which is described in the following article.

In 'Scholarship and Evangelism: Oil and Water?' Lynne Price tells the story of the staging of one of Hollenweger's evangelistic plays, 'The Adventure of Faith', which was performed in the Selly Oak Methodist Church the day after the consultation ended. In this narrative, Price describes Hollenweger's 'dialogical' method, in which scholarship and evangelism can be effectively combined. In 'Global Pentecostalism in the New Millennium', I make some concluding reflections on the issues raised and add some further observations gleaned from recent academic work by pentecostals themselves and their self awareness in their missionary task. This publication is to some extent an attempt to further air Hollenweger's thought and to discuss the contribution that Pentecostalism makes to our understanding of world Christianity and its relevance for the next century. It is hoped that readers will reflect seriously about the issues raised here, and that pentecostal and charismatic readers in particular will better understand themselves and their role in the new millennium.

THE BLACK ROOTS OF PENTECOSTALISM

Walter J. Hollenweger

Introduction

Pentecostalism has come to a crossroads. From its own ranks there comes the challenge first for a critical historiography, and some critical historical description is found in this publication. Secondly, there is a challenge for a social and political analysis. Juan Sepúlveda, who writes here on Chilean Pentecostalism, reflects the thinking of several pentecostal scholars who are asking very searching social and political questions. Then thirdly, there is the challenge for a more differentiated treatment of the work of the Spirit and for a spirituality which does not blank out critical thinking—it is now possible to speak in tongues and to be a critical thinker at a university at the same time—this was not possible in the past. Pentecostals are asking for a new appraisal of pre-Christian cultures in their own Third World sister churches, such as the relationship between Pentecostalism and Korean shamanism or African traditional healing, the influences on this movement from different kinds of Caribbean religions or native American religions in Latin America. All these religious expressions have been taken in and transformed by Pentecostalism, which is a mark of its strength. Finally, there is a challenge for ecumenical dialogue and openness. There are four scholarly pentecostal periodicals in the English speaking world that discuss these and related topics: *The Journal of Pentecostal Theology* (Sheffield Academic Press), *Pneuma* (Society for Pentecostal Studies), *EPTA Bulletin* (European Pentecostal Theological Association), and *Asian Journal of Pentecostal Studies* (Asia Pacific Theological Seminary, Baguio City, Philippines).

The details of these topics are worked out in this publication. There are three branches of Pentecostalism, namely: (1) the Classical Pentecostals, like the Assemblies of God world-wide or the Elim Pentecostal Church in Britain; (2) the Charismatic Renewal Movement, different groups appearing in older churches like the Anglican, Presbyterian or Methodist churches; (3) the pentecostal or pentecostal-like 'non-white indigenous churches'[1] in the Third World, usually called African independent churches in Africa, of which Allan Anderson is a specialist and for which probably the best documentation in Europe is found in the Research Unit for New Religions and Churches at the University of Birmingham, England. All three of these branches belong to the pentecostal movement. The question to be asked today is which way will these three branches of Pentecostalism turn?

In the meantime, the military have discovered the significance of Pentecostalism and have infiltrated it in certain countries of the world in order to use it as a tool for winning the hearts of people. For instance, to make the people open for the North American way of life, well-trained people are sent into pentecostal churches where they get 'converted' and become pastors, and so influence the whole movement. This has happened in many parts of the world, where the strategic social and political importance of Pentecostalism has been recognized. Pentecostals are now sitting in state parliaments in the United States (where significantly, these are usually black pentecostals), and in the Brazilian parliament and other parliaments of the world. Pentecostal televangelist Pat Robertson played an important role in US American politics, helping Ronald Reagan to become president.

Ethnologists, anthropologists and sociologists also study the pentecostal movement in detail, as it does not only have religious importance. Theological faculties in general, however, excel in incredible ignorance. In Europe in particular, we have specialized institutes and libraries on all kinds of topics, but not on the most important missionary movement of our time. There is no specialized institute or library in the whole of Europe, and sometimes even the specialized scholarly periodicals on Pentecostalism are not available in our libraries. All this shows how much theology slumbers and is seemingly oblivious to this important phenomenon. Yet, 'a religious movement that already encompasses nearly half a billion people and is multiplying geometrically should not be dismissed so easily', says Harvey Cox,[2] who points out that eminent

    1.   D.B. Barratt, *World Christian Encyclopedia* (Oxford: Oxford University Press, 1982), pp. 60-63.
    2.   H. Cox, 'Why God Didn't Die: A Religious Renaissance Flourishing around the World. Pentecostal Christians Leading the Way', *Nieman Reports* (The Nieman

sociologists project that 'by early in the next century, pentecostals in all their variegated manifestations will outnumber both Catholics and Protestants'. Pentecostals are already more important than any denomination in the Protestant world, and they are continuing to grow. In countries like Brazil there are more pentecostal worshippers on Sunday mornings at church than Catholics. Eight thousand people are leaving the Catholic Church *daily* in Latin America, and most of them join pentecostal churches. The real growth areas of Pentecostalism are not in North America and certainly not in a fashionable white suburb in Britain or Switzerland, not on television and not among white people, but in the Third World, where the millions are. Once these millions enter the World Council of Churches, the whole ecumenical movement will be changed fundamentally. When that happens, the Third World will have a majority in the form of Pentecostalism and independent churches, and the older western churches will no longer be the ones who call the tune. We will have to play the tune together then, and this may be one of the reasons why the present ecumenical movement is not very eager for pentecostals to come into its midst in any great force.

Pentecostalism has a certain down-to-earth this-worldliness secularity, and that makes it attractive. Werner Hoerschelmann from Hamburg says, 'Pentecostal spirituality is the future'.[3] John A. Mackay said that 'the true hope of ecumenism is the charismatic renewal', for 'uncouth life is better than aesthetic death'.[4] The World Council of Churches[5] and some pentecostals[6] realize that a systematic dialogue between Pentecostalism and Ecumenism is a must for the future. That is the single most important topic for the church of the twenty-first century, both for theology, for mission and for ecumenicity.

Foundation at Harvard University 47/2, Summer 1993), pp. 3-8 (8). See also H. Cox, 'Some Personal Reflections on Pentecostalism', *Pneuma* 15 (1993), pp. 39-44.

3. W. Hoerschelmann, 'Der Heilige Geist als Machtfaktor: Pfingstfrömmigkeit verändert die ökumenische Landschaft', *Luth. Monatshefte* (1990), pp. 67-70 (67).

4. M.R. Curlee and R.R. Curlee, 'God's Springtime: John A. Mackay, David J. Du Plessis and Presbyterian Charismatic Origins' (unpublished MS, 1993), p. 79. See also J.A. Mackay, *Ecumenics: The Science of the Church Universal* (Englewood Cliffs, NJ: Prentice–Hall, 1964) p. 198.

5. 'Interview with Konrad Raiser', *Der Säemann* 109 (1993), p. 5.

6. C.M. Robeck, Review of Jerry L. Sandidge, *Roman Catholic/Pentecostal Dialogue (1979–1982): A Study in Developing Ecumenism* (2 vols.; Frankfurt, 1987), in *Pneuma* 11 (1989), p. 135.

Characteristics of the Black Oral Beginnings

In overview, Pentecostalism has five roots, consisting of the catholic, evangelical, critical, and ecumenical roots and the black oral root—the main focus of this article—coming through African American slave religion. Pentecostals have yet to act on the ecumenical theology of their founder, William Joseph Seymour.[7] Two world-wide Christian movements were founded by non-Europeans. One is the global pentecostal movement, the other is Christianity itself. The founder of Pentecostalism was a black ecumenist from the United States; the founder of Christianity was a story-telling rabbi who belonged to the oral culture of the Middle East. Jesus was not a European and he never wrote a book, but taught with stories. Both movements owe their initial growth to the oral structure of their origins. The reason for Pentecostalism's breathtaking growth does not lie in a particular pentecostal doctrine, in spite of what the pentecostals think. Doctrinally, Pentecostalism is not a consistent whole, still less if one subsumes under Pentecostalism the independent non-white indigenous churches and the Charismatic Movement. There are trinitarian and non-trinitarian churches, there are infant baptizing and adult baptizing pentecostals, and many other variations. There are even pentecostal denominations that have accepted state subsidies. The reason for its growth lies in its black roots, which can be described as follows.

First, their *liturgy is oral*, unlike other churches whose liturgy is written and sounds written too. This fact does not preclude pentecostals from writing down their liturgy, but it is produced in an oral way. It is very clearly structured and is not chaotic, but like a jazz concert, which also originates from black oral culture, it has its structure in music, the so-called 'choruses' which are indicators of which part of the liturgy one is now in. Secondly, their *theology and witness is narrative*. Dietrich Bonhoeffer was one of the first, and for at least 40 years the only western theologian, who saw the political and theological relevance of the spirituality of these black churches. The following reconstruction is based on both Bonhoeffer's notes and my own knowledge of these

---

7.   D.T. Irving, 'Drawing all Together in One Bond of Love: The Ecumenical Vision of William J Seymour and the Azusa Street Revival', *Journal of Pentecostal Theology* 6 (1995), pp. 25-53, esp. p. 53.

kinds of churches.[8] The whole sequence is what I would call a true story, even though it is reconstructed.

When Bonhoeffer arrived to speak at the black Church of God in Christ in Harlem, New York, service had already begun. A young person sang:

> When the Holy Ghost fills you, you can smile
> When the blood of Jesus cleanses you, you can smile
> When you feel like the Baptist ...

Bonhoeffer was taken by surprise. What should he say? Fortunately, these people were thoughtful. First they sang another hymn, one of those famous spirituals about the final liberation of all people, although superficially it was a hymn about heaven: 'I'm going to lay down my heavy load'. Bonhoeffer listened carefully. 'What, brothers and sisters, shall we lay down?' In full harmony the congregation replied: 'I'm going to lay down my heavy load'. A well-endowed elderly woman sang the next stanza. She not only sang with her mouth, which she could open unbelievably wide, but *everything* about her sang—the well upholstered hips, the thick legs, the strong arms, even the big, swaying bosom sang the rhythm of the hymn: 'I know my robe's going to fit me well; I've tried it on at the gates of hell'. And again the whole congregation joined her in unison: 'I'm going to lay down my heavy load'. Bonhoeffer thought, how true. We stand at the gates of hell, but the assurance of a coming morning gives us strength. Unbidden prayer rose in him: 'Thy kingdom come'. But he also thought of his teachers in Germany and of his colleagues who in clever formulations tried to justify the German Nazi policy of aggression. He thought of those Lutheran theologians who tried to keep out of the battle by making correct, yet irrelevant definitions on the Holy Spirit. It was almost laughable, if it were not so tragic. But these Christians here did not need any teaching on the Holy Spirit. They experienced him; he talked to them. But what should he, Bonhoeffer, tell them? He did not think that he had anything to say, at least not for the moment.

8.   D. Bonhoeffer, 'Bericht über den Studienaufenthalt im Union Theological Seminary zu New York', in *Gesammelte Schriften*, I (Munich: Kaiser Verlag, 1958), pp. 84-103. See also W.J. Hollenweger, 'Dietrich Bonhoeffer and William J.A. Seymour: A Comparison between Two Ecumenists', *Norsk Tidsskrift for Mision* 39/3-4 (1985), pp. 192-201.

When the hymn was finished the pastor asked him to come to the pulpit. Bonhoeffer stood up. 'Brothers and sisters',—Bonhoeffer was just beginning to understand the meaning of this way of addressing the church—'brothers and sisters, I want to thank you for your invitation. I hear your songs and your prayers. I cannot sing them and I do not know your prayers.' (In fact, he thought, that was not quite true. But he could tell them for the moment what was troubling him about the gates of hell in Germany, about the Blacks in Germany who were not only oppressed but killed.) 'But I thank you for your spirituals. That is all.'

He sat down. The congregation was a little astonished. The pastor grasped the situation immediately. 'Brothers and sisters, Dr Bonhoeffer is a German theologian and as you know, such theologians usually speak with a paper in front of them on which is written their speech. You must understand. That is what they learn at the university.' Everyone laughed. 'Give him a hand', he said, and all clapped. 'Yes, brothers and sisters', the pastor continued, 'we shall wonder, wonder and marvel, when at last we shall overcome, when all the saints are marching into the city of golden streets ...' He had hardly finished when the trombone began to play: 'Oh when the saints ...', and again the congregation stood up and danced and marched through the church. The theme was continued by an old grey-haired preacher: 'Brothers and sisters, when the saints march into the new Jerusalem, do you think there will be Catholic saints, Lutheran saints, Pentecostal saints?' 'No, no', the church shouted. 'Will there be black saints and white saints?' And again the whole congregation responded enthusiastically: 'No, no'. 'No', the preacher said in a hoarse voice in a way that cut rut through the entire building.

> No, there will only be saints. Saints who have washed their garments. Hallelujah! But some of us will marvel, I tell you. In heaven we will marvel even more than down here. You know, in heaven it will become clear, very clear indeed, what we worship. Whether we worship Jesus the manual worker, Jesus our saviour or whether we worship our own fears and our own impulses. Yes, brothers and sisters, it will become clear whether we worship our own race, our nation, our money (even if we don't have much of it)—praise God—or whether we worship Jesus. I wouldn't be a bit surprised in the least if all white people would be confronted with a black Jesus, and all black people with a white Jesus. Let us pray.

Bonhoeffer folded his hands, but these black Christians obviously had a different understanding of prayer from his, for they began to sing again. Bonhoeffer did not know whether they had invented the song or whether it was a song known to them. Anyway, they did not use a hymnal. In the song they asked for God's blessing for their work, for their church. They had a special stanza in which they prayed for their German guest and his students and then for a whole verse they sang 'Amen'. Bonhoeffer did not know whether white Christians would meet a black Christ on the Last Day of Judgment. Possibly—but surely *Aryan* Christians would meet a *Jewish* Christ!

This is what I mean by 'narrative theology', of which we do not have enough at our western universities. One can be very critical and very scholarly and still be narrative—Jesus is the proof of this. This narrative theology is also illustrated by a performance of my biblical drama, *The Adventure of Faith*, which Lynne Price describes in her article in this book and which demonstrates stories based on critical New Testament exegesis.

The third characteristic of the black oral culture we are describing is *maximum participation* at the levels of reflection, prayer and decision making and therefore a form of community that is reconciliatory. This means, for instance, that 'majority decisions' are not made in a western, white fashion; instead a matter is talked over repeatedly until agreement or consensus is found. This belongs to black culture. The first thing that Nelson Mandela did after his release from a cruel South African prison was to talk about reconciliation. The second thing he did was to ask his archenemy De Klerk to become second in command of his government. That had never happened before—but it illustrates what I mean by maximum participation at the level of decision making. Can you imagine the Conservatives and the Labour Party forming a government together in Britain? It was quite normal in an African situation, made possible by Mandela's African roots.

Then fourthly, the *inclusion of dreams and visions* into personal and public forms of worship—just like in the life of Jesus, who taught using images (not illustrations) which needed no explanation but spoke for themselves, functioning as a kind of icon for the individual and the community. Finally, a fifth characteristic is an *understanding of the relationship between the body and the mind* that is informed by experiences of correspondence between body and mind. The most striking applications of this insight is the ministry of healing of the sick by prayer, which one finds in most pentecostal churches, and the wonderfully liturgical pentecostal dancing, especially found in black churches.

William Joseph Seymour

In Europe and North America, Pentecostalism is fast developing into an evangelical middle-class religion. There, many of the elements that were vital for its rise and expansion into the Third World are now disappearing. They are being replaced by efficient fund-raising structures, a streamlined ecclesiastical bureaucracy and a pentecostal conceptual theology. In Europe and North America this theology follows the evangelical traditions to which is added the belief in the baptism of the Spirit, mostly but not always characterized by the 'initial sign' of speaking in tongues. Things were different at the beginning of Pentecostalism, during the Azusa Street revival in Los Angeles under the black leader William Joseph Seymour. His story was told for the first time by my doctoral student John Douglas Nelson's thesis 'For Such a Time as This'.[9] James Cone stated: 'The histories are going to have to be rewritten after reading Nelson'.[10]

Who was William Joseph Seymour? He was born the son of former slaves from Centerville, Louisiana. He taught himself to read and write and was for a time a student in Charles Fox Parham's Bible School in Houston, Texas. Parham (1873–1929) is often described as a pioneer of Pentecostalism, but was also a sympathizer of the Ku Klux Klan and therefore excluded Seymour from his Bible classes. Seymour was allowed only to listen outside the classroom through the half-open door. Nevertheless, Seymour accepted Parham's doctrine of the baptism of the Spirit and began to teach it in a Holiness church in Los Angeles.

Seymour and his black brothers and sisters suffered bitterly. During Seymour's adult lifetime three and a half thousand black persons were known to have been lynched, averaging two a week. Innumerable brutalities took place around him, many of them instigated by Christians. In spite of constant humiliation he developed a spirituality that in 1906 led to a revival in Azusa Street, Los Angeles, which most pentecostal historians believe to be the cradle of Pentecostalism. The roots of Seymour's spirituality lay in his past. He affirmed his black heritage by introducing spirituals and music into his liturgy at a time when this

9. J.D. Nelson, 'For Such a Time as This: The Story of Bishop William J. Seymour and the Azusa Street Revival. A Study of Pentecostal/Charismatic Roots' (PhD thesis, University of Birmingham, 1981).
10. Quoted by I. Clemmons in, 'True Koinonia: Pentecostal Hopes and Historical Realities', *Pneuma* 3 (1981), pp. 44-56 (52).

music was considered inferior and unfit for Christian worship. At the same time he steadfastly lived out his understanding of Pentecost. For him Pentecost meant more than speaking in tongues. It meant to love in the face of hate, to overcome the hatred of a whole nation by demonstrating that Pentecost was something very different from the success-oriented North American way of life. In the revival in Los Angeles, white bishops and black workers, men and women, Asians and Mexicans, white professors and black laundry women were equals—and that was in 1906. It was little wonder that the religious and secular presses reported the extraordinary events in detail. But as they could not understand the revolutionary nature of this pentecostal spirituality, they took refuge in ridicule and scoffed: 'What good can come from a self-appointed Negro prophet?' and the *Los Angeles Times* constantly made fun of this revival. The mainline churches also criticized the emerging pentecostal movement. They despised the pentecostals because of their lowly black origins. Social pressures soon prompted the emerging pentecostal church bureaucracy to tame the Los Angeles revival, and pentecostal churches segregated into black and white organizations just as most other churches had done. This did not hinder the pentecostal denominations from developing on a world wide scale. They are strongest in those countries of the Third World where an oral mode of communication is an important way to communicate.

Parham or Seymour?

There is a debate as to whether Charles Parham or William Seymour is the founder of Pentecostalism. Some pentecostals were ashamed of their black origins and looked for another founder. Charles Fox Parham was the first to invent the doctrine of the baptism of the Spirit with speaking in tongues as the 'initial sign'. And so, James R. Goff said: 'It is Parham alone who formulated the distinguishing ideological formula of tongues as initial evidence of the Holy Spirit baptism. That discovery, in effect, created the Pentecostal movement.'[11] For him Parham, and Parham alone, is the founder of Pentecostalism. Seymour is excluded because his race- and class-transcending spirituality was soon dismissed in North American Pentecostalism and has consequently since died out.

11.   J.R. Goff, *Fields White unto Harvest: Charles F. Parham and the Missionary Origins of Pentecostalism* (Fayetteville: University of Arkansas Press, 1988), p. 7.

What is there to say about Goff's analysis? First, I do not want to quarrel with him on facts. He presents a number of issues that are important, for instance that for Parham glossolalia was *always* xenolalia (that is, speaking in an existing human language) and served as evidence of a candidate's mission call, indicating to which country the candidate was called according to the particular language given[12]—which of course proved to be nonsense. This understanding of tongues has also died out in Pentecostalism, after several embarrassments in the mission field by people claiming to speak foreign languages which no one could understand. Secondly, if you take this yardstick, then Christ is not the founder of Christianity, because many of the things he taught and lived have not been taken seriously in Christianity, such as his teaching that we should be non-violent and that we should be poor and give away all our things—even the churches do not follow Christ. Thirdly, Parham was also a racist, although not the most racist of all the pentecostal pioneers. For him the Jews, Anglo-Saxons, Germans and Scandinavians, the Aryan Indians and Japanese—in short Jews and Aryans—are the master race. Under them are the Gentiles: French, Spanish, Italians, Greeks, Russians and Turks. At the bottom are Africans and Malays, Mongolians and indigenous Indians. That race theory (which he took from the Bible) fitted well into the background of the southern United States at that time. Fourthly, Parham was accused of homosexuality, although the charge was never proven. Goff maintains that because Seymour's ecumenical vision did not survive in America, he could not be the founder of Pentecostalism. Following this argument also means that Christ could not be the founder of Christianity, as most of the things he taught have not been taken seriously by Christianity, such as his teaching on non-violence and on poverty. Furthermore, most of the doctrines of Parham have not survived in Pentecostalism anyway, such as his racist theory, his doctrine of the 'Destruction of the Wicked' and his understanding of speaking in tongues as actually speaking existing human languages.

It all depends on what we consider to be the essence of Pentecostalism. If Pentecostalism is qualified by a religious experience (Spirit baptism and speaking in tongues) then one might consider Parham as its founder. If, however, it is the oral missionary movement, with spiritual power to overcome racism and chauvinism, then there is only one can-

12. Goff, *Fields White*, p. 75.

didate left and that is Seymour—which of course does not exclude speaking in tongues but gives it its rightful place in spiritual life. After a long hesitation, the North American Assemblies of God have cast their lot with Seymour:

> The Azusa Street revival witnessed the breakdown of barriers which normally divided people from one another... And this was decades before the civil rights movements. Parham denounced the mingling of races in Los Angeles because he was racially prejudiced. God will not bless such hostility toward anyone for whom Christ died.[13]

To sum up: one important root of Pentecostalism is black orality and ecumenism.

Black Pentecostals in the United States

One of these black pentecostals, Arthur Brazier, said that the United States 'must choose between democracy and repression, between the republic and a police state: for America cannot keep down thirty million people who are moving up, without destroying the entire nation in the process'.[14] This is the general tone of black pentecostals in the USA who reject the purely spiritual unity with other pentecostals. They supported Martin Luther King. Black pentecostal Bishop Golder said:

> If the white pentecostal brethren would have stood firm against prejudice and racial injustice, having the most powerful authority (the Holy Spirit) and the most powerful message (the Gospel of Jesus Christ), they could have been the instruments of God for the destruction of this hideous ideology. But instead of fighting against it, they submitted to its influence and have been affected by it even until now.[15]

Black pentecostal Leonard Lovett said: 'No man can experience the fullness of the Spirit and be a *bona fide* racist'.[16] These comments amount to a very interesting doctrine of the baptism of the Spirit which may

---

13. An official report of the Assemblies of God, 'Being the People God Called', *Pentecostal Evangel* (1991), pp. 3-7 (6).

14. A.M. Brazier, *Black Self-Determination: The Story of the Woodlawn Organization* (Grand Rapids, MI: Eerdmans, 1969), p. 5.

15. M.E. Golder, *History of the Pentecostal Assemblies of the World* (Indianapolis: Morris E. Golder, 1973), p. 80.

16. L. Lovett, 'Perspectives on Black Pentecostalism' (unpublished paper, 1972). See also Lovett, 'Black-Holiness Implications for Ethics and Social Transformation' (PhD thesis, Emory University, 1979), p. 165.

create a fascinating question to ask at white charismatic conferences held in international hotels. Samuel Solivan observed: 'We have justified, sanctified, and have baptized our racism and we have fooled ourselves into believing that the Spirit has led us. A spirit has, but which one?'[17]

For almost a century, white American pentecostals ignored these signals from their black brothers and sisters. African Americans were even excluded from the North American Pentecostal Fellowship, even though the black Church of God in Christ was one of the biggest pentecostal churches in the world. Black pentecostals were just wiped out from history. And because the white pentecostals dominated the media, the rest of the world followed them. Due to the work of some black scholars, the generally changing climate and the white pentecostal theologian at Fuller Theological Seminary, Cecil M. Robeck,[18] the situation is changing slowly. In the autumn of 1994 the old Pentecostal Fellowship of North America with its racist ideology was dissolved. A new organization was founded in which black and white pentecostal churches were equal members, but without the 'Oneness' pentecostal churches. With explicit reference to the founder of Pentecostalism, William Joseph Seymour, who saw in the integration of black and white people in his church an essential characteristic of the work of the Holy Spirit, the race-war between black and white pentecostals was ended. A symbol of this was that a white Assemblies of God pastor spontaneously washed the feet of black bishop Ithniel Clemmons—a gesture whose significance cannot be underestimated and which would have been impossible a few years ago. White pentecostals confessed their guilt, 'our participation in the sin of racism by our silence, denial and blindness'.[19] This is only a beginning, but at least it is a beginning.[20]

17. S. Solivan, 'Cultural Glossolalia in Acts 2: A Theological Reassessment of the Importance of Culture and Language' (paper for the Society for Pentecostal Studies, 1994), p. 25.

18. C.M. Robeck, 'Taking Stock of Pentecostalism: The Personal Reflections of a Retiring Editor', *Pneuma* 15 (1993), pp. 35-60. See also the bibliography in W.J. Hollenweger, *Pentecostalism: Origins and Development Worldwide* (Peabody, MA: Hendrickson, 1997).

19. 'Racial Reconciliation Manifesto', *Pentecostal Evangel* 4205 (1994), p. 25.

20. For a detailed documentation and discussion on the substance of this article see Hollenweger, *Pentecostalism*, pp. 18-53.

RESPONSE

Errol Oliver

Inevitably, I am compelled to begin my response from a position of experience rather than from an academic perspective. I do this at the risk of reinforcing the stereotypic image that some non-Pentecostals and academics have of Pentecostals. It is true that on the whole, Pentecostals believe that its better to do more and talk less, and to live a good Christian life than to be endowed with knowledge of what it means to be a Christian and yet avoid its experience. Practical Christianity is usually far more important to black Pentecostals than a theoretical framework of what it means to be a Christian. Black Pentecostals feel that practical Christian experience outweighs the academic pursuit of theology. This perspective may give the false impression that black Pentecostals are not interested in formal theology. On the contrary. In the past, due to a denial of access to academic institutions, which situation originated from poor educational opportunities and racial discrimination, blacks have remained outside the centres of learning. This has hindered formal training in theology and restricted the emergence of black theologians equipped to present the black perspective in the development of Pentecostal Theology. Thankfully, things are beginning to change, enabling blacks to participate more fully in the evolutionary development of the Pentecostal Movement.

Hollenweger claims that Pentecostals taught him to love the Bible while the Presbyterian church taught him to understand it. Because Pentecostals love the Bible they take a practical perspective to an understanding of the Bible. This has often led to the perception by non-Pentecostals that they have an inferior understanding of the Bible. This misunderstanding persists simply because non-Pentecostals have failed to understand the approach of Pentecostals to hermeneutics. On the whole, Pentecostals are more appreciative of Christians living by the Bible than those with only an intellectual understanding of the Bible.

For example, Pentecostals acknowledge the practicality of their faith when they quote the Apostle Paul, 'Not that we are sufficient of ourselves to think anything of ourselves; but our sufficiency is of God' (2 Cor. 3.5; KJV) and they believe in the ability of God to heal the sick in response to prayer.

There is an incompatibility between Christianity and the passive (and even active) support for injustice that is sometimes found in so-called 'Christian' circles. The Gospel demands justice in race relationships and we should not separate theology from racism. Hollenweger states that the North American Assembles of God have now accepted William Joseph Seymour, the black leader used mightily by God to lead the Azusa Street revival in Los Angeles, as the father of Pentecostalism and not Parham, a white racist who supported the Ku Klux Klan and rigidly practised segregation. The Assembles of God logically and correctly argued in favour of Seymour and against Parham citing, 'God will not bless such hostility toward anyone for whom Christ died'. However, I wonder whether this decision was motivated primarily by a response to be reconciled to black brothers and sisters in support of natural justice, or was it a public relations exercise to ease the conscience troubled by the silent sin of white racism? Nevertheless, I take the view that this is an important step towards repentance and the beginning of doing what is right and theologically sound. The Azusa Street experience saw the integration of blacks and whites and for a moment, Seymour thought that the Azusa Street revival was on the verge of the greatest miracle the world had ever seen in the racial integration and ecumenical fellowship experienced by these early Pentecostals. Seymour's short-lived vision still has validity today, but in a sense, black Pentecostals still struggle to be accepted as equals by white Christians, although this is changing as the barriers of separation are reduced and integration is seen as the relationship God intended for us.

In September 1995, I attended the 17th World Pentecostal Conference in Israel. What was very clear during the theological discussions was the heterogeneous nature of Pentecostalism. I am sure we would all agree with Hollenweger that Pentecostalism is not homogeneous and therefore, consistency in doctrine is not a factor for its growth. Unquestionably, the growth of Pentecostalism should be attributed to its black, oral roots. The absence of an agreed set of doctrines in which all Pentecostals share is both a strength and a weakness. It is a strength because it provides the opportunity for spiritual innovation and variety, and a weakness because it reinforces inconsistencies in some doctrines within the Movement. The Pentecostal Movement is indeed at a crossroad. In addition to the key challenges identified by Hollenweger, I feel that we will one day need to deal with the issue of defining the boundary of Pentecostalism in terms of its teachings (e.g. Trinitarian or non-Trinitarian), core values (e.g. living by the principles of Scripture) and practices (e.g. acceptance or lack of acceptance of infant baptism).

I agree with Hollenweger's analysis of why Pentecostalism is worth the attention of critical academic study. However, it may well be studied for the wrong reasons. If white authority figures in the movement with control over the instruments of history fail to continue with the step taken by the North American Assemblies of God, then the Pentecostal Movement will carry on its development along racial lines. The consequences of this development will exacerbate the diverging theological and historical perspectives of black and white Pentecostals. And with the exception of worship and a belief in the work of the Holy Spirit, there may be very little oral, visual or textual evidence remaining that might support a common history or a corporate view of Pentecostalism. Furthermore, the growth of Pentecostalism within the Third World may well provide the catalyst for true reconciliation between black and white Pentecostals, as white Pentecostals seek to reposition themselves in a movement in transition from positional power held by whites to legitimate power assumed by blacks.

Finally, the Pentecostal Movement has a responsibility to rewrite its own history to accurately reflect its black roots and to formally accept William Joseph Seymour as its founder. Failure to do so may result in a continuation of the unhealthy tension that exists between black and white Pentecostals. The opportunity for realizing the ecumenical theology of Seymour has never been better, as we enter a soul-searching period of historical reflection. The Pentecostal Movement must progress from saying the right things and begin to do what is right and just.

BLACK PENTECOSTALS AND BLACK POLITICS

Robert Beckford

Introduction

If liberation theology begins with the concrete concerns of marginalized people, then let me begin with a question that arises out of my context as a black urban pentecostal in Britain. 'Is it possible to be a black pentecostal and black conscious—concerned with black mobilization in Britain today?' This question expresses an existential concern of many second- and third-generation black Pentecostal Christians in Britain for whom the type of black Pentecostalism their parents brought with them from the Caribbean was and is still politically quiet. Growing up in the 1970s and 1980s, I witnessed two manifestations of political quietism: 'spiritualization' and 'pacification'. By spiritualization I refer to the way that concrete concerns confronting the black community—and indirectly the black church community—were interpreted as cosmic concerns only changed by consulting God through prayer. Consequently, if family security was threatened by a racist attack, our most effective response was prayer. We believed that God would fight our battles and after long, sincere and dynamic family or church prayer sessions we not only felt better but believed that God had heard and was dealing with our concerns. Racism was never explicitly mentioned, but sometimes implicit within our oral communication to our deity. Despite the psycho-social satisfaction we experienced from prayer, spiritualizing reality promoted socio-political passivity—there was no external protest or challenge to the white supremacist powers within our town.

By pacification, I refer specifically to our commitment to a particular domestic neo-colonial social mentality where we dealt with oppression by living with dignity, pride and self-respect. For example, my father experienced intimidatory behaviour from the local police force when they stopped and searched his car for no apparent reason. Faced with this situation, rather than express his anger verbally and possibly violently, his response was the opposite. Calmly and with dignity he answered their questions and showed the appropriate documents. He believed that by not displaying anger he had shown the police that he was above intimidation and had 'won a moral victory'. A passive sociopolitical response to our existential concerns was related to our faith in a God of order, who governed our behaviour. Consequently, we did not engage in social analysis and we certainly did not think about political action. Juxtaposing these family experiences with the praxis of black consciousness occurring simultaneously within the African Caribbean British community in the 1970s and early 1980s reveals a dialectical tension. Black consciousness opposed the political quietism of my parents and our black Pentecostal Church tradition.

British black consciousness of the 1970s and early 1980s as a social and political philosophy was concerned with black empowerment through the vehicles of cultural appreciation, social and historical recovery and collective political action. Cultural appreciation was taking black culture seriously in a context where appreciation and development of one's blackness was to be oppositional both politically and socially. Cultural appreciation was an inherent feature of the Rastafarian movement in the 1970s. Social and historical recovery was the excavation and recontextualization of black traditions of emancipation. These traditions and perspectives were considered to be hidden from the consciousness of black peoples by centuries of European socio-historic hegemonic control. Social and historical recovery in the 1970s and 1980s was manifest in the explosion of black newspapers and publishing houses concerned with developing community identity, and black psychological and social development through strategies of self-love. Political action as a component of black consciousness was concerned with self and group mobilization—that is, the emancipation of the black community from oppressive forces such as structural racism. It involved political education (decolonization) and political mobilization (marches, boycotts, etc). In the 1970s and 1980s the growth of independent black political organizations, political parties and numerous black women's groups alongside black gay and lesbian action movements typified the political action of this period.

However, it would be wrong to assume that the tension between black British pentecostal faith and black consciousness is irreconcilable.

For instance, there are schools of thought that present the conservative behaviourism of the black church movement in Britain as a form of black resistance. In short, the establishment, proliferation and consolidation of a black institution of black empowerment in the midst of white oppression represents a form of black resistance. That is, a conscious attempt to resist oppression. This view is argued by scholars such as Valentina Alexander, Roswith Gerloff and Iain MacRobert.[1] For example, Alexander suggests the black church movement displays the characteristics of passive and active radicalism in response to oppression in Britain:

> The notable feature of *passive radicalism*, is that whilst it is encouraged within a collective context; for example through communal worship or Bible study etc., it is, nonetheless, meant to serve the practical interests of the individual believer. It gives them the strength and incentive to cope with the ideological and material disadvantages which confront them ... *active radicalism* is so called because, whilst emanating from the same source as passive radicalism, it nonetheless attempts a more systematic and, above all, corporate attack against the oppression experience ... to challenge and eventually dismantle the structures of society from which oppression is manifested and maintained ...[2]

Out of passive radicalism emerges a tradition of active radicalism. Alexander continues to say that 'Active radicalism forms explicit political, economic and social allegiances, uniting them into a single active theology of liberation which aims to benefit church members and the wider community.' Significantly, Alexander eventually states that active radicalism has 'not been fully authenticated by the main body of leadership'[3] within most of the black churches. Alexander's 'passive/active' dichotomy draws upon the survival/liberation paradigm of black Christian faith found in the work of the African American religious historian Gayraud Wilmore.[4] Her analysis suggests that the horizons of

---

1.   See V. Alexander, 'Breaks Every Fetter' (PhD Thesis, University of Warwick, 1996); R. Gerloff, *A Plea for British Black Theologies: The Black Church Movement in Britain in its Transatlantic, Cultural and Theological Interaction* (Peter Lang: Frankfurt, 1992); I. MacRobert, 'Black Pentecostalism: Its Function and Theology' (PhD Thesis, University of Birmingham, 1991).
2.   Alexander, 'Breaks Every Fetter', p. 123.
3.   Alexander, 'Breaks Every Fetter', p. 123.
4.   G. Wilmore, 'Survival and Liberation in Black Faith', in S. Maimela and D. Hopkins (eds), *We are One Voice: Black Theology USA and South Africa* (Johannesburg: Skotaville, 1989), pp. 1-33.

black pentecostal faith and black consciousness intersect in a limited manner.

My concern here is with the politico-ideological distance between survival and liberation in black British Christian faith.[5] I contend that, despite the arguments of Alexander, Gerloff and MacRobert, black faith and black consciousness in the black British context remain oppositional approaches in their response to oppression. Consequently, those within the church concerned with black liberation must find a way to reconcile black faith with radical black consciousness. In this article, I would like to reconcile these antithetical responses to black oppression by making use of resources that emerge from the black British communities. This is so that a black British methodology is used to evaluate a black British situation.

My approach is to develop a black Christian cultural theory as a methodology for interrogating the black Christian experience—in short, to make use of aspects of black culture to radicalize black British pentecostal church culture and theology. This is not a new phenomenon in black Christian circles. The combination of black expressive culture and the Christian gospel produced gospel music with its radical and political quality.[6] Moreover, in recent times black Christians have selectively appropriated aspects of black popular culture in order to enhance and enrich black faith. In the mid-1980s, the gospel group, 'The Winans' used the 'soul-gospel-funk' genre in a song, 'Let my people go'. The song was a critique of Apartheid. What I am suggesting is that we correlate radical and rebellious aspects of black culture with the black pentecostal understanding of the gospel in order to devise a rebellious black British Christian faith. I propose to show that there is a distinctive element of resistance imbedded within black popular culture that can be used to reflect critically upon the faith and praxis of the black Church movement in Britain. There are three aspects of this quest. First, I will define some of the contours of black British culture in order to identify its radicality. Second, I will search for a system of resistance within the black church movement. Finally, I will attempt to correlate cultural resistance with black Pentecostal theology through the matrix of Christology.

5.   For a discussion of the difference between survival and liberation see G. Wilmore, *Black Religion and Black Radicalism* (Maryknoll, NY: Orbis Books, 1987).

6.   J. Cone, *The Spirituals and the Blues* (Maryknoll, NY: Orbis Books, 1971).

Black Culture

What do we mean when we talk about black culture? The 'black' component in black culture is difficult to define. Stuart Hall suggests that its 'black' component is located exclusively within the black communities where the experience of struggle and resistance against oppression produces distinctive 'cultural repertoires' from which popular representations emanate. For Hall, this communal-organic understanding of blackness defines and authenticates black popular cultures. Furthermore, he outlines three expressive repertoires within black culture that signify its difference or Otherness. The first concerns style. For black popular culture, style is 'not a mere veneer or coating but the subject itself'. Second, black popular culture is deeply attached to music in contrast to mainstream culture's logo centrism. Third, the body is used as canvas.[7] We are concerned with the configuration of these expressions in Britain. Recent studies suggest that black cultural expression is influenced and reshaped by experience, syncretism, plurality and ideology.

1. *Experience*
First, as mentioned by Hall, black culture is intimately related to experience. Black culture is the creation of the concrete experience of being black. Examples of this inter-relatedness of culture and experience exist in studies on the relationship between Jamaican society and the emergence of reggae culture[8] and the Civil Rights Movement and the development of 'Soul' culture in North America.[9] The organic relationship between experience and culture is taken seriously in black theology, because black theology emerges out of a distinctive black experience. According to James Cone, black culture is the creative response of trying to 'carve-out an existence in dehumanised white society'. For Cone,

    7.   S. Hall, 'What is the "Black" in Black Popular Culture?', in G. Dent (ed.), *Black Popular Culture* (Seattle: Bay Press, 1992), pp. 27-29 (27).
    8.   See S. Hall, 'Religious Ideologies and Social Movements in Jamaica', in R. Bocock and K. Thompson (eds.), *Religion and Ideology* (Manchester: Manchester University Press, 1985), pp. 276-77 (276).
    9.   See P. Gilroy, *There Ain't no Black in the Union Jack* (London: Unwin Hyman, 1987), pp. 153-222.

black culture is mobilized in response to white racism.[10] Similarly, religionist Theo Smith suggests that the experience of black people in the African diaspora produced a culture of conjuration. Conjuration is geared towards total liberation of the black subject.[11]

2. *Syncretism*

Black expressive cultures are not static but syncretistic. Because culture is dialogical it is also both profane and promiscuous. According to black British cultural critic Kobena Mercer, cultural syncretism is one way in which black communities develop ways of 'surviving and thriving in conditions of crisis and transition'.[12] A good example of the black cultural syncretism is found in the lateral exchanges between black diasporan communities, particularly between Jamaica, Britain and the United States—for instance, the emergence of the 'rap' genre in the 1970s and 1980s. The entry of black sound systems from Jamaica with their stylistic lyrical commentary or 'toasting' over reggae music's dubbed soundtracks inspired African Americans to inflect this style and produce their interpretation called 'rap'. Further recontextualization in Britain completed rap's historic journey. Hence, the network that once shipped black slaves and commodities for exploitation in the New World, is now made use of to communicate through a common language.

3. *Diversity*

Third, because black culture is syncretistic, one ensuing corollary is its diversity. Black diversity means we can no longer speak of one distinctive homogeneous black British experience or singular cultural identity. As one critic states, 'Black communities are internally divided: by class, sexuality, gender, age, ethnicity, economics, and political consciousness.'[13] Therefore, attempts to unify black experience through

---

10. J. Cone, *A Black Theology of Liberation* (New York: Orbis Books, 2nd edn, 1987), p. 27.

11. T.H. Smith, *Conjuring Culture: Biblical Formations of Black America* (Oxford: Oxford University Press, 1994), pp. 5-6.

12. K. Mercer, *Welcome to the Jungle: New Positions in Black Cultural Studies* (New York: Routledge, 1994), pp. 4-5.

13. P. Gilroy, *The Black Atlantic: Modernity and Double Consciousness* (London: Verso, 1993).

processes of cultural homogeneity ignores the black diversity and mul-
tiplicity. This issue is raised by the black philosopher Victor Anderson
in *Beyond Ontological Blackness*. Anderson argues that we must move
beyond an ontological blackness that essentializes black experience.
For Anderson, we live in an age of postmodern blackness.[14] Here blackness is continually undergoing change and producing hybrid forms.
Therefore black culture is never singular.

4. *Ideology*

Fourth, culture is ideological. That is to say, cultural repertoires can
be used to construct cultural systems to cope with the strains of life
(Geertz) and also to represent interests (Marx).[15] In black diasporan cultures one ideological form of culture is 'resistance'. For example, Rastafarians grow 'dreadlocks' to symbolize identification with the African
past and identify themselves as representatives of mental decolonization. Dreadlocks signify black resistance to white supremacy. Similarly,
the 'Funki Dread' genre that emerged in the 1980s in London and other
urban areas decontextualized dreadlocks from their Rastafarian origins.
Funki Dread became a recontextualization of Rasta ideology among
Britain's urban black males. Black hair styles are forms of political
resistance.[16] However, cultural ideology can be sinister. This is because
cultural systems may also be used to legitimize oppression. For example, the African American philosopher Cornel West identifies nihilistic
tendencies within contemporary African American culture, particularly
within the emergence of West Coat 'Gangster Rap' in the late 1980s.[17]

   In summary, the discourse of black culture does not occur in a vacuum. Culture is hotly contested and a strategic ideological battleground.
How then does it function as a source for the development of a theology
of liberation for the black Pentecostal Church movement in Britain?
Black cultural resistance unites the black church with resistance in black
culture. By locating the cultural resistance (passive) within the black
pentecostal church we can locate some 'ideological space' for developing a theology of liberation. There are several areas in which the
black Pentecostal Church movement exhibits survival.

   14. V. Anderson, *Beyond Ontological Blackness* (New York: Continuum, 1995),
p. 1.
   15. See Bocock and Thompson (eds.), *Religion and Ideology*, p. 276.
   16. Mercer, *Welcome*, pp. 4-5.
   17. C. West, *Race Matters* (New York: Beacon Press, 1994), pp. 1-20.

First, the gospel music tradition is a form of cultural resistance within black churches. The gospel genre, is multiple in meaning. It is both spiritual and political.

> Press along saint, press along in God's own way (repeat)
> Persecution we must face, trial and crosses in our way
> But the hotter the battle, the sweeter the victory.[18]

When black people sing this song, their singing expresses interest in both eschatological and existential realities. The militaristic emphases of many black church songs are often misunderstood: I would contend that when black people sing about the 'battle' they refer not only to the spiritualized forms of struggle but also to the struggle for authentic existence as black people. When they sing of the 'victory' they refer to the imminent return of Christ and the realization that it is possible to press along and 'make it through the most difficult time' despite the dehumanizing forces unleashed against the black community. When things go wrong in the black community, the church's response for 'someone to raise a song' is an act of defiance!

A second example of cultural resistance within the black church is the persistence of 'black talk'. The black Pentecostal church in Britain has been one of the few social spaces where black people can gather and participate in the expressive orality of black language. As a child growing up in Britain during the 1970s, apart from the home, the church was the only place where black talk was acceptable and fully utilized with all its stylistic devices. Creole maintenance and development within the church is resistance on two levels. *First*, it provides a semantic field where black people can share their language (being) in solidarity without the presence of the white language systems (nonbeing). *Second*, black talk is black creative expression. Take for example black prayer styles where prayer is a rich tapestry of song, exaltation and intercession. Black prayer is extemporaneous, eclectic, corporate and polemical. The orality of this prayer tradition underlines the social-psychological legacy of black talk: creativity affirms self-worth. When black people pray with passion and expression, this symbolizes divine participation in being black. Praying to God in black talk makes Jesus a Creole speaker and ontologically black.

Third, the body plays an important role in the articulation of resistance. Style and 'dressing up' for Sunday has been a central part of

18. Black pentecostal church chorus.

church life. In a context of black dehumanization, through negative representation of black people in white popular culture, black dress styles permit black Christians to express their 'somebody-ness' through a visual aesthetic. It is a counter statement affirming the black body and black style. In *In Search of Our Mother's Garden*, Alice Walker argues that the desire for freedom and resistance to oppression is historically expressed in the production of domestic art. Domestic art is whatever you can get your hands to create. In the traditions of the black church movement, dress has been utilized in a similar form of creative expression and cultural resistance.[19]

If the black church displays the trappings of a culture of resistance, how then can cultural resistance be the basis for developing a theology of liberation? I propose that we make use of black language. Language can be used to express desire, resist domination and maintain dignity. Hence, dialogue between radical language in black experience and the 'God talk' of the black church is one way to develop a 'God talk' of liberation. The form of language I have in mind is found in 'dread' culture.[20] 'Dread' culture emerged with the Rastafarian movement in the Caribbean Diaspora in Britain in the early 1970s. Despite the decline of Rastafarianism as a movement in Britain today, 'dread' culture is still present, reconfigured in black popular culture, and it continues to play an integral role in black cultural resistance. I propose that 'dread' culture provides a way of talking about black liberation. Dread culture is political and social. Politically, dread culture is concerned with rebellion. It is the language of resistance and the aesthetics of mental decolonization. Socially, dread culture is responsible for the symbols of the existential longing for black freedom. Therefore, historically speaking, we may say that dread culture has a long history that predates black British history. We can describe it as the residuum of African traditional religion that captured Africans in the Caribbean used to resist enslavement and incite rebellion. Its essence was utilized in the anti-slavery and anti-colonial movements in the Caribbean islands. However, in postwar Britain it is found in Rastafarianism where being 'dread' is about self-emancipation and self-definition and freedom. 'Dreadness' is therefore the recognition of the quest for freedom within the black soul. Dread culture today is represented in a variety of cultural

19. See J. Cone and G. Wilmore (eds.), *Black Theology: A Documentary History*. I. *1966–1979* (Maryknoll, NY: Orbis Books, 1979).
20. Gilroy, *There Ain't no Black*, pp. 197-209.

expressions under various titles. It is exhibited in the concerns for community togetherness in the music and philosophy of the black group 'Soul II Soul'. It is represented in black organizations working for intellectual decolonization within the black community and articulated by insurgent black British intellectuals. It is expressed within the power and creativity of black urban pirate radio stations that play music, discuss issues, and 'conscientize' their communities. It is found in the unquestionable quest for black liberation in Britain.

Towards a 'dread' Jesus for the Black Pentecostal Church in Britain

What happens when 'dread' culture meets the Christ of the black church? In other words, what happens when we use a cultural system of liberation to interpret who Jesus is for the black British community to-day? The answer lies within a rethinking of what we mean by Chris-tology. Here, Christology is not concerned with European christological formulations as expressed in the Nicene/Chalcedonian articles of faith. Instead, Christology is influenced by what it means for Jesus to be Christ for oppressed people in Britain. A black Christology must sup-port the dual task of resisting systems of white supremacy as well as developing a political and social structure that is capable of challenging the domestic neocolonial situation faced by black British people. The way I suggest that we begin this task is by calling Jesus 'dread'. Nam-ing Jesus 'dread' utilizes the power of 'black talk' in the black church where language is used as a form of empowerment. This is the point of correlation between black radicalism and the traditions of resistance within the black church.

I use 'dread' here as an ontological symbol. Linguistically, I draw on the semiotic tradition of Ferdinand de Saussaure[21] that understands symbolic language as signifiers, conveying a hidden meaning. Theolog-ically, I draw also on the work of Paul Tillich where ontological sym-bols are used to point us to the divine, using limited human language to describe the infinite being we call God. For Tillich, ontological symbols point beyond us and participate in that reality, as well as unlocking truths about both the divine and human beings.[22] Consequently, to talk

21. F. de Saussure, *A Course in General Linguistics* (New York: McGraw Hill, 1966).

22. P. Tillich, *Dynamics of Faith* (New York: Harper Colophon Books, 1957), pp. 42-43.

of a 'dread' Christ points us to an existential black freedom; a place where we are equipped to face and destroy the structures of multi-lateral oppression. 'Dreadness' or being 'dread' is to engage in the struggle for black freedom. Furthermore, to say that Christ is 'dread' is to unveil a Christ of black uplift, black empowerment and black progress.

Similarly, a 'dread' Christ tells black British people that the Jesus of history is with them as they protest, fight, boycott, march and work for black freedom. In short, a 'dread' Christ is a black Christ participating in black lives and black struggles. In the context of Britain, a 'dread' Christ is the focus of our socio-political struggle against lateral and vertical systems of discrimination. If the 'dread' Christ becomes the norm or the hermeneutical paradigm by which we do theology in the black church, we can begin to develop a theology of black British liberation that works for black freedom in Britain.

Conclusion: Beyond the 'dread' Christ

As mentioned above, the remnants of 'dread' culture remain in recontextualized forms in black popular culture in Britain. Even so, we must recognize the limitations of 'dreadness'. First, 'dread' as a concept is time-bound and in some sense, outdated. Therefore, it is necessary to find new ways of talking about Christ and the work of God in this black community that take us beyond 'dread'. For example, we must note the cultural significance in the emergence of postnationalist movements in Britain as well as the contextualization of Afrocentrism in the black British context. In short we must ask whether 'hip-hop' cultures and Afrocentric cultures affiliate or disaffiliate with narratives of resistance found in 'dread' culture. Second, 'dread' as a concept is underpinned by black masculinist existential presuppositions: 'Dread' emerges from the contexts of resistance of black men in the Caribbean and its diaspora in Britain. Therefore 'dread' must be critiqued by black feminist and other voices to challenge the patriarchal hegemony of a 'dread' Christology.

Returning to my original question, Can one be black conscious and a black pentecostal? The answer is a resounding yes. Correlating the revolutionary aspirations of the black community found in dread culture with the theology of the black church is one avenue by which we produce a theology that seriously engages with black consciousness in

Britain. Moreover, while the black pentecostal church displays the trapping of survival (passive resistance), in a time when more than a passive response is possible from black churches, not to develop strategies of liberation (active resistance) is to validate our own oppression! A church that refuses to speak out and represent the black quest for freedom is a church that continues to be a church of the slavemaster.

My experience as a black British person in this country has taught me that being committed to the 'dread' Christ means that I advocate active resistance to oppression as well as praying and expecting God to act, as was the case with my parents. I act first and reflect theologically afterwards. I am committed to confronting racist attacks and other vicious onslaughts made upon the black community. Similarly, rather than 'living a quiet life of dignity' as a means of resistance, I speak out, stand out and rage against injustice in whatever form it is manifest. The 'dread' Christ as a symbol of resistance proclaims that to be an acceptable friend of the black community inevitably means to struggle against black oppression in Britain.

Roswith Gerloff

Robert Beckford's paper is a challenging and passionate piece of work. As a member of the young Black second and third generation of African Caribbean pentecostal Christians in Britain, faced with perpetual racism and social injustice, it begins and ends with an existential question: Is it possible to be a black pentecostal and black conscious? Is it possible as a committed Christian and postmodern theologian to confront, and if necessary, to 'rage' against the onslaught made upon marginalized and deprived communities? I honour and respect this existential concern in the name of both humanity and the Christian faith.

1. *Agreements*

Let me first state on which points I am in agreement with the analysis and argumentation of the paper:

Yes, there has been the danger of spiritualization of the pentecostal message within black majority churches in Britain from the 1950s until recently, or the internalization of hope and confidence, as if we could leave it all to God, he would fight our battles. Years ago, I myself turned passionately around to a member of the Cherubim and Seraphim Church: 'Because in Germany Christians left it all to God, millions of Jews were killed in the Shoah!' This is to say, without undermining specifically black issues, that this risk has been inherent in almost all renewal movements within Christian history: the Reformation (e.g. Luther's stance against the revolting peasants and the Anabaptists), the Society of Friends (Quaker philosophy versus the rather radical christological position of George Fox), the Holiness movement (the individualization of values such as the liberation of slaves and women, or non-hierarchical structures of the church), and even early Pentecostalism (the departure of white pentecostals who began to utilize the revival for their own religious edification instead of community building). This may be a weakness within Christianity itself: Martin Luther King, Jr. versus Stokeley Carmichael or Malcolm X; non-violent resistance versus militant liberation movements; the confessing church versus Dietrich Bonhoeffer—a 'dialectical tension' that at least theoretically has never been solved. What aggravates it in this context is that people most adversely affected by racism and impoverishment have for a long time not mentioned these issues explicitly, certainly not to their white Christian counterparts. Hence there is the danger of pacification, which attempts to overcome predicaments and attacks by personal 'dignity, pride and self-respect'. That is, of course, linked to a very subtle and complex psycho-social development of 'superiority' and 'inferiority', from the history of slavery, the theology of the slave masters, the ideological misdirection by colonial missions, to the imposed Victorian values in the Caribbean aftermath, internalized 'Christian' quietist perceptions and entirely unrealistic expectations in the 'motherland's Christianity' upon arrival in this country. In comparison, Pentecostalism as such, especially when already indigenized in the Caribbean, was in essence a departure from such colonial mentality in the way it eased the transition from a rural peasant to an urban industrial society, widened the world view, and encouraged the search for a new cultural personality enabled to integrate disparate trends in society and 'gain a sense of power and self-esteem'.[1] Pride, dignity and self-respect were also part and parcel of survival tactics in oppressed communities, symbolized by Anansi, the Spiderman or trickster, in Caribbean folklore, and in Highjohn de Conquer in African-American folklore.

> Winning the jackpot with no other stake than a laugh. Fighting a mighty battle without outside-showing force, and winning his war from within. Really winning it in a permanent way, for (John) was winning with the soul of the black man whole and free. So he could use it afterwards. 'For what shall it profit a man if he gains the whole world, and loses his own soul...' He who wins from within is in the 'Be class'. *Be* here when the ruthless men come and *be* here when he is gone.[2]

Dialectical tension between religious quietism and radical consciousness, certainly: There has been a kind of 'heavenmindedness' or 'indulgence in powerlessness' in many black majority churches, more recently

1. Bedanoya, quoted in Gerloff, *Plea*, p. 152.
2. Z.N. Hurston, *The Sanctified Church* (Turtle Island; Berkeley, 1983), pp. 70-71.

heavily criticized by church leaders themselves, in that it prepared Christians for the 'Day of the Lord' but not for tackling the economic and political issues here and now. This is, of course, a legacy of slavery. That African traditional religion has always addressed this world's problems is reflected in the African independent churches. And black theological imagery, as James Cone has ascertained for the Spirituals,[3] has always relied on the Bible as symbolic and functional language in the way Africans understand God, Gospel, Spirit, Worship, Community and Politics now and here.

Thus I cannot regard the positions of Valentina Alexander, Iain McRobert and myself so far from Beckford's own critique and his search for developing a black British theology of liberation. If he is right that 'black faith and black consciousness in the British context remain oppositional approaches to oppression' then, consequently, those within church and theology concerned with the black quest for freedom 'must find a way to reconcile black faith with radical black consciousness'. I myself, for instance, have never claimed that examples of 'conservative behaviourism' in the black church movement in Britain are a 'form of black resistance'. What I have analysed and still would insist upon is that within both the history and the presence of black religion (even in Britain) there is a revolutionary potential that is extremely radical compared with some parts of white Christianity. This has to be freed from white and otherwise fundamentalist superimpositions to find its fulfilment. I can observe this clearly in the ongoing struggle within the Churches of God as two of the largest black Pentecostal denominations in the country.

I therefore agree with Alexander that there is an 'active radicalism' which can emerge from black congregations and form political, economic and social alliances. I disagree with her that this will result in a 'single active theology of liberation'. I rather follow Beckford that black culture and black churches will be always diverse and contextual, that is a concert of 'multi-layered voices', historical, denominational, generational and regional. I also agree with him that any step forward can only be drawn from resources within the black communities themselves. However, I do not observe these in Britain alone but maintain that these are nourished by strong and older cultural and spiritual forces.

3.   Cone, *The Spirituals*.

Altogether, there has been a positive process of black majority churches increasingly tackling social issues and uniting against continuing discrimination and exploitation. However, with Beckford, there has so far been a lack of theological reflection on social actions. This worries me. The best example last year was the sermon preached by one outstanding black pastor and social worker, known for his empathy with the community, on the day of the uprising of Asian youths in Bradford: no word about the events in Manningham, instead a critique of the Church of England tolerating homosexuality.

2. *Disagreements*

The following critique is not intended to undermine Beckford's radical position, but rather to strengthen his arguments and add a historical and biblical dimension. Although I have lived with the black church movement in Britain over the past 25 years, I speak from outside and as a missiologist. He argues from within as a cultural critic and black theologian who seeks a language of liberation for his own people. His analysis of British black culture therefore stands as it is, especially in relation to style, music and body language. My critical suggestions refer to the three headings of the exploration: Black culture, black Pentecostalism and Christology as a vehicle to correlate the two. They claim that historically and biblically speaking, black faith and black consciousness are not necessarily, and have not always been, oppositional approaches to oppression.

1. *Black Culture*
Beckford's analysis would be greatly enhanced by drawing on historical forces, both cultural and spiritual, or in what Gayraud Wilmore, Theo Smith and others claim to be the foundation of black resistance in the New World, namely a unique and distinctive culture emanating from the encounter between African and Euro-Christian sources and traditions. They illustrate the 'black to black theological exchanges' of which Beckford speaks, not only as a modern phenomenon but also of the past centuries. As Leonard Barrett argues, black religion and black resistance have been often *one*, vehicles for both survival and active rebellion.[4] I refer to George Liele as the 'Prophet of Deliverance' and his

---

4.   *The Rastafarians* (Sangsters Bookstore Ltd, Jamaica, in association with Heineman, 1977).

Ethiopian Church in Kingston, his close links with independent Christianity in North America, his impact on white baptists and the abolitionists, the Jamaica Revival and later outright political revolt. Sam Sharpe, who started a non-violent resistance which ended in a violent slave-rebellion, Paul Bogle and William Gordon who opposed the Jamaican Governor, were all people nourished by the fervent spirit of Baptist prayer-meetings, and were all executed. I also refer to the various African Caribbean religions (long before Rastafari) such as the Shouters, Spiritual Baptists and others, whose faith and defiant music were the vehicles of surviving in dignity and freedom from the colonial powers. I refer to pan-Africanists such as Martin Delaney or Edward Wilmot Blyden who developed a black theology of 'missionary emigrationism'[5] and became, together with hundreds of black preachers, the forerunners of a pan-African philosophy of people like Marcus Garvey. This means that there was that constant 'cultural fusion' and 'recontextualization' of new identities in diverse circumstances.

Henry Mitchell speaks of 'immemorial existential situations' and a 'multi-channel awareness' underlying this experience and informing black music from the spirituals and the blues to gospel and reggae and rap. I have therefore encouraged a number of my students to explore the role of music in the liberation of black people.

2. *Black Pentecostalism*

It appears as if Beckford, apart from gospel music, does not draw much upon the history of early Pentecostalism as a contribution of the black oppressed to the church worldwide, an expression of black leadership and a community of defiance against the dominant, monocultural, legalistic and dogmatic nature of established Christianity. Nor does he investigate the clashes and splits between black and white elements within different Pentecostal churches. However, it was precisely at Azusa Street that 'black talk' arose publicly, in the midst of vehement opposition, that the 'expressive orality of black language' gave way to creative forms in worship and mission and that people began to share their struggles collectively—from speechlessness and for healing. Energetic black prayer became an inspiring force and body language such as dancing, rolling, dramatizing was allowed 'back' into church. That Pentecostal history did not result in active political resistance is due to many

    5.   Gayraud S. Wilmore, *Black Religion and Black Radicalism* (Maryknoll, NY: Orbis Books, 1983).

reasons, to misconceptions of its white adherents, yes to some 'heaven-mindedness' of black churches and to their overall socio-economic powerlessness. However, William J. Seymour created a racial climate that would outdo all discrimination. Figures such as Charles H. Mason, Thomas Garfield Haywood or Robert C. Lawson would actively carry the burden of their communities, and Smallwood Williams would join the Civil Rights movement. None of these have ever been the focus of black intellectual research. However, there are innumerable practical examples such as Arthur Brazier's Woodlawn organization, the African indigenous role in the struggle against colonialism, and even projects in our very midst.

What, perhaps, is more, is that early Pentecostalism drew on African traditional religion with its 'we' feeling, a spirituality of belonging, the bringing of self into worship, the enrichment of community life, and the discovery of God's actions in the socio-economic milieus of oppressed people.

3. Christology
This of course is at the core of Beckford's paper and it is a very authentic approach to find a black theological language of resistance and decolonization. I agree that black Pentecostalism has to speak in a language to be understood by the 'dread culture' of black youths. However, as it stands, I have difficulties in three directions. One is the total lack of biblical references both from the Hebrew Bible and the New Testament, for example concentrating on the Messiah as 'Suffering Servant', the Liberator of the Oppressed (Mt. 11) and the Magnificat. This is what Womanist theology has achieved and why it seems to be listened to by both black male theologians and white feminist theologians. In the pentecostal context, to forget about the Scriptural foundations can only be counterproductive and does not give due credit to the inspirational biblical language for freedom from enslaving human forces.

The other problem lies, in agreement with Beckford's own claim of 'multi-layered voices' in the black communities, in the use of one particular cultural concept. As far as I see, quite apart from denominational and generational conflicts, there is also a continuous debate among black youths about how to formulate their identity, Black Atlantic, Afrocentrist or what? Beckford says himself that the term is 'time-bound' and, with the decline of Rastafari in favour of the Nation of Islam, in some sense 'outdated'. Again, it appears as if Womanists have done better. They too have applied a term, 'womanish', drawn from the black experience—someone who dares to speak and to do what is improper; yet, they have succeeded in turning it into a concept understood by many. Black novelists such as Alice Walker and others may have supported this development. 'Dread', on the other hand, is not only not understood or rejected by the older black generation, but also by Africans and many young pentecostals. What would be necessary is to develop a Christology that is nourished by African perspectives in general, that is outdoing the Euro-Western 'ruling mentality' in favour of a humanity that fosters sharing and mutuality.

This is the third direction: To speak of Christ today in a world of global capitalism that constantly violates worth and dignity of individuals and communities, means, yes, to speak of Christ as the emancipator or liberator of the excluded and oppressed. Yet it also means, as in early Pentecostalism, to speak of him as the one who breaks down all our barriers. This precisely was one aspect of the 'new issue' controversy between the Assemblies of God and what later emerged as 'Apostolic' or Oneness Pentecostalism, not so much the debate about the baptismal formula, but about who Jesus is: the traditional Christ of 'divide and rule'—or the Jesus in whose power we can overcome destruction. Or with the words of Lawson of Harlem, to have a 'Jim Crow Pentecostal Church' is to behold a 'spiritual monstrosity'. I therefore do not and can not apply the word 'ontological' to blackness nor to any christological concept, for example Cone's insistence on the ontological blackness of Jesus. Again, I have encouraged a number of my students to look into Cone's and similar concepts in comparison with black Pentecostals' preaching and the theology of Martin Luther King, Jr.

What I am opting for are not answers but the dialogue between different christologies including 'dread', in which each and everyone can uplift Christ in their own language in correlation with others. This would free all of us from a slave master's mentality.

PENTECOSTALS IN THE AFRICAN DIASPORA

Roswith Gerloff

Two Clarifications

'Two worldwide Christian movements were founded by non-Europeans, Walter Hollenweger affirms, 'one is the global Pentecostal Movement, the other is Christianity'.[1] To this statement I add those non-white or rather, black and African derived movements which are in content and structure closer to the New Testament and patterns of thought in the Bible as a whole than many Western interpretations of doing theology after Christopher Columbus. On one hand, they arose from the spiritual, cultural and social contexts of people from the Third World; on the other hand, they respond to global issues vital for the future of human-kind. They offer experience instead of dogmas, songs of love instead of rhetoric, signals of friendship instead of complicated books. As people with a painful past, a present often without prospects, and a sense of hope in resurrection against all odds, they offer us a theology from grassroots communities, contextual and diverse. They demonstrate a faith in God and the goodness of human existence which helped them to survive the Middle Passage, the forcible removal from their African homelands, continuous oppression and exploitation, and further migra-tion and perpetuated racism—faith of an existential character, not borrowed from the slave masters. Henry Mitchell, the African Ameri-can theologian, therefore speaks of a 'faith-genius, right through slav-ery, to believe in the providence and justice of God', by which 'no amount of absurdity and injustice seemed capable thereafter of discour-aging this profound affirmation of the goodness of life'.[2] And Leonard

---

1. W.J. Hollenweger, *Pentecostalism: Origins and Developments Worldwide* (Peabody, MA: Hendrickson, 1997), p. 18.
2. H.H. Mitchell, *The Recovery of Preaching* (London: Hodder & Stoughton, 1977), p. 17.

Lovett of the Church of God in Christ wrote more than 20 years ago that 'categorically stated, Pentecostalism emerged from the brokenness of black human existence' and thus grew into a living witness of the liberating work of the Holy Spirit in the twentieth century.[3]

African and African Caribbean churches in Britain from the 1950s and 1960s, with all their limitations, struggles, splits, isolation and failures to address social politics, still bear witness to such a history of solidarity in faith, prayer and action. In discipleship to Christ as liberator, they refused to add to further segregation, bitterness and hatred and as such made an essential contribution to the wellbeing of British society. Although, as Robert Beckford rightly says, in constant danger of 'pacification' in the midst of struggle and resistance against oppression, they have revitalized something of the Spirit's ingenuity in early Pentecostalism. This article pays tribute to the early pentecostal message, or the boundary-breaking and unifying power between diverse cultural and ethnic groups in the Azusa Street Revival, as well as to its firm grounding in African roots or retentions. It testifies to the lived-out theology of a similar spirit still existent in black majority churches today. Furthermore, it allows us to include not only African Caribbean and those pentecostal bodies linked to white North American headquarters but also the various 'pentecostal-type' African initiated churches now present in Britain and Europe. This is the first clarification.

The second one refers to the term 'Diaspora', which has been recently challenged by European scholars on linguistic and historical grounds.[4] With a view to its origins in the Jewish community, and to the obvious difference between the history of slavery in the Americas and the history of colonialism and neo-colonialism and their varied migration patterns from Africa to other parts of the world, they query it as a viable description to enhance the diversity and contextuality of such different experiences. However, the term 'African Diaspora' was coined by African American scholars such as Gayraud S. Wilmore, Albert Rabo-

3.   L. Lovett, 'Perspectives on Black Pentecostalism' (unpublished MS, 1973), p. 8.

4.   'Religious Communities in the Diaspora', International Conference at the Theological Faculty in Leiden, Netherlands, December 1995; G. ter Haar, *Chosen People: The Concept of Diaspora in the Modern World*, Seventh Annual BASR Lecture, *British Association for the Study of Religions* 16 (1996), pp. 2-5; M. Spindler, 'The Impossible Quest for a General Theory of the Diaspora', *Exchange* 27. 1 (1998), pp. 8-10.

teau and others to describe the global scattering of Africans outside the
continent of Africa as the historical consequence of the transatlantic
slave trade, of the mutual encounter of black and white communities
under such adverse conditions, and of subsequent perpetuated racism
within the northern hemisphere. Theologically, it came to describe the
consistent patterns of African 'survivals' or retentions, even when fam-
ily-bonds, language and religion were ruthlessly broken up. This continuum refers to belief in a spiritual reality, narrativity of theology,
empowerment by the spirit, music and rhythms, dreams and visions, or
healing in belonging which were not destroyed but rather began to
influence the 'host-societies'. Melville Herskovits, in his eager search
for the unbroken cultural forces in music and religion, mapped out the
scales of their intensity from the Latin American continent to the
Caribbean islands, the Sea Islands and Southern parts of the United
States, and the 'free Negroes' of the Northern American regions.[5] What
once was mainly concentrated in the Americas has now become alive in
Europe. Descendants of African and African Caribbean immigrants into
Britain may have been geographically and historically the farthest ex-
tension on these scales, but the intensity of their religious experience,
even via New York, Kingston or Georgetown, is still informed and supplied by African culture and religion, even more so among the newly
arrived genuinely African indigenous churches.

As much as there are apparently great differences liturgically, theologically and culturally between African and African Caribbean Christian communities, there is also much common ground which has turned
Britain into a unique meeting-point between very diverse traditions.[6]
The recovery of African elements in the Azusa Street Revival under the
leadership of the black Holiness pastor William J. Seymour in 1906,
and its undeniable impact on both West African independent churches
from the 1920s and the black church movement in Britain from the
1950s, proves my point. Ghanaian indigenous groups in London such as
the Musama Disco Christo Church call themselves unashamedly 'pentecostal' and ask for a redefinition of Pentecostalism in view of the

5. M.J. Herskovits, *The Myth of the Negro Past* (Boston: Beacon Press, 1944).
6. R. Gerloff, *A Plea for British Black Theologies: The Black Church Move-
ment in Britain in its Transatlantic Cultural and Theological Interaction* (2 vols.;
Frankfurt a.M.: Peter Lang, 1992); cf. World Council of Churches, *Report on the
Consultation with African and African Caribbean Church Leaders in Britain 1995*
(R. Gerloff and H. Van Beek, eds.; Geneva: WCC, 1996).

freedom of language and culture at Pentecost, and therefore of a shared African Biblical heritage.[7] Research into the relationship between early integrated and black Pentecostalism on the one hand and the African initiated churches on the other still remains to be undertaken, as does an enquiry into the relationship of both to the white Pentecostal/Charismatic movements including North American headquarters with black overseas churches and also to the more recent development of 'prosperity' religion.[8] My most recent visit to Latin American pentecostal and charismatic congregations in Buenos Aires and Mexico has even further confirmed how urgent and complex such investigations would be. They will become increasingly important for historical, missiological, theological and economic-political reasons. Historically, interaction between diverse African expressions in the transatlantic cycle between America (including Latin America), the Caribbean, Europe and Africa is significant as a counter-experience to the European monocultural shape of Christianity. This means that their value lies precisely in their diversity and contextuality. Regarding mission, African indigenous Christianity, African American and Caribbean Pentecostalism, and the American-based Charismatic Renewal increasingly and continuously now criss-cross each other across the Atlantic Ocean, and even British blacks have long established missions in Africa, the Caribbean and North America. Theologically, the impact of a religious tradition grown from both African traditional religion and the common experience of oppression, poverty and exploitation in Africa, the Americas and Europe, is of great relevance for the reformulation of the Christian message and its biblical roots. Politically and economically, as blacks in Europe form such a small minority, they need mutual exchange for the common good of their people.

I therefore regard the term 'African Diaspora' as a powerful instrument for redefining black international identity. Biblically and historically, it points to the Diaspora experience of the Israelites with whom blacks in the 'New World' began to identify, or to the history of people with whom God wandered through light and darkness, cloud upon the tent by day and pillar of fire at night (Num. 9.15-23; Exod. 40.34-38). Missiologically, it evokes hope and courage, as the wilderness begins

7.   J. Jehu-Appiah, WCC Consultation , pp. 32, 63.
8.   R.I.J. Hackett, 'New Christian Identities in Africa: The Pentecostal/Charismatic Reenvisioning and Reordering of the World', *Passages: North Western University African Studies Bulletin* (1995), pp. 199-214.

to make sense; migration turns into mission; and the land of broken promises becomes, by the grace of God, the 'promised land', if only by a deepened understanding and testimony to her inhabitants. Theologically, it gives meaning to a distorted and painful history of voluntary as well as enforced exile, so relevant in a century of the uprooted, displaced and refugees: powerlessness then turns into empowerment, meaninglessness into a holistic human message. Socio-politically, it puts people on a common ground and supports them to reclaim their rightful place and spiritual-cultural identity. This is the second clarification.

Historical Discoveries and Theological Insights

Research in the churches of the African Diaspora, and generally in oral cultures within Christianity, is relatively new. Research in Black Pentecostalism, which forms the greater part of black majority churches in Britain, began only 25 years ago. Until then, white historians of the pentecostal and charismatic movements falsified the issue by evaluating Pentecostalism from their limited literary and racist perspectives.[9] Anthropologists and sociologists of religion considered Pentecostalism to be a North American cultural import and imposition on indigenous people, in line with the colonial type of mission which for centuries used places like the Caribbean islands as 'happy hunting-grounds' for proselytization and westernization—an interpretation, of course, by no means untrue for a number of white North American headquarters.[10] Only the Birmingham school under Walter Hollenweger introduced quite different historical and theological insights.[11] The historical ignorance and cultural arrogance of western Christians rendered churches which are part and parcel of world Christianity as 'sects' and 'cults', as I experienced myself in Jamaica.[12] Misinterpretations still circulate—such as

9. Compare R.M. Anderson, *Vision of the Disinherited* (Oxford: Oxford University Press, 1979).

10. W. Watty, *From Shore to Shore: Soundings in Caribbean Theology* (Kingston, Jamaica: UTC, 1981), pp. 73-74; Gerloff, *Plea*, pp. 156-58, 194-96.

11. D.J. Nelson, 'For Such a Time as This: The Story of Bishop W.J. Seymour and the Azusa Street Revival' (PhD thesis, University of Birmingham, 1981); I. MacRobert, *The Black Roots and White Racism of Early Pentecostalism in the USA* (New York: Macmillan, 1988); K.D. Gill, *Towards a Contextualised Theology of the Third World* (Frankfurt: Peter Lang, 1994).

12. Gerloff, *Plea*, pp. 139-59.

the 'otherworldliness' or the preponderance of 'fundamentalism' in all black majority churches—which views have little or no foundation in the faith and social life of groups which stem from a history of exploitation and suffering. African American scholars such as C. Eric Lincoln have therefore spoken of 'Black oblivion'—the invisibility of communities of African heritage in white-dominated societies and the ensuing failure of white theology to include black people in its 'universe of discourse' and its 'area of meaningful concern'.[13]

The rise of Pentecostalism however, in particular in the racial climate of the United States at the turn of the century, cannot be truly interpreted without such insights, or without attending to the reality of oppression and suffering, more concretely to the history of colonialism by which millions of Africans became enslaved or dehumanized in the name of the Christian nations. In obliterating this, history becomes perverted, as we read from the 'apartheid' development within North American and South African Pentecostalism.[14] Or the message becomes spiritualized by losing its connection with essential cultural and sociopolitical roots—the very soil from which it grew, namely the longing of people for greater love, mutuality and justice in a humane society.[15]

In an essay published by the European Pentecostal Theological Association, I have briefly summarized in six statements the historical discoveries and theological insights by research undertaken in the past 20 years. I will repeat them here and then throw light on them in the specific context of Pentecostalism in the African Diaspora in Britain and Europe. A more detailed description and illustration relating to Pentecostal history can be gathered from the full paper.[16]

1. The early pentecostal movement was the contribution of the African scene to the church universal, or the spiritual and social-political departure of black Christians from physical and cultural bondage.

2. Early Pentecostalism—and subsequently also the charismatic movement—owe their origin, proliferation and growth to an integrated Christian fellowship under black inspiration and leadership, or to quite

13. C.E. Lincoln, *The Black Church Since Frazier* (New York: Schocken Books, 1974), p. 145.

14. Compare, *A Relevant Pentecostal Witness* (no author given) (Durban: Relevant Pentecostal Witness, 1988).

15. See Nelson, 'For Such a Time', pp. 202-205.

16. *EPTA Bulletin* 14 (1995), pp. 85-100.

different communication structures from those of white established churches.

3. Pentecostalism shares with all Christians the biblical foundation of faith in the gospel of Jesus Christ. However, it presents in its original lived-out pneumatology as well as in its modern black and Third World expressions, a different concept of the Holy Spirit or the power of God in the life of the believers than that of traditional theologies.

4. Black Pentecostalism—largely from ignorance rather than lack of access to different resources—has been taken captive by fundamentalist tendencies. However, it is in a slow but persistent process of shaking off this disastrous white rational legacy.

5. Black and white pentecostals use the same biblical symbolic language and employ similar ecstatic or enthusiastic expressions, yet they represent quite different realities under such stories, paradigms and manifestations. This we can clearly read from a comparative analysis of sermons, liturgies, community life styles and diverse, sometimes contradictory attitudes to social and ecumenical issues.

6. The churches of the African Diaspora have been one of the main forerunners of the modern pentecostal/charismatic movement on the one hand, and of pop culture on the other. The religion and music of Africans in the 'New World' were the two areas that the slave master could not control nor exploit. They formed the 'heart' of the black church as the vibrations of spiritual, cultural and socio-political survival. Yet, in the twentieth century, the white charismatic movement and the mass media run the risk of further exploitation by integrating these elements into their respective systems. This raises the delicate question whether or not there is still a subtle supremacy at work, or rather the perpetual co-option of the black religious experience into western Christian and secular structures.

Contribution to the World Church

'Pentecostalism developed on the black scene and became a contribution of the ghetto to the Christian nation at large', contends the late James Tinney, then a pentecostal scholar at Howard University.[17] Meanwhile this had been ascertained in much of the scholarly work done under the supervision of Walter Hollenweger. In my own words, the

17. J.S. Tinney, 'Black Origins of the Pentecostal Movement', *Christianity Today* 16 (1971), pp. 4-6.

Pentecostal movement signifies how an African oral culture became the pioneer of a worldwide movement not in spite of but because of its intermediary role between African and European theologies and cultures. Black Pentecostalism, in particular, as the Christian community grown from the 'underside' of human life, forms today one of the most significant integral parts of the ecumenical dialogue, unless the ecumenical movement wants to be further dominated by the North Atlantic family of churches. This is behind the decision taken by the Canberra Assembly of the World Council of Churches in 1991 to promote efforts 'to establish and strengthen relationships with evangelical, pentecostal and independent churches' worldwide, highlighting the fact that more than half of the non-Roman and non-Orthodox churches do not belong to the world organization.[18] With Douglas Nelson in his dissertation on William J. Seymour, the pentecostal movement emerged 'for such a time as this', meaning at the start of a century which increasingly showed the ugly face of racism and ethnocentrism and is in need of a 'new reformation'.[19]

Such insights are naturally based on much wider research findings than those in Pentecostalism alone. One is the discovery in black culture and black religion that the African heritage had never been lost in the lives of the slaves, when languages, family bonds and ethnic belongings were unscrupulously destroyed.[20] Interwoven with biblical imagery, it contributed to the physical and spiritual survival of a people. This is immensely relevant for an understanding of the 'inculturation' of a religion, and it is also important for the beginning of a dialogue between African Caribbean and African indigenous churches in Europe[21] in view of their common legacy, oral modes of communication, belief in spiritual power and a ministry to the whole person. Another insight is the interplay between early Pentecostalism and the Holiness movement, still reflected in the black majority churches in Britain—not only in terms of the doctrine of Christian perfection, but

18. See Reports on WCC Consultations: Lima, Peru 1994; Leeds, England 1995; Ogere, Nigeria 1996; Limuvu, Kenya 1997.

19. Nelson, 'For Such a Time'; H.P. Van Dusen, 'Caribbean Holiday', *Christian Century* (1955), pp. 946-48.

20. W.E.B. Dubois, *The Souls of Black Folk* (London: Constable, 2nd edn, 1969 [1905]); Z.N. Hurston, *The Sanctified Church* (Berkeley: Turtle Island, 1983); Herskovits, *Myth*.

21. Jehu-Appiah, WCC Consultation, pp. 61-65.

also in terms of the social and communal content of 'Holiness' and of the influence blacks had on whites in the camp-meetings of the Great Revival of the nineteenth century. This synthesis between black and white elements, or a first kind of a lived-out and acted-out intercultural articulation of the Christian faith, was also reflected in the Jamaica Revival of 1861–62, when Christian and African elements entered a fruitful symbiosis or a fresh articulation of reality, by some dismissed as 'syncretistic', by others greeted as genuine indigenized Christianity with a long-lasting impact on the Caribbean islands, including Native and Spiritual Baptists, Revivalists, Zionists and Pentecostals.[22] A third insight is the insistence that the religion of the slaves and the religion of the slave masters were never identical, even when both referred to the same Bible.[23] Africans in the 'New World' identified with the Israelites under Egyptian bondage and with the apostles after Christ's crucifixion: Exodus and Resurrection as the non-violent victories over evil and enemies, and Pentecost as the renewed power of communication, became the theological imagery for a people with whom God wandered through the desert and the 'valley of death' (Ezek. 37). Albert Raboteau speaks of the 'invisible institution',[24] Gayraud Wilmore of an 'aggressive thrust of folk religion'.[25] This is significant in view of the younger black generation, as Louis Chase expressed it in the 1970s: Young African Caribbeans in England would become aware of the 'unbroken journey toward the Kingdom of God' , and therefore speak with pride and self-respect of their ancestors who made it through a brutal history.[26]

Remembering such historical connections relates to most recent developments. The WCC Consultation with African and African Caribbean Church leaders in Britain (Leeds 1995) reflected on the need for British Black Theologies, including a Black Pentecostal theology.

22. F.J. Osborne and G. Johnston, *Coastlands and Islands* (Kingston, Jamaica: UTC, 1972); G.E. Simpson, *Black Religions in the New World* (New York: Columbia University Press, 1978).

23. MacRobert, *Black Roots*, pp. 90-93.

24. A.J. Raboteau, *Slave Religion: The 'Invisible Institution' in the Antebellum South* (Oxford: Oxford University Press, 1978), pp. 190, 320-21.

25. G.S. Wilmore, 'The Black Religious Experience in a Cross-Cultural Perspective' (unpublished; Northampton: Overstone College, 1983).

26. *Der Bischof tanzt vor dem Altar* (West German Broadcasting Corporation, 1980).

Black Theologies, one workshop stated, reflect and express black peoples' experience with a God who affirms the identity of all and seeks justice for all. In Britain they are therefore theologies of the inner cities or 'urban ghettos'. They have to deal with the lives of black youths, their language, their frustration and with the question of how to 'tell one's own story' as the experience of struggles in a variety of contexts: generational, denominational and regional. This includes the need for affirming the dignity of each and every individual in the community, for recovering and reinterpreting the Bible in a post-modern context and for asserting God as real in African lives. It involves space for both redefining and presenting theologies from an African perspective, that is, the liberation of the pentecostal/charismatic message from white exclusivist interpretations.

Movement Organization

The origin, proliferation and growth of Pentecostalism in North America and worldwide, including the black majority churches in Britain, are due to an integrated fellowship under black leadership, and to 'movement organization',[27] that is, entirely different organizational and communication structures from those of the centralized, bureaucratic western denominations. The distinctive characteristics according to Gerlach and Hine are outlined in my book[28] as follows:

- A reticulate (or polycephalous) organization, linked together by a variety of personal, structural and ideological ties, which is not linear but can be likened to a cellular organism and, such as life itself, cannot be suppressed.
- A mission that travels along pre-existing daily social relationships such as family, friendship, village or island community, trade or work companionship, and shared migration, thus carrying its message like reliable and comforting luggage.

27. L.P. Gerlach and V.H. Hine, *People, Power, Change: Movements of Social Transformation* (Indianapolis: Bobbs-Merrill, 1970), p. 78.
28. L.P. Gerlach and V.H. Hine, 'Five Factors Crucial to the Growth and Spread of a Modern Religious Movement', *Journal for the Scientific Study of Religion* 7 (1968), pp. 23-40 ; Gerlach and Hine, *People, Power*, p. 78; Gerloff, *Plea*, pp. 178-80.

- The personal commitment of leaders, 'witnesses' and members generally: charismatic leadership which identifies with the needs of people, demonstrates spiritual maturity and personal integrity, and lets the charisma of each individual 'flow freely through the ranks' of the movement.[29]
- A change-orientated and action-motivating message which is not abstract but can be easily communicated, verbally and non-verbally through words, music, dance and body-language.
- Opposition from the established order, that is, resistance against inhuman forces, in favour of the worth of grassroots communities, and the relevance and human power of each individual.

All these elements can be verified over and over again in Caribbean, African and British Black Pentecostalism.

Early black pentecostal leaders such as William J. Seymour, Charles H. Mason, Garfield T. Haywood and others, stood for more 'Holiness', meaning wholeness of the person and of the community, and a gospel of love for other human beings. Regarding their descent and lifestyle, they embodied the 'protest against the highbrow tendency in Negro Protestant congregations',[30] that is, the alienation of black intellectuals from the impoverished masses. In a climate of outright racial discrimination and murder, they preached racial redemption in the name of Jesus Christ.[31] They were not heroes or personal gurus but leaders of oppressed communities, and they perceived themselves as mediators in a process of interracial, intercultural, interlinguistic and intercreedal reconciliation. They followed, in discipleship to Christ, an outsider-centred concept of mission.[32] Seymour, according to Nelson, 'saw the church as a new body of equals both interracial and glossolalic' to whom power was granted to build a unified fellowship, thus counteracting the distortion of the gospel in racially divided churches.[33]

This is not the place to go deeper into early pentecostal history with both its intercultural 'success' and its betrayal of the Spirit in a segregated history. We only refer to it in the light of still existing tensions.

29. Gerlach and Hine, 'Five Factors', p. 32.
30. Hurston on Black American preachers, in Gerloff, *Plea*, p. 123.
31. Gerloff, *Plea*, pp. 121-24.
32. K. Koyama, 'New World: New Creation: Mission in Power and Faith', *Mission Studies* 10 (1993), pp. 74-75.
33. Nelson, 'For Such a Time', p. 203.

Any interactions between cultures, more so between dominant and subordinate ethnic groups, is a power struggle. As Tinney rightly pointed out, different interpretations and clashes between conflicting interests are inevitable. Azusa was an attempt to overcome these by the power of God's Spirit. It brought into existence a kind of 'marriage' between two cultural traditions, one African (modified under slavery), the other Euro-American; one oral and multifaceted, the other literary and more or less one-dimensional: 'What now seems clear is that black participants at Azusa demonstrated a very different set of values and beliefs and needs than did the white participants'.[34] As I have elsewhere pointed out:

> Black Pentecostals such as Seymour or Haywood represented a Black religious position which was extremely radical compared with White Christian standards and which bore in itself a revolutionary potential. Their religious expressions were community-orientated and, in fact, an outright protest against the prevailing social order, including the Black middle class which had adapted itself, both doctrinally and liturgically, to White American main-line Protestantism ... In a nutshell, Black Pentecostals attempted to change the world—if only in their alternative communities of faith—by the power promised to them in the New Testament. White Pentecostals tended to reject the world and confine the spiritual power to a merely religious area ... For Blacks, the Church—and indeed the community—had the loose network of assemblies with a charismatic leadership, an itinerant ministry, an unsophisticated message, and the quite natural opposition to the status quo; for Whites, the Church—and indeed Pentecostalism—had slowly but persistently to adapt to society as it stood, with its linear understanding of authority, its pecking order, its rationalistic language, and its bureaucratic form of organization.[35]

Some of this still applies today, not only with regard to the relationship between black and white pentecostal denominations (and the threat the latter felt when black congregations began to mushroom in England), but also to those between black and white churches in general—made even more intricate by the complex nature of pentecostal history, varied migration patterns, black pentecostal bodies linked to white American headquarters, white pentecostals influenced by blacks and still existing interracial campaigns and congregations. My many years'

---

34. J.S. Tinney, 'The Significance of Race in the Rise and Development of the Apostolic Pentecostal Movement' (unpublished paper, Harvard, Boston: Symposium on Oneness Pentecostalism, 1984), pp. 2-3.

35. Gerloff, *Plea*, pp. 100-104.

long examination of tensions of such kind in North America, the Caribbean and Britain—clashes, splits and hopeful intercultural ventures—has sharpened my eyes for similar mechanisms, power struggles and victories in our own society, including the British established churches and the Centre for Black and White Christian Partnership.

The WCC Consultation in 1995, in a second workshop on mutual sharing and resourcing, said that true interaction must be built on a mutual spiritual basis. Black churches in Britain came into being out of necessity, to serve in the first instance their own cultural and spiritual constituencies. Nevertheless, they themselves often displayed features bound up with the legacy of adaptation and a colonial mission and did not engage in genuine partnership. What then are the best means and structures for relating to the English churches, pentecostal/charismatic and otherwise? How can there be solidarity in tackling poverty, racism and injustice? In obedience to the Spirit of Pentecost, a culture of increased sharing on all levels is not a matter of purely technical management. It must have a spiritual foundation. African and African Caribbean congregations have much to offer: a spirituality of belonging, so relevant in a fragmented Europe; the bringing of self into worship; the enrichment of community life; theologizing at the grassroots, full of vibrancy and meaning of life, of discovering God's actions not just in remote sacred or academic spheres but in very down-to-earth places; a healing ministry which seeks salvation for the whole person; and pastoral care identical with social action and evangelism. I consider the test case for such mutual relationships whether or not white Christians learn to accept Black inspiration and leadership, something already proven difficult in Azusa Street.

An Energetic Concept of the Holy Spirit

The Pentecostal movement shares with all Christians the biblical foundation of faith in the gospel of Jesus Christ. Yet it represents in its beginnings—as well as in many modern Third World developments and expressions—a quite different concept of the Holy Spirit than that of traditional theologies.[36] The rebellion which white members of the Azusa Mission staged against what Charles Parham described as the 'unintelligent, crude negroism of the Southland'[37] grew not only from

36. Gerloff, *Plea*, pp. 264-71.
37. Quoted in Anderson, *Vision*, p. 190.

cultural, racial and social dissatisfaction but more deeply from different
pneumatological understandings. Again and again, white Christians distance themselves from the enthusiastic expressions of black and integrated worship and attempt to deprive the Spirit experience of both its
bodily and communal manifestations. Conversely, almost all black independent churches today, even with Methodist, Baptist, Adventist or
Anglo-Catholic leanings, turn charismatic. Even in Ethiopia, charismatic renewal is welcomed 'everywhere in all the Christian communities, the Ethiopian Orthodox Church included'.[38] The Spirit of God in
these lived-out, not necessarily verbally defined theologies is first and
foremost a living power, or—in quite biblical as well as African
expression—'power-in-participation', power of continued interdepen-
dence of all creation; ' travelling power' from generation to generation,
continent to continent; embodied in Jesus of Nazareth and at work not
only in the church but in the world. With the words of a woman evangelist in Birmingham in the early years of black pentecostals there:
'There has been always this demonstration of the divine power or energy, and this life-giving force has travelled down through the ages
when Moses, Elisha, Peter and Paul, and many more prophets and apostles demonstrated the healing wonders God has given us'.[39]

In contrast, white charismatics in building religious communities are
often in danger of instrumentalizing gifts by which they are revived, for
the purpose of insider-centred religious edification and personal piety,
in violation of Paul's teaching about the charismata as diversely acti-
vated gifts for the good of the whole community (1 Cor. 12). With Fred
Foster, in his history of Oneness Pentecostalism:

> Azusa Street is commonly looked upon as the stroke God used to spread
> the influence of the baptism of the Holy Ghost experience to much of the
> United States and several countries of the world. Yet, after some time,
> Seymour was replaced by men of more natural ability, and the races no
> longer mixed in services, but the flame was spreading far and wide(!).[40]

According to my findings, only the Third World and black Oneness
Apostolic Pentecostals have so far developed a new oral pentecostal
pneumatology,[41] largely overlooked in the hot controversies about the

---

38. 'Charismatic Renewal', in *Crossings* (St Louis, MI, 1995).
39. International City Mission, quoted in Gerloff, *Plea*, p. 15.
40. F.J. Foster, *Think it not Strange: A History of the Oneness Movement* (St
Louis, MI: Pentecostal Publishing House, 1965), p. 36.
41. Gerloff, *Plea*, pp. 251-71.

'New Issue' and ensuing enmities within the movement. Whereas pentecostal denominations like the Assemblies of God or the Churches of God borrowed their theological language, without further reflection, from the Trinitarian tradition of historic Christianity, black Apostolic pneumatology is rooted, quite true to the New Testament, in a Spirit-Christology which perhaps in a post-Hellenistic era, offers better categories for the Christian mission than the traditional Logos-Christology. Jesus becomes the 'Great Emancipator from within',[42] or with James Cone, the 'Deliverer of humanity'[43]—the embodiment of unsentimental love within ourselves, which appears to be constitutive for all black theologies from slave religion to William Seymour, Martin Luther King or the African indigenous churches.[44] The Holy Spirit then is experienced and articulated:

> not just as the third person of the trinity (where it can then conveniently be tamed and marginalized through categories of theology, ecclesiology, and above all categories of so-called decency) ... [but] as a cosmological reality for life and liturgy, for politics and prayer, for healing and wholeness, for unity in diversity.[45]

Although at face value the teachings of Oneness and Trinitarian black pentecostals in the Caribbean and Britain appear to be different, in my observation there is more affinity than generally admitted. The controversy is of North American provenance. In black pentecostal worship of all kinds, it is Jesus or Jesus' name which is exalted, and this Jesus is present as liberator indwelling the believers and inspiring them to do the same or even greater works (Jn 14.12). Also, in both traditions the Spirit is not just energy but a person, not passively but very actively working through us.

This again is illustrated in the 1995 WCC Consultation's recommendation on Mission and Evangelism. Evangelism means pastoral care in a specific local context, just as Jesus 'went about all Galilee, teaching in their synagogues and preaching the gospel of the kingdom and healing every disease and every infirmity among the people' (Mt. 4.23). Mission is broader, covers the world and can never be separated from

42. Malachi Ramsay, JMCGB, 'United we Stand, Divided we Fall' (unpublished, 1976) in Gerloff, *Plea*, p. 234.
43. Cone, *The Spirituals*, p. 47.
44. Nelson, 'For Such a Time', pp. 202-205; N.L. Erskine, *King among the Theologians* (Cleveland, OH: Pilgrim Press, 1994).
45. Hollenweger in Foreword to Gerloff, *Plea*, p. ix.

politics. It is grounded in a serving not a ruling mentality, that is, in mutual respect and sharing. It has to be dialogical, as demonstrated in Jesus' life and teaching and in church history. Most important, it is rooted in spiritual empowerment, as manifested in Jesus' baptism, in prayer and undivided attention to people. This includes observing revivals that are already happening instead of concentrating on narrow agendas; the recognition of the black independent churches' contribution to mission in Europe and world-wide; and the exploration of a joint agenda in mission which transcends self-interests and attends to the overall human crisis.

Freedom from Fundamentalism

Pentecostalism, including black churches—largely from lack of access to different resources—have been taken captive by fundamentalist tendencies. However, it is fascinating to see how in the past 25 years, African and African Caribbean Pentecostals, including the Churches of God linked to white evangelical headquarters in the USA, have shaken off these impositions from a captivity which kept them apart from society and ecumenism. Rational Fundamentalism, which preserves the status quo, is in the long run incongruous with the faith of peoples who in past and present struggle against social injustice and racism (or—as black women—against the unholy alliance between racism, sexism and classism) resist class divisions, act and preach through self-help projects, care for the identity of the young, strive for the wholeness of the person in the community and—increasingly in Britain—speak out against inequality and injustice in church and society. If anything, then theirs is a liturgical fundamentalism',[46] a poetry which preserves the beauty of the scriptural word in worship and a theology which firmly centres in the Bible and not in a foreign superimposition.[47] 'Born Again', for example, means being the 'new creature' in Christ which is no longer racist—the very opposite of some white 'born again' Christians.

Black majority churches in Britain have been criticized for their 'heaven-mindedness' and their 'indulgence in powerlessness'.[48] Evi-

46. J. Barr, *Old and New Interpretations* (Currie Lectures; London: SCM Press, 1964).
47. Gerloff, *Plea*, pp. 194-95.
48. Mainly criticisms launched by scholars and clergy outside the movement.

dently in the early years of migration the newly founded congregations had no power and were literally confined to the four walls of a school or sports hall, without resources and premises. Furthermore, the black church's hope lay (and still lies) in the imminent return of Christ, the final judgment and the restoration of all things. This, however, had the 'unintended negative effect' that the Church failed to prepare members 'to live and participate in the affairs of this society'.[49] From the mid-1970s, with social unrest in the inner cities, the rise of Rastafarianism and the influence of the Civil Rights movement and Black Power, the 'very bible-based black-led denominations underwent some form of scriptural analysis as to the way forward on these issues'.[50] Faced with a political machinery which failed to 'integrate' people from other shores, and a democracy which could not protect minorities, they have increasingly set up their own programmes relating to supplementary education, underachievement, single parent households, old age pensioners, prisons and mental health institutions, and have begun to analyse the reasons underlying these everyday experiences.

The 1995 World Council of Churches Consultation, in another workshop, tackled the issues of racism and social injustice. It criticized all churches (regardless of denomination or culture) for failing to put these issues openly on their agendas, to exert pressure on the government, and to ally with all like-minded agencies, be they churched, unchurched or of other religions, against the evil forces that degrade human beings. I consider the next urgent step in Black Pentecostalism to be to reflect theologically on these actions in the light of the revolutionary potential of early Pentecostalism and the Holiness movement, with even further reference to the African 'we'-feeling as a total concern for people leading to a prophetic and healing ministry. This includes dialogue with other black theologies such as those of King, Cone or Malcolm X. This certainly is in an embryonic stage.

Same Biblical Language but Different Realities

Black and white pentecostals use the same biblical symbolic language and employ similar enthusiastic expressions, yet they represent in wor-

---

49. S.E. Arnold, *From Scepticism to Hope* (Birmingham: Grove Books, 1992), p. 11.

50. T. Parry, *Black-led Churches in West Yorkshire* (Leeds: Barnados; CANA, 1993), pp. 45-46.

ship and teaching quite different realities in conflicting cultural and social milieus. Whereas black Christians, faced with adversity, are often
necessarily led to gain new insights through both the impact of biblical
paradigms and community experiences, many white middle-class Christians, including pentecostals and charismatics, can lose the dynamics of
their faith by clinging to status propositions, security and possessions.
Kosuke Koyama has identified this as the difference between an outsider-centred and an insider-centred concept of mission.[51] Black pentecostal denominations in Britain which turn middle-class run the risk
of a similar development, but they are increasingly challenged by a
more radical generation.

This, of course, relates back to the conflict between cultures, which is
not an issue of colour but of milieu. Unity in diversity, or between overt
socio-economic disparities, is never cheaply acquired but needs the
conversion experience of Pentecost, the 'hearing miracle' (Acts 2) by
which we learn to listen to the different realities behind the same words
and images. In our context, this would imply that white pentecostals
and charismatics (and Christians generally) would identify with those
affected by disadvantage and exclusion. It would lead to the search for
a Church 'in dynamic transition, crying for reality and relevance'.[52] As
an example, the African Caribbean Evangelical Alliance has dedicated
itself 'to be in the vanguard of community building and development ...
to enhance the economic regeneration of inner-city communities; to
create strategies to deal with the endemic social injustices and disparities associated with urban decay; and to provide moral and spiritual
leadership and direction'.[53]

The workshop on Church, Culture and Identity in the WCC Consultation in 1995 formulated this in the following way: black churches
necessarily know the connection between faith, culture and identity.
Culture is intrinsic to humanity, and if people's culture is not affirmed,
they become dehumanized, as colonial history has demonstrated. Culture is linked with people's past, present and future, carried as a bag-
gage by a group, family or society. It therefore is dynamic, constantly
evolving around the particular needs of a community. For people of
African descent it is interrelated with the experience of oppression,

51. Koyama, 'New World', pp. 74-76.
52. Joel Edwards in a sermon at the West Yorkshire African Caribbean Council
of Churches Convention 1996.
53. ACEA advertising leaflet, 1995.

racism and injustice. Therefore, pentecostal churches have to reassess the problems and aspirations of black youths who are born and educated in Britain as Ronald Nathan observed. They have to rediscover the church as an 'extended family' or vehicle for community building and community capacity building.[54] They have to proclaim a holistic interpretation and incarnation of the Christian gospel that crosses the boundaries that divide human beings.

Danger of Further Exploitation

The churches of the African Diaspora have been the main forerunners of the pentecostal-charismatic movement on the one hand and of pop culture on the other. The religion and music of Africans in the New World were the two important instruments for spiritual, social and cultural survival, the rhythms of life and the 'dances of assurance' to Christ Jesus in a world that worships foreign gods.[55] The modern charismatic movements and the secular mass media, however, are in danger of further exploiting the black religious experience. By integrating it into their respective systems, by manipulating and instrumentalizing it, they often deprive it of its genuine content. Without the Spirituals and the Blues, the 'Soul' of an oppressed people, there would be no modern entertaining music on multifaceted channels. Without the discovery of African elements in North American society, there would be no charismatic movement. Black majority churches therefore emphasize that they are no 'disco church', but that their music is carried by prayer and a search for more love and 'holiness'. The Gospel music of young African Caribbean choirs in Britain is a conscious attempt to counteract commercialization and trivialization.

If not the mass media, at least the church circles should remember their historical roots. Besides our common heritage in Apostolic faith and early Christianity, there is also to be observed a complex common history of intercultural and interreligious exchange in church history. Johann Baptist Metz speaks of the need for an 'anamnetic culture' by which we remember to whom we owe certain insights and expressions: 'Christianity originally is a community of remembering and storytelling

54. WCC Consultation, Workshop IV.
55. J.H. Cone, 'Sanctification and Liberation in the Black Religious Tradition with special reference to Worship' (Oxford Institute of Methodist Theological Studies, unpublished paper, 1977), p. 4; Gerloff, *Plea*, pp. 64-65.

in discipleship to Jesus who first attended to the suffering of foreigners. This supposedly "small" and "weak" … definition is presumably the most promising description of Christianity for our times.'[56]

In the pentecostal/charismatic context, we owe insights and expressions to Africans whose humanity has been kept alive in the furnace of suffering, although it was constantly undermined by the colonial mission of western Christianity. It is reverse mission which has brought about a third wing of Christianity soon outnumbering the 'historic' churches. I have often been asked in Germany how the mass campaigns of Reinhard Bonnke, who styles himself as 'Apostle to Africa', relate to the humble black congregations in the inner cities on the one hand and to the mass psychosis of a *Reichsparteitag* on the other. My answer has always been that the characteristic of black pentecostal and African independent churches is 'Just be yourself', and that 'spiritual gifts' in their midst are a life reality and not something staged on the platform of a Congress Hall. Eventually we have to decide on whose side we are: on the side of those who still believe in the justice of God and the goodness of life, or of those who continue to co-opt the power of the marginalized into their system of profit and control.

56. J.B. Metz, 'Kirche in der Gotteskrise', *Frankfurter Rundschau* (1994). Translated by R. Gerloff.

RESPONSE

Joseph Aldred

Bishop Joe Aldred of the Church of God of Prophecy and presently Director of the Centre for Black and White Christian Partnerships at Selly Oak Colleges, responded to Roswith Gerloff's, 'Pentecostals in the African Diaspora', and what follows is taken from a tape recording of that response. He said that black pentecostals, like the Christians in the book of Acts, had been 'scattered abroad', and that it was this 'scattering' that created the black churches as Christians almost impulsively 'gossiped' the gospel wherever they went. He was concerned about the danger on the one hand of an attempt to portray the black church today as 'victim', because this perpetuated the idea of an underclass, and on the other of the tendency among white researchers to make 'grandiose claims' on behalf of the black pentecostals, a 'love affair' with the church that failed to recognise the significant 'scratch marks'. This could be seen in the portrayal of black Pentecostalism as having bridged cultural gaps and boundaries and the raising up of Azusa Street as its pinnacle—whereas probably the largest black pentecostal church in the world today, the Church of God in Christ, preceded Azusa Street historically. The divisions and racism that so quickly followed Azusa Street made him wonder why this was always held up as *the* model. Racism that existed then and still existed today cast doubt on the propriety of holding up black Pentecostalism as making any difference to the black/white divide either then or now.

The hegemony of white leadership in Britain and the segregation on colour lines on both sides of the Atlantic remained 'untarnished', he said. The setting up of 'decidedly black' churches in Britain had probably contributed to the segregation in British Christianity by not engaging with the white structures which had said 'no' to blacks. These churches 40 years later were still black, whether in the USA or in Britain. Charles Mason of the Church of God in Christ, and William

Seymour later, had recognized that the idea that whites would be led by blacks was something that would probably not happen. Mason was probably a better example of what was more likely to succeed in this divided world than Seymour was, as he had set up a black church, aiming to make it succeed. Aldred did not think that it was helpful to be making it the aim of the black church to chase 'white acceptance'. The determination of many black congregations (including some very small and poor ones) to own their own buildings was an example of the need for them to reaffirm their own sense of dignity to themselves and the God whom they served—and not to anyone else. Black Christians now said to others: 'We are here; learn from us if you will but if you don't, then God bless you!'[1]

1.   Adapted from a taped recording of Bishop Joseph Aldred's response, June 1996.

DANGEROUS MEMORIES FOR SOUTH AFRICAN PENTECOSTALS

Allan Anderson

Truth and Reconciliation

It was estimated that pentecostals and those African initiated churches (henceforth AICs) with affinities to the pentecostal movement, together referred to here as African pentecostal churches,[1] accounted for over 30% of the total South African population in 1991. It is collectively one of the most significant expressions of Christianity in Africa today. There are now at least six thousand churches comprising some ten million people in South Africa who can be identified with a form of Pentecostalism, especially in the experiential emphasis on the Holy Spirit and practices such as divine healing, exorcism, prophecy, revelation and speaking in tongues.[2] The growth of these churches is much more rapid than that of the older churches; the AICs (most of which are churches of the pentecostal type) presently incorporate almost half of the black population of South Africa.[3]

---

1. Following W.J. Hollenweger, *The Pentecostals* (London: SCM Press, 1972), p. 151, the term 'African pentecostal churches', in addition to those churches which are similar to the pentecostal movement in the rest of the world, includes those African initiated churches with historical, theological and liturgical affinities with the pentecostal movement. These 'pentecostal type' churches, which constitute one third of the black population of South Africa and are usually called Zion and Apostolic churches, have an emphasis on the Holy Spirit, especially manifested in prophetic healing practices, and other pentecostal beliefs like adult baptism by immersion and speaking in tongues.

2. These AICs, particularly the indigenous pentecostal churches, multiplied from some 30 churches in 1913 to 3,000 in 1970, and probably to well over 6,000 by 1990.

3. A.H. Anderson, 'African Pentecostalism in a South African Urban Environment: A Missiological Evaluation' (DTh thesis, Pretoria, University of South Africa, 1992), pp. 23-24. Figures quoted are taken from the official 1991 South African Census report.

Unfortunately, so little has been written on the history of black pentecostals in South Africa. Sometimes the histories of white pentecostals are written as if they represent the whole pentecostal movement. The tragic consequence of South Africa's socio-political context in the twentieth century is that white pentecostals often assumed that the growth of the movement was almost wholly the result of the labours of white pentecostals. Nothing could be further from the truth. In fact, Pentecostalism developed spontaneously among the African population as an authentic African expression of Christianity, usually (in the case of AICs) without any assistance from white churches, and sometimes (in the case of pentecostal churches founded by whites) despite such 'assistance'. The history of South African Pentecostalism is fraught with 'dangerous memories', and it is on these memories that I wish to concentrate in this article. Just as the recent Reconciliation and Truth Commission has tried to bring reconciliation through a confession of the truth, so Pentecostalism in South Africa with its painful divisions for most of its existence, needs to acknowledge the truth about its origins and development, these 'dangerous memories', if meaningful reconciliation is to be achieved.

The Coming of Zion

Many AICs and pentecostal churches in South Africa have their roots in events that occurred in Wakkerstroom in Mpumulanga province. In 1902 or 1903 Pieter le Roux, a Dutch Reformed missionary working there, joined the Zion movement founded in Chicago, Illinois, together with some 400 African coworkers and converts. He had become aware of the Zion movement through its founder John Alexander Dowie's magazine *Leaves of Healing*, and had requested membership in his Christian Catholic Apostolic Church in Zion, while inviting Dowie to send a representative to South Africa. In 1904 Daniel Bryant arrived as Dowie's appointed overseer of the church, which by this time already had a considerable number of African members.[4] Soon after his arrival, Bryant baptized 141 converts at Wakkerstroom, including le Roux. The Wakkerstroom group grew to five thousand members by 1905,[5] and was the source out of which eventually the whole series of Zion and

4.   Anderson, 'African Pentecostalism', p. 18.
5.   B.G.M. Sundkler, *Zulu Zion and some Swazi Zionists* (London: Oxford University Press, 1976), p. 30.

Apostolic AICs would emerge.[6] Wakkerstroom was to South African pentecostal churches what the Azusa Street revival in Los Angeles was to the world-wide pentecostal movement. The fact of continuity between the early Zion movement and the pentecostal movement in Southern Africa is crucial to our understanding of subsequent developments, and places African pentecostal churches within their correct historical and theological context.[7]

The Arrival of Pentecostal Missionaries

In 1908 pentecostal missionaries arrived from the USA, led by Thomas Hezmalhalch and John G. Lake, who had had connections with the Azusa Street revival under black preacher William Seymour and with the Zion movement in Chicago. Le Roux thereupon discovered that 'Zion taught immersion and divine healing, but NOT Pentecost'.[8] Lake and Hezmalhalch soon took over the 'Zion Tabernacle' in Johannesburg for services,[9] and were largely identified with the Zion movement. Pentecostalism in South Africa thus began in a black church with fully integrated services. A number of other pentecostal missionaries arrived from 1908 onwards, mainly from North America and Britain, some of whom were to fulfil significant roles in the formation of various pentecostal denominations, including the Assemblies of God[10] and the Full Gospel Church of God. Le Roux joined Lake's new movement[11] called the Apostolic Faith Mission (hereafter AFM), and soon became a leader there. The name of this church was modeled after the name of the mainly black Azusa Street mission; a considerable irony when subsequent events made the white AFM one of the staunchest supporters of apartheid among South African pentecostals. Le Roux's African fellow-workers remained Zion members to all intents and purposes, whilst they embraced the doctrine of the Holy Spirit emphasized by the pente-

6. B.G.M. Sundkler, *Bantu Prophets in South Africa* (Oxford: Oxford University Press, 1961), p. 48.
7. Sundkler, *Zulu Zion*, p. 51.
8. Sundkler, *Bantu Prophets*, p. 48.
9. Sundkler, *Zulu Zion*, p. 52.
10. P. Watt, *From Africa's Soil: The Story of the Assemblies of God in Southern Africa* (Cape Town: Struik, 1992), pp. 20-21.
11. Sundkler, *Zulu Zion*, p. 53.

costals. They did not consider themselves separate from the pentecostals; and le Roux was still one of their leaders. In fact, a meeting
between representatives of the 'Zion Church' and the AFM executive in
1909 agreed that le Roux was in charge of the Zion mission work in the
Transvaal, and that these two organizations would 'mutually acknowledge each other's certificates' of membership and ordination.[12]

The pentecostal movement initially grew mainly among the disen-
franchised black people and the poor white Afrikaners reeling from the
aftermath of the Anglo-Boer War of 1899–1902.[13] African leadership,
however, was not given freedom to emerge in the early years, and leadership was kept firmly in the hands of white men,[14] resulting in the
eventual separation of the independent Zionist and Apostolic churches
from the pentecostals.[15] A 1911 edition of the AFM magazine *Comforter* makes the revealing statement that 'A fact not duly appreciated is
that the vast majority of native work is being conducted by natives
themselves without white assistance ...' [16] These African leaders, however, only leaders in their local constituencies, were not permitted to
emerge on a national level, even though they were largely responsible
for the spread of the pentecostal message throughout the country. White
dominance was true of most established churches in South Africa at this
time and for at least another seventy years.

Segregation and Secession

The first pentecostal services held in Doornfontein, Johannesburg in the
Zion church were racially integrated, so that Burton reported that 'all
shades of colour and all degrees of the social scale mingled freely in

12. C.R. de Wet, 'The Apostolic Faith Mission in Africa: 1908–1980. A Case
Study in Church Growth in a Segregated Society' (PhD thesis, University of Cape
Town, 1989), p. 64.
13. De Wet, 'Apostolic Faith Mission', p. 39.
14. De Wet, 'Apostolic Faith Mission', p. 161.
15. There was no perceived schism between Le Roux (and by implication, the
AFM) and the African Zion members at this stage. It would appear that Pente-
costalism did not take the place of Zionism; it was simply added to it. In 1910 the
AFM executive committee decided that 'whereas the natives deem the name of
Zion so essential that this portion of our Mission be known henceforth as the Zion
Branch of the Apostolic Faith Mission' (de Wet, 'Apostolic Faith Mission', p. 161).
16. De Wet, 'Apostolic Faith Mission', p. 311.

their hunger after God'.[17] The white pentecostals, however, decided soon after the missionaries arrived to separate the races in baptisms.[18] The pentecostals, like other churches in South Africa at this time, yielded to the pressures of white society and developed segregated churches. The AFM grew especially among African people in these early years partly through the remarkable work and healing ministry of Elias Letwaba, and the growth among white Afrikaners was given impetus by the 'Central Tabernacle' in Johannesburg, regarded as the 'mother church' of the movement.[19] Le Roux was president from 1913, when the AFM was officially registered, until 1943, by which time it was an established denomination. By 1918 there were about 13,000 black and 5,000 white people in the church, and ten years later these figures had trebled. Most white members were and are still Afrikaners. In 1928 a schism in the white church led by Maria Fraser, who felt that the AFM had departed from its holiness roots, resulted in the Latter Rain Mission, and another major schism in 1958 resulted in the formation of the Pentecostal Protestant Church, a group which felt that the AFM had departed from its pentecostal roots.[20] The white AFM was to become increasingly identified with and subservient to the apartheid policies of the white regime.

The African pentecostal churches, initially called the Zion Apostolic Church, continued to work together with the white AFM at first.[21] Early white pentecostal leaders actually encouraged independent African groups to join the AFM,[22] and estrangement between black and white pentecostals occurred only gradually. Although it appears that one of the Zion leaders, Daniel Nkonyane, had broken with le Roux as early as 1910,[23] the earliest recorded secession took place in 1917, when Elias Mahlangu (one of the first African Zion members) founded the Zion

17. De Wet, 'Apostolic Faith Mission', pp. 51-52.

18. I.S. v.d.M. Burger, *Geloofsgeskiedenis van die Apostoliese Geloofsending van Suid-Afrika 1908–1958* (Johannesburg: Evangelie Uitgewers, 1988), p. 175.

19. I have adapted from two unpublished manuscripts by Drs Isak Burger and Christo de Wet in this paragraph.

20. In 1955 G.R. Wessels, a senior pastor in the AFM and its vice-president, became a senator in the ruling National Party. This event contributed to this schism, in which liturgical issues and academic qualifications for ministers also played a part.

21. Sundkler, *Bantu Prophets*, p. 48.

22. De Wet, 'Apostolic Faith Mission', p. 63.

23. Sundkler, *Bantu Prophets*, pp. 55-56 n. 54.

Apostolic Church of South Africa.[24] But by 1917 there may have already been numerous black pentecostal churches in existence.[25] Out of Mahlangu's Zion Apostolic Church, Edward Lion's Zion Apostolic Faith Mission seceded in 1920—the name showing an obvious desire to maintain continuity with the AFM. Engenas Lekganyane's Zion Christian Church (ZCC) seceded from the ZAFM in 1925 and is now one of the largest churches in South Africa—bigger than all the white-founded pentecostal churches combined.[26] The white AFM was either not aware of these later secessions or did not recognize them. For instance, in 1921 the AFM executive council considered Edward Lion as 'leader of the (AFM) work in Basutoland' (Lesotho), whereas Lion did 'not want to submit himself to the Mission as other native leaders do'. It was therefore 'necessary', the AFM stated, 'for us to get a white man to go and settle there and take control of the work'.[27]

Pentecostals and Apartheid

Although the first pentecostal meetings in South Africa were racially integrated, only four months after the founding of the AFM in 1908 its all-white Executive Council minuted 'the necessity of getting adequate accommodation for the holding of services in Doornfontein especially for the coloured people'.[28] Less than two months later it decided that 'the baptism of Natives shall in future take place after the baptism of the white people'.[29] In February 1909 it was resolved that the Superintendent over the 'Native work' had to be a white man.[30] The minutes of July 1909 read: 'In future, the baptism of Whites, Coloured and Natives shall be separate'.[31] A year later separate annual national conferences for white and black people were held.[32] In 1910, a 'Native Council' was formed consisting of three white and three black members. All decisions

24. De Wet, 'Apostolic Faith Mission', p. 63.
25. De Wet, 'Apostolic Faith Mission', p. 63.
26. The ZCC puts its official beginning at 1910, which appears to be the year that Lekganyane received his divine call.
27. De Wet, 'Apostolic Faith Mission', p. 126.
28. De Wet, 'Apostolic Faith Mission', p. 60.
29. De Wet, 'Apostolic Faith Mission', p. 160.
30. De Wet, 'Apostolic Faith Mission', p. 161.
31. Sundkler, *Zulu Zion*, p. 54.
32. De Wet, 'Apostolic Faith Mission', p. 93.

of this council had to be ratified by the Executive Council.[33] By 1915
no ordination or leadership appointment could be made by a black
church official except with the consent of the white Superintendent.[34]
This lack of trust in black leadership in the AFM contributed to the
many schisms that took place from this time onwards. In 1917 the following ambiguous resolution was adopted by the Executive Council,
which illustrated clearly the prevailing prejudices:

> … we do not teach or encourage social equality between Whites and
> Natives. We recognise that God is no respecter of persons, but that in
> every nation he that feareth Him and worketh righteousness is acceptable
> to Him. We therefore preach the Gospel equally to all peoples, making
> no distinctions. We wish it to be generally known that our white, Col-
> oured and Native peoples have their separate places of worship, where
> the Sacraments are administered to them.[35]

In 1925 the Executive Council decided that all black districts should
be under the control of a white overseer or district superintendent.[36] On
several occasions during this period decisions were made for black people by whites; and they had simply to obey, or leave the church.[37]
Things did not get better. In April 1944 the following resolutions
revealed that the white AFM supported the emerging apartheid structures of the National Party, which would become government policy
after 1948:

> (1)   Race Relations: The mission stands for segregation. The fact that the
>   Native, Indian and Coloured is saved does not render him European …
> (3)   Native education: The mission stands for a lower education [for black
>   people] but is definitely against a higher education.

These resolutions were reaffirmed in April 1948, when the 1917 resolution cited above was virtually repeated. A revealing article on 'The
church and racism' by C.P. du Plessis appeared in the AFM's magazine
The Comforter in September 1955,[38] in which the author, *inter alia*,
affirmed his belief in the mental, emotional and spiritual superiority of
the white race, all based on the Scriptures! The article is replete with

33. De Wet, 'Apostolic Faith Mission', pp. 95-96.
34. De Wet, 'Apostolic Faith Mission', p. 100.
35. De Wet, 'Apostolic Faith Mission', p. 165.
36. De Wet, 'Apostolic Faith Mission', p. 135.
37. De Wet, 'Apostolic Faith Mission', p. 163.
38. De Wet, 'Apostolic Faith Mission', pp. 179-80.

racial arrogance and slurs. In the same year the white AFM supported
the appointment of its Vice-President Gerrie Wessels as a National
Party Senator.

African pastors in the white-led pentecostal churches seem to have
accepted this situation. The AFM pioneer Elias Letwaba, like many
Africans of his time, raised no objection to the indignities placed on
him because of the colour of his skin.[39] Towards the end of his life, he
wrote the following in the AFM magazine *Die Trooster*:

> ... I pray for our benefactors, the white people, who have brought the
> Eternal Light to us. My nation must learn to love our benefactors ... and
> be obedient to them, because there would be no heaven for us poor
> Blacks if it were not for the white man.[40]

Letwaba's subservience was probably one of the reasons he remained
in the AFM—unlike his contemporaries Edward Lion and Engenas
Lekganyane and many other black leaders, who chose to leave and
found their own churches. Letwaba had the dubious distinction of being
one of only two black district overseers ever to be appointed in the
AFM's first 50 years; and he was even allowed to speak at white conferences!

The widely influential Zulu AFM leader in the 1970s, Richard Ngidi,
was known for his opposition to involvement in politics, which fur-
thered the traditional apolitical feeling in the AFM. Ngidi would not
allow any discussion on what he perceived to be political matters.
Christo de Wet feels that this was probably due to the prevailing view
in the AFM (and, in fact, in most pentecostal circles) that involvement
in politics was sinful.[41] Ngidi was, therefore, a product of his pietistic
environment.

---

39. On one occasion he was reported to have been preaching on a farm where he
was told to sleep in the fowl-house. In the middle of the night he was wakened by
the white farmer and asked to pray for his sick wife. This he did, and the farmer
thereupon apologised for having put him in the fowl-house. To this Letwaba replied:
'It is all right, sir, to put me there, my Master slept in a stable, and I am only a black
worm' (in De Wet, 'Apostolic Faith Mission', p. 70).

40. Translated from original Afrikaans by the author from De Wet, 'Apostolic
Faith Mission', pp. 69-70.

41. De Wet, 'Apostolic Faith Mission', p. 143.

The Reaction of African Independent Churches

The founder of the Zion Christian Church, Engenas Lekganyane (c. 1885–1948), met Le Roux in Johannesburg in 1908,[42] and was subsequently healed and baptized in the Spirit. He joined a congregation of the Zion Apostolic Church near his home. Lekganyane, a powerful preacher and evangelist, soon became leader of the church in the north. He appears to have been one of the many who reacted to white domination, as he continued with Elias Mahlangu after his break with the AFM in 1917. Subsequent differences between them resulted in Lekganyane's visit to Lesotho in 1920 and his joining Edward Lion's Zion Apostolic Faith Mission, which had just seceded from the AFM. There he was ordained a bishop. Once again, differences emerged, and at the end of 1924 he returned home and with over 900 members founded the ZCC.[43] By 1943, only 18 years later, there were over 40,000 members and the ZCC under Lekganyane's remarkable leadership had already become one of the largest AICs in Africa, and is now by far the largest in South Africa.

Divine healing and miracles were the main characteristics of Lekganyane's ministry; in this respect he was a true pentecostal.[44] The ZCC, like most other AICs, does not have a written 'dogma' by which it may be assessed, but its theology may be said to be continuing in the pentecostal oral and narrative tradition, with an emphasis on healing, exorcism and prophecy. Its distinctive prophetic healing practices and the adaptations to traditional life and rituals, however, make it a church that has developed beyond its pentecostal roots. The ZCC has also experienced various splits. The St Engenas ZCC was founded after the death of Engenas Lekganyane in 1948 by his son Joseph, continuing as a similar movement to the larger ZCC led by Engenas's other son Edward. In 1962 a former ZCC minister in Soweto, Frederick Modise,

42. C. Hanekom, *Krisis en kultus* (Pretoria: Academica, 1975), p. 39.
43. Hanekom, *Krisis*, p. 41.
44. From the beginning of his ministry Lekganyane emphasised divine healing. He healed by the laying on of hands but as the church developed he also began to 'bless' various objects like strips of cloth, strings, papers, needles, walking sticks and water to be used for healing and protective purposes. Several remarkable and miraculous incidents are attributed to the latter part of Lekganyane's life. See A.H. Anderson, *Bazalwane: African Pentecostals in South Africa* (Pretoria: University of South Africa Press, 1992), p. 44.

commenced the International Pentecost Church, a Sabbatarian church which emphasizes faith healing but outlaws the use of prophetic healing practices and speaking in tongues.

The African pentecostal movement in South Africa had its share of remarkable women founders. One of these was Christina Nku of the St John Apostolic Faith Mission,[45] which like the ZCC, had pentecostal beginnings in the AFM, where Nku was baptized in 1924, but which she left to start her own church. Mrs Nku became well-known as a healer and, within a few years, gathered thousands of people into her church. The name, St John Apostolic Faith Mission, like that of Lion's Zion Apostolic Faith Mission, showed the perception of continuity with the AFM and the pentecostal movement.[46] These churches were just a few of the more prominent examples of the many hundreds of AICs that were to emerge either directly or indirectly from the pentecostal movement, today generally known in Southern Africa as Zionists and Apostolics.[47]

Movements towards Unity and Freedom

There are today three significant pentecostal churches founded by western missionaries: the Assemblies of God (AOG) and the Apostolic Faith Mission (AFM), each with about a quarter of a million members in the early 1990s, and the somewhat smaller Full Gospel Church of God (FGC). There are several other much smaller churches and a number of new independent charismatic churches. These pentecostal churches have continued to grow in South Africa, having overcome their pariah image in the white community by successful evangelistic and healing campaigns. In the 1950s two leading North American pentecostal evangelists, William Branham followed by Oral Roberts visited South Africa, and thousands who had never been in a pentecostal service before were attracted to these sensational meetings. Tent crusades have remained an integral part of the culture of South African Pentecostalism. Nicholas

45. Sundkler, *Zulu Zion*, pp. 79-82.

46. Some of her practices (particularly her healing practices using holy water) brought increasing distance between her church and the pentecostal churches.

47. More information on the history and beliefs of the churches outlined in this section is to be found in Anderson, *Bazalwane*, pp. 36-44, 98-114; and A.H. Anderson and S. Otwang, *Tumelo: The Faith of African Pentecostals in South Africa* (Pretoria: University of South Africa Press, 1993).

Bhengu and Richard Ngidi were particularly effective in this regard in the black communities, and in the 1980s German evangelist Reinhard Bonnke commenced 'Christ for All Nations' in South Africa, with an emphasis on tent evangelism in black townships. Resulting from these and other campaigns many thousands were attracted to these pentecostal churches.

From the founding of the AFM in 1908, white members had determined the constitution, and power had been vested in the all-white executive council. The three separate, racially determined black, so-called 'Coloured' (mixed race) and 'Indian' sections of the church that developed were controlled by a Missions Department and a Missions Director appointed by the white church.[48] These three sections were to have no legal standing, as only white persons could become 'legal' members of the AFM—which situation remained until 1991. In 1985 the white Executive Council called the leaders of the three black sections of the church together to discuss the future of the AFM.[49] A proposed Declaration of Intent was agreed on for acceptance by the four racially divided Workers Councils (the conference of representatives from all local churches). The main provisions of this document declared that the AFM accepted 'the Biblical principles of unity', rejected 'the system of apartheid based on racial discrimination as a principle in the Kingdom of God and within the structure of the Church' and accepted that 'the Church should operate as a single structural unit'.[50]

The Declaration was approved by the four separate Workers' Councils by June 1986 and a committee was appointed to work towards unity. It soon became apparent, however, that the majority of white AFM members interpreted 'unity' differently from the black members.

48. The terms 'Coloured' and 'Indian' used widely in the South African context were used at the time to divide people on racial grounds. In this paper they are used as convenient terms to describe the historical realities, although I do not agree with the ideology behind their original use! During the 'struggle' many so-called 'Coloureds' and people of Indian origin used to refer to themselves simply as 'blacks', to identify with the oppressed 'non-white' majority.

49. The information obtained here on the recent history of the AFM results from interviews during July and August 1991 with Edgar Gschwend, first President of the AFM Composite Division, George Mahlobo, General Secretary, and Japie Lapoorta, Vice-President. I also had access to an unpublished secretarial report of the Committee for Unity of the AFM for the period 1985 to 1991.

50. Quotations taken from the Declaration of Intent, unpublished MS.

To the white members 'unity' meant the 'equality' before God of all its members in *separate* church structures.[51] An interim constitution for a united AFM was drawn up and presented to the four Workers' Councils in April 1987. The three black sections accepted it; but the white section proposed two divisions, and a stalemate resulted.[52] In 1988 it was agreed that although continuing to negotiate with the white section, the black sections should now unite, and in 1990 they combined to form the Apostolic Faith Mission, Composite Division. The white churches remained separate, but for the first time in the 80-year history of the AFM, black people were legal members. There were now two presidents of the AFM: in 1993 Frank Chikane was elected president by the Composite Division of the church,[53] and Isak Burger had been elected by the all-white Single Division a few years earlier. Political and not theological factors kept the two sections apart. In 1995 it was agreed to unite the two divisions as a single church, but whites were negotiating greater local church autonomy in order to protect themselves from the imagined 'black danger'.[54] In May 1996 the unity between the two divisions was formally approved amidst great media attention as Frank Chikane and Isak Burger embraced in front of the cameras.

The Full Gospel Church of God (FGC), unlike the AFM, has many English-speaking members and a large number of members of Indian origin, but apartheid structures also exist in this church.[55] The FGC is the largest Christian church in the South African Indian community; and approximately 80% of its total membership is black. The first open

---

51. During the ensuing negotiations the white Workers' Council unilaterally changed the wording of the Declaration, including the deletion of the word 'apartheid' to read that the AFM 'rejects all systems of discrimination'.

52. The white church still controlled the finances, including the support given to black pastors. They were still the only section legally recognised in the constitution.

53. In 1996 Chikane was appointed personal assistant to South Africa's Deputy President Thabo Mbeki, later Director General in the Office of the Deputy President. His 1999 appointment as Director General in the Office of the President has implications for his future leadership of the AFM.

54. Afrikaans, *swart gevaar*, a slogan during the apartheid era.

55. This church commenced with the arrival of the North American missionary George Bowie to South Africa in 1910, sent by the Bethel Pentecostal Mission in Newark, New Jersey. Bowie was soon joined by other missionaries, the most notable being Archibald Cooper, who immigrated to South Africa from England in 1902. This mission in 1921 united to form the Full Gospel Church, and is now associated with the Church of God (Cleveland).

agitation for a united church began in 1975, initiated by the three black sections.[56] Like the AFM, however, the white section was the exclusive decision-making body and had the sole right to change the constitution. Negotiations took place until 1986, when an umbrella legislative body was formed purporting to be non-racial. But the black churches continued to exist as separate bodies, and black leaders (especially Africans) were not adequately represented. Negotiations resulted in a 'Statement of Intent' to unite being drawn up in 1986.[57] The pressure by the black churches against white control increased, and May 1990 was set as the final date for a united church. The white churches, however, asked for an indefinite period to 'prepare' their members for such unity. White leaders could not obtain the required consent of their General Conference. In May 1990 two separate associations were formed, each with its own ecclesiastical government. The mostly black organizations together united to form the United Assemblies Association of the FGC, and most of the white churches formed a separate association known as the Irene Association. Effectively these associations now form two separate church bodies which legally constitute the FGC. The black church gave the white FGC a maximum of four years (until February 1994) to resolve the differences. In fact, the first step towards unity was only achieved in October 1997, when the two associations formed a federal system with separate Moderatures and Executive Councils, and at the local level, separate regions and districts. One observer said 'nothing has changed', and in the election of the office bearers the two most senior posts went to representatives of the conservative white constituency. The church was aiming at complete unity 'by about 2000', the spokesperson added. It is too early to know what impact these events might have upon the black FGC.

The work of various missionaries from North America and Europe resulted in the South African District of the Assemblies of God (AOG) being formed in 1925.[58] This umbrella organization served pentecostal missionaries from various countries, but by 1932 the AOG in South

56. This information results from telephone interviews during 1991 with Cornelius van Kerken, then General Overseer of the United Assemblies Association, Henry van der Vent, Secretary General of the same Association, and Lawrence Rowlands and Marius Herholdt of the Irene Association.

57. The FGC was to have a single General Conference, with one Executive Council acceptable to all four sections of the church.

58. Watt, *From Africa's Soil*, p. 23.

Africa was recognized as a separate national church. There were no white congregations until 1935, and it was initially a black church controlled by white missionaries. In 1938 it was decided to make provisions for the different sections under different leaders to have complete autonomy. That year Nicholas Bhengu joined the movement, and the stage was set for the future participation of black leaders in the national executive, a unique feature among white-founded pentecostal churches in South Africa.

The revival that followed the ministry of Bhengu, especially in the Eastern Cape, lasted until the late 1950s and resulted in the AOG becoming the fastest growing pentecostal mission church at that time. In 1950 Bhengu launched the 'Back to God Crusade', an evangelistic and church planting body that developed quite independently from the churches under white missionaries. The churches that sprung up from Bhengu's movement soon constituted the majority in the AOG. Inevitably, conflicts arose between expatriate missionaries and South African leadership (particularly in the Bhengu group) leading to a split in 1964.[59] Several other divisions occurred in the AOG, and in the 1990s attempts were being made at reconciliation.

The AOG has generally been more open to integration than other white pentecostal churches have been.[60] Nevertheless, some of the tensions described in those churches are found here, although to a much smaller degree. Unlike the other white-led pentecostal churches, the AOG was not divided into 'mother' (white) and 'daughter' (black) churches. As Watt points out, it 'was a black church before any white congregations were formed'.[61] The division of the organization into different autonomous associations or 'groups' was the result of the work of particularly gifted leaders and missionaries. Bhengu, for example, was the founder and head of the largest group, the Back to God

59. The missionaries were disturbed by what they perceived as Bhengu's autocratic leadership style. James Mullan and John Bond were the two white AOG leaders who supported Bhengu against expatriate missionaries. A minority group of black leaders and the American missionaries withdrew from the AOG to form the International Assemblies of God.

60. The information here is as a result of conversations during 1991 with several AOG leaders, including Chairman John Bond, General Secretary, Victor Nkomonde; an executive member and chairman of the predominantly 'Coloured' and Indian 'Association', Colin La Foy; and another executive member, Dan Lephoko.

61. Watt, *From Africa's Soil*, p. 22.

Crusade, known after 1990 as the Assemblies of God Movement. The AOG 'groups', however, are mostly divided along racial lines and reflect the divisions in South African society;[62] although some AOG leaders contest this assessment.[63] The 'group' division may be construed as lending support to racial segregation, and has been the main criticism of the AOG by some of its younger black leaders. Nevertheless, the remarkable fact is that for much of its history the executive has had a majority black leadership, presided over by a white Chairman, John Bond (who held this position from 1967–1995) elected by an 85% black General Conference in an open ballot.[64] Isaac Hleta from Swaziland became the first black Chairman of the AOG General Executive in 1995, with Colin La Foy, a 'Coloured', Vice-Chairman, and the constituency of the Executive changed to 16 of the Bhengu group to eight from the other groups. This was a significant step forward.

Pentecostals and the 'Freedom Struggle'

Pentecostals were seldom in the forefront of the 'freedom struggle', although there were a few exceptions. Bhengu pioneered the Assemblies of God's transformation to a truly African church, but did not often make socio-political pronouncements.[65] According to Watt, however, Bhengu was quite clear on such issues, as he believed 'that black people would be brought to liberation from political and economic oppression through the gospel' and that 'by coming back to God, blacks would be prepared for nationhood and political power'.[66] Bhengu's stance on these issues was apparently one of 'self-confidence and sense of equality'. He and other black AOG leaders 'refused to allow the prevailing social context to separate them from Whites and to shape the

62. Watt has in effect side-stepped the issue with his emphasis on what he terms the division between 'indigenous' (including white) and 'expatriate' (including black) streams. He calls this 'a pragmatic response to the South African situation'.

63. Watt (*From Africa's Soil*, p. 39) for example, says that this is a 'simplistic view'. He thereupon proceeds to admit that 'some groups were limited to a racial group' but that 'others were not'.

64. A fuller discussion of the events which led to the unity talks between the divided white-dominated pentecostal churches can be found in Anderson, *Bazalwane*, pp. 78-88.

65. Watt, *From Africa's Soil*, p. 178.

66. Watt, *From Africa's Soil*, p. 112.

Church'.[67] But Bhengu, a political activist before his conversion, did not challenge the status quo, was described by some African nationalists as a 'sell-out' (traitor) and received several threats to his life.[68] He believed that political activity was futile, forbade his members any political affiliation,[69] believing that liberation would only come through God. As Dubb states, his belief in national redemption was 'through non-violence, good relations with Whites, obedience to the laws of the land and, above all, through faith in God rather than in political action'.[70] In this respect Bhengu followed the stance of most pentecostals of the time.

The best-known example of the struggle against apartheid in the white-led pentecostal churches is the former General Secretary of the South African Council of Churches, and President of the AFM's Composite Division, Frank Chikane. Chikane was very active in the AFM in Soweto as a young man, and was involved in evangelism. While at university, he followed former African National Congress general secretary Cyril Ramaphosa as chairman of the Student Christian Movement. He joined the organization 'Christ for All Nations' led by German evangelist Reinhard Bonnke, and in 1976 was given an AFM congregation, as well as responsibility for evangelism. He became involved in a community project, and between 1977 and 1982 was detained four times by police, during which he was interrogated and tortured, on one occasion by a white AFM deacon.[71] During the first of his several months of detention during 1977–1978, the church district council removed him from his congregation.

In 1980 he was ordained an AFM pastor; and one of the conditions of his ordination was that he should not participate in politics. For Chikane this condition was not a problem; he had not joined any political organization. But his continued involvement in the freedom struggle and community projects got him into trouble with the church leadership. In August 1981 the West Rand district council suspended him. This 'suspension from full-time service', confirmed by the national Executive

67. Watt, *From Africa's Soil*, p. 149.

68. A.A. Dubb, *Community of the Saved: An African Revivalist Church in the East Cape* (Johannesburg: Witwatersrand University Press, 1976), pp. 119-120.

69. Dubb, *Community of the Saved*, p. 120.

70. Dubb, *Community of the Saved*, p. 27.

71. R. Sider, 'Interview with Rev Frank Chikane', *Transformation* 5 (1988), pp. 9-12.

Council, was for one year. The reasons given for the suspension were that 'he did not keep the promise he made regarding the conditions of his ordination' and that 'there is no change in his attitude'.[72] He was not reinstated the following year; and he was asked to return his credentials. In fact, only intense agitation by an unofficial organization within the black AFM forced the lifting of the suspension in 1990. On 20 May 1993 he was elected President of the Composite Division of the AFM, and he had come a full circle from excommunication in a church to its highest office bearer. In 1996 he became personal assistant to Deputy President Thabo Mbeki, and he now holds the position of Director General in the President's Office.

But there were other, less high profile struggles against white hegemony in South African Pentecostalism. At least half of the signatories of *The Evangelical Witness* were pentecostals, drawn up by the 'Concerned Evangelicals' in 1986 as a reaction to the political conservatism of Evangelicalism. This was 'an important document in the struggle of Pentecostals against apartheid'.[73] In 1988 a group of pentecostals drew up a similar document called *The Relevant Pentecostal Witness*, which was more specifically a pentecostal stance against apartheid and the theology justifying the status quo. Part of the driving force behind this movement was a reminder of the non-racial origins of the pentecostal movement and a theology of the Spirit motivating a preference for the poor and oppressed. In many of the younger generation of black pentecostals there was a similar identification with the struggle for freedom. Among other things, this manifested itself in student protests against racism in white controlled Bible colleges in 1989 (in the case of the International Assemblies of God college in Rustenburg) and in 1991 in the AFM Central Bible College in Soshanguve. In both cases, students were expelled and numbers decimated, but many of these students were accommodated at Tshwane Theological College outside Soshanguve, where I was Principal at the time. One of these so-called 'rebels' and pastor of an AFM church in Winterveld (one of the poorest and largest informal housing areas of South Africa) Jan Mathibela, was leader of the local civic association and was elected African National Congress mayor of Winterveld in 1995.

72. De Wet, 'Apostolic Faith Mission', pp. 77, 182.
73. J.N. Horn, 'The Experience of the Spirit in Apartheid South Africa', in *Azusa* 1 (1990), pp. 19-40 (31).

Dangerous Memories

White South African pentecostals do not always acknowledge their own non-racial beginnings—for these, and the origins of Pentecostalism in Azusa Street, are indeed 'dangerous memories' for them. Former AFM President Francois Möller, who was obviously aware of the implications for South African Pentecostalism, dismissed the black origins of the pentecostal movement in Los Angeles as follows: 'Later Seymour was replaced by more able people and the different races ceased worship together'.[74] The current President of the AFM, Isak Burger, also found it expedient to dispense with this view, saying that the idea that pentecostalism originated in a black church was a 'warped, one-sided conclusion' and that the pentecostal movement developed a 'natural and spontaneous segregation'. Burger went on to attribute the segregation that developed in the AFM 'to the fact that some Afrikaners who understood (*sic*) the history, nature and the attitudes of race relationships in South Africa better than the Americans were elected on the Executive'.[75] This so-called 'understanding' led to black members being accorded no legal status in the AFM for over 70 years.

The South African pentecostal movement, in spite of its witness to spiritual freedom, acquiesced in the midst of the social evils in South Africa. The original integration and fellowship were short-lived; and black people were denied basic human rights in the very churches in which they had found 'freedom' in the Spirit. Many African pentecostals silently withdrew to the independent church movements or to their new-found pentecostal 'spirituality' that remained 'other worldly' for the most part. African Pentecostalism in South Africa has its roots in a marginalized and underprivileged society struggling to find dignity and identity. It expanded initially among oppressed people who were neglected, misunderstood and deprived of anything but token leadership by their white pentecostal 'masters', who had apparently ignored biblical concepts like the priesthood of all believers and the equality of all people in Christ. But the ability of Pentecostalism to adapt to and fulfil African religious aspirations was its main strength. African pentecostal churches (particularly those without any 'white' influence whatever) have contextualized and indigenized Christianity in Africa.

74. Horn, 'Experience of the Spirit', p. 29.
75. Horn, 'Experience of the Spirit', p. 29.

The unique contribution of the pentecostals in the early years of this century to a multitude of AICs in South Africa, and their common roots are highly significant facts. The independent African pentecostal churches have in turn made their own distinct contribution to African theology, to the extent that these churches have developed along quite different lines from the more western pentecostal churches. These churches demonstrate what happens when Pentecostalism, unencumbered by western forms, encounters the traditional spirituality of Africa. Holistic, ecstatic, and experiential religious practices are still found in pentecostal liturgy throughout the world, as they were borrowed from the nineteenth-century African American Holiness movement, which in turn had roots in traditional African religion—the shout, antiphonal singing, simultaneous and spontaneous prayer, dance and motor behaviour—are all essentially African practices. Early pentecostals emphasized the freedom, equality, community and dignity of people in the sight of God. The pentecostal experience of the power of the Spirit can be a unifying factor in a deeply divided society, and the catalyst for the emergence of a new community.

Patrick Kalilombe

Allan Anderson's article is of great interest to us here in Britain in that
it reflects on the relationship between black and white pentecostals in
South Africa at this time when officially the apartheid system has been
abandoned. Pentecostalism has been closely related to the African Insti-
tuted Churches whose rise and development has, in the South African
context, been seen as largely due to that system of racist discrimination.
We in Britain have wanted to learn what effect the socio-political
changes in South Africa, as indeed in the whole of Africa, will have on
these independent churches and on their role and significance in the
new situation. This was one of the aims of the Nairobi Consultation of
1995. We wanted to find out whether there were any lessons we could
learn from the African scene for our own understanding of the future of
black churches and the relation between black and white churches in
this country, but also in the countries of continental Europe where it is
now clear that the Black Church movement is spreading fast in its cities.

This article goes a long way towards giving us some matter for reflection, which we in Britain have been looking for. Most of the reflections
are based on the author's recent research as reported in his two books,
where Anderson also is forced to look at historical factors. When black
churches were just beginning in Britain, there was already a long history of these churches in South Africa, and therefore studies from South
Africa may give us some idea of where the black-led churches in Britain
might go. The main theme is an examination of the relationships between the involvement of white and black Christians in Pentecostalism.
This seems to be addressing a similar question to the one Iain Mac-
Robert, encouraged by Hollenweger, together with others, sought to
investigate, namely, 'the reasons for the non-integration of the black-

led and white-led pentecostal congregations in England'.[1] Anderson's conclusion for the South African scene is very similar to the one for the British situation, as summarized by Hollenweger, namely, that white and black 'are two cultures, an oral, narrative, inclusive black culture and a literary, conceptual, exclusive white culture. The two integrate very badly and only if some of the black and white Christians become "bilingual" '.[2] This is demonstrated in the two cases by recalling the history of the early years of Pentecostalism. We see how already then white pentecostals had to struggle with what Anderson calls 'dangerous memories' of the non-racial beginnings of Pentecostalism and of the fact that most of what is distinctive in pentecostal style and practice derives from African black cultural and religious traditions.

The tendency to wish to suppress or side-step the African cultural roots of Pentecostalism has resulted in the introduction into the Pentecostal movement of 'problems' that keep bedevilling it: among others, the rigidity of doctrinal and organizational structures that encourages partisan and exclusive fundamentalist dogmatism and serves as a backhanded device for racially motivated so-called 'natural and spontaneous segregation', which was not natural nor spontaneous at all. It is also largely responsible for the proliferation of the new types of narrowly conceived 'charismatic', televangelistic faith healing campaigns, and the capitalism-influenced 'prosperity' gospel trends described in J.N. Horn's *From Rags to Riches*,[3] as well as the tendency to break down the holistic vision of human life by separating the spiritual from the temporal, socio-economic and political realities.

What I find most instructive, then, in the article is the fact that it highlights the problems that result in Pentecostalism from the attempt to underplay its African origins and to impose on it other world-views that militate against those black cultural roots, I think that the future of black churches here in Britain, most of which belong to Anderson's general 'pentecostal-type', will be determined mainly by whether or not these churches own their African origins and avoid being co-opted by other cultural trends which seek to discredit whatever is black or African. The fact that a growing number of young blacks are becoming disenchanted

1.   I. MacRobert, *The Black Roots and White Racism of Early Pentecostalism in the USA* (Basingstoke: Macmillan, 1988), p. ix.

2.   MacRobert, *Black Roots*, pp. xiii-xiv.

3.   J.N. Horn, *From Rags to Riches* (Pretoria: University of South Africa Press, 1989).

with the black churches which meant so much to their elders and seem to find them irrelevant may be a sign of warning in this sense.

Anderson's article seems to allude, at several points, to a fundamental problem in the general study and description of black religious experience, pentecostal or otherwise; but it does not deal with it explicitly. And that is that, by and large, these studies are made from the point of view of non-blacks rather than that of blacks themselves. Until now such studies are predominantly attempts to help the white-dominated establishment to begin to understand and make sense of the black experience. The questions and issues that are raised, the kind of analytical tools and even the language that are used, assume that the point of reference is primarily the white experience and that the blacks themselves are mainly seen as the object of study. I am thinking of questions like syncretism, which is a problem that one likes to raise about black Christianity, as if it is not a question that has to be raised for any and every cultural incarnation of the Christian faith. Similarly, the construction of typologies for analysing black religious trends, the classifications that are made, and even the names applied to these religious trends are largely imposed unilaterally from outside. One wonders what the blacks themselves would say about them and the title 'pentecostal' which is applied to them. It would be interesting to find out, for example, how the African Independent Churches interpret the dynamics of their expansion, the motivations for their activities and practices, the reasons for which people join this or that church or decide to change over to another, or how they assess the 'truthfulness', the 'goodness' or otherwise of their beliefs and practices. This would surely lead us to a better understanding of what is going on. I have attempted elsewhere to show, for example, how the question of ecumenism could be understood in a new light if we took into serious consideration the understanding of religious belonging in the African Traditional Religion.[4] In his conclusion, Anderson remarks quite rightly that independent African pentecostal churches have made their own distinct contribution to African theology, as 'these churches have developed along quite different lines from the more western pentecostal churches'. This should mean that henceforth our progress in understanding these churches will depend on how much, and how authentically, the black participants begin to speak for themselves.

4. P. Kalilombe and M. Santer, 'Unity from Below: Lessons from African Traditional Religion' (Selly Oak Colleges Occasional Paper 11, 1993).

INDIGENOUS PENTECOSTALISM AND
THE CHILEAN EXPERIENCE

Juan Sepúlveda

Introduction

The increasing interest that the growth rate of Protestantism in Latin America has awakened among scholars was made apparent with the publication in 1990 of two very much commended books, David Stoll's *Is Latin America Turning Protestant? The Politics of Evangelical Growth*,[1] and David Martin's *Tongues of Fire: The Explosion of Protestantism in Latin America*.[2] As the title of the latter suggests, this 'explosive' growth is attributed mainly to the pentecostal-type churches. Since then, quite a number of new articles and books have been published, both in English and Spanish, so that the bibliography on Latin American Pentecostalism is getting bigger and bigger. However, the dominant perspective of researchers on Latin American Pentecostalism since the ground-breaking works of Emile Willems and Christian Lalive d'Epinay[3] 30 years ago has remained mainly sociological. As Francisco Cartaxo Rolim, himself a sociologist, put it, scholars have been more interested to know what Pentecostalism *does* (or does not) in society as a whole, than to know what Pentecostalism *is in itself*.[4]

---

1.   D. Stoll, *Is Latin America Turning Protestant? The Politics of Evangelical Growth* (Berkeley: University of California Press, 1990).
2.   D. Martin, *Tongues of Fire: The Explosion of Protestantism in Latin America* (Oxford: Basil Blackwell, 1990).
3.   E. Willems, *Followers of the New Faith: Culture Change and the Rise of Protestantism in Brazil and Chile* (Nashville: Vanderbilt University Press, 1967); C. Lalive D'Epinay, *Haven of the Masses: A Study of the Pentecostal Movement in Chile* (London: Lutterworth, 1969).
4.   F.C. Rolim, 'Pentecostisme et société au Brésil', *Social Compass* 26 (1979), pp. 345-372 (346).

Consequently, Pentecostalism has often been seen as a sort of mechanism of social adaptation in a time of rapid and conflictive social changes, overlooking and underestimating its religious and theological significance.

Without underestimating the valuable insights contained in the abundant sociological literature on Latin American Pentecostalism, the purpose of this article is to highlight another perspective, namely, the attempt to understand pentecostal growth in Latin America as the emergence of a search for an indigenous Christianity. This perspective was suggested by Eugene Nida as early as 1961,[5] and has been clearly present in Professor Hollenweger's writings on Latin American Pentecostalism,[6] but was only partially considered by Lalive's and Willems' classic works. During the 1970s and the early 1980s, this perspective was almost totally obscured because of the dominance of the so-called conspiracy theory, which interpreted the growth of pentecostal-type churches and other 'sects' in Latin America as the product of a strategy of the USA Department of State to counterbalance the influence of liberation theology, and to provide a religious legitimisation for US American imperialism.[7] These churches, therefore, were seen as anything but foreign. More recently, a number of case studies in different Latin American countries, chiefly by anthropologists, have related the adoption of pentecostal-type expressions of Christianity by sections of the indigenous population, to new processes of 'ethnic revitalization', bringing new light to the interpretation of Latin American Pentecostalism as the emergence of an indigenous Christianity.[8]

5.   E. Nida, 'The Indigenous Churches in Latin America', *Practical Anthropology* 8 (1961), pp. 97-105.

6.   W.H. Hollenweger, *The Pentecostals* (London: SCM, 1972); *idem*, 'Methodist's Past in Pentecostalism's Present', *Methodist History* 20 (1982), pp. 169-82.

7.   The 'conspiracy theories' brought together old allegations of traditional Catholicism against Protestant missions in Latin America, and new ideological confrontations. See S. Escobar, 'Conflict of Interpretations of Popular Protestantism', in G. Cook (ed.), *New Face of the Church in Latin America* (New York: Orbis Books, 1994), pp. 112-34. A well known representative of the 'conspiracy theories'' was A.M. Ezcurra, *The Neoconservative Offensive: US Churches and the Ideological Struggle for Latin America* (New York: Circus Publications, 1983).

8.   See literature quoted by J.-P. Bastián, 'La mutación del protestantismo Latinoamericano', in T. Gutierrez (ed.), *Protestantismo y cultura en América Latina* (Quito: CLAI-CEHILA, 1994), pp. 115-35.

My own contribution here is an attempt to look at Chilean Pentecostalism, which, along with Brazilian Pentecostalism, represents the
earlier expression of a Pentecostalism of local origin and independent
development in Latin America, from the perspective of the search for
an indigenous Christianity.[9] The article will conclude with some reflections on the relevance of this perspective both as a complementary
explanatory factor of Latin American Pentecostal growth, and for the
understanding of the religious and theological significance of Pentecostalism in itself.

The Methodist Revival and the Birth of Pentecostalism in Chile

It is generally considered that the famous revival of Azusa Street in
1906 is the cradle of modern Pentecostalism. 'As Aldersgate Street,
London was to Methodism, so Azusa Street, Los Angeles was to Pentecostalism'.[10] Chilean Pentecostalism is, however, the result of an
independent development, contemporary to that of Los Angeles.[11] Most
of the descriptions of the Chilean revival follow the testimony written
by one of its key protagonists, Willis C. Hoover.[12] Born on 20 July
1858 in Freeport, Illinois, Hoover studied medicine in Chicago. Out of
personal dissatisfaction, in 1889 he gave up medicine and applied to
William Taylor's self-supporting mission. The same year Hoover was
sent as teacher to the Iquique School in northern Chile, where he
worked until 1893 when, disappointed with its evangelistic results, he
decided to dedicate himself entirely to the Spanish preaching work. He

---

9.   The core of this analysis is part of Chapter 3 of my doctoral thesis:
J. Sepúlveda, 'Gospel and Culture in Latin American Protestantism: Toward a New
Theological Appreciation of Syncretism' (PhD thesis, University of Birmingham,
1996).
10.   Martin, *Tongues of Fire*, p. 29.
11.   I am of the opinion that the recognition that modern Pentecostalism developed from revivals occurring more or less at the same time across the Americas,
Europe, Asia and Africa, should replace the image of a single birth place from
where Pentecostalism spread all over the world. C.M. Robeck, 'Pentecostal Origins
from a Global Perspective', in H. Hunter and P. Hocken (eds.), *All Together in
One Place* (1992 Brighton Conference Papers; Sheffield: Sheffield Academic Press,
1993), pp. 166-80, however, thinks that there is not enough historical evidence to
dismiss the theory of a single origin.
12.   W. Hoover, *Historia del avivamiento pentecostal en Chile* (Valparaiso:
Excelsior, 1948).

soon succeeded in forming churches in two little towns outside Iquique. The following year, he was made pastor of the Spanish-speaking church of Iquique.[13] Trying to find a date that could be rightly marked as the beginning of the process toward the revival, Hoover mentions a number of events that occurred during his Methodist ministry.

During a furlough between November 1894 and September 1895, he visited a 'pre-Pentecostal' church in Chicago 'which was living in a constant state of revival'. Such an experience left a lasting impression on him.[14] In 1902, he replaced E. Wilson as pastor of the Church of Valparaiso. There he found that the members of the church, although fervent and well-organized, had little idea about the meaning of sanctification. Soon after his arrival, a series of studies on the Acts of the Apostles for the Sunday school's teachers was organized. When studying Acts 2, the question emerged about what prevented them from receiving the Holy Spirit as the primitive church did. Hoover's answer was that the only impediment lay in themselves.[15] That moment triggered an intense search for sanctification involving most of the congregation. Between 1905 and 1906, two tragedies affected Valparaiso: a smallpox epidemic, and a devastating earthquake followed by fires. The earthquake destroyed the church building, so the congregation had to be divided into small clusters worshipping in some homes, each one under the care of a lay exhorter. These events did nothing but increase the longing for a spiritual revival.[16]

The first contact with the 'Pentecostal doctrine' as such occurred in 1907, when Mrs Hoover received a pamphlet describing a revival that had taken place in the girls' home of Pandita Ramabai at Mukti, India. It had been written and sent by Minnie Abrams, Mrs Hoover's old classmate at the Chicago Training School. According to Hoover, the pamphlet spoke of a 'clear and distinct baptism of the Spirit, as a complement to justification and sanctification which we had hitherto believed to comprise the whole of Christian experience'.[17] The pamphlet

---

13. J.B.A. Kessler, *A Study of the Older Protestant Missions and Churches in Peru and Chile* (Goes: Oosterbaan & le Cointre, 1967), pp. 101, 108.

14. Hoover, *Historia*, p. 9.

15. Hoover, *Historia*, pp. 10-11.

16. Hoover, *Historia*, pp. 13-16.

17. Hoover, *Historia*, p. 14. C.M. Robeck ('Pentecostal Origins', p. 177) finds in the fact that Minnie Abrams, the author of the pamphlet, 'had received her Pentecost at Azusa Street', enough evidence to suggests that the Chilean revival was also

also reported that some of the girls baptized by the Spirit had seen visions, fallen into trances and spoken in languages other than their own. The congregation continued its services in a large tent erected with the help of the mission, and after collecting money from local sources it started to build a new temple. Meanwhile, Hoover corresponded with several early pentecostal leaders to find out more about the Baptism of the Holy Spirit. On 7 March 1909, the new building, which could seat 1,000 people, was dedicated by Bishop Bristol.[18] So, the stage was set for the special blessings for which they were all waiting.

Up to that moment, Hoover's gifts to build up a fervent congregation and to motivate their giving so that a large building could be erected with no money from the mission Board, made him appear as a very successful Methodist pastor. In fact, in 1906 he was made Superintendent of the central Methodist district of Chile.[19] Representatives from other Methodist and even Presbyterian churches[20] would visit Valparaiso's church to learn from the experience going on there. But troubles were not far ahead.

On the initiative of lay members of the congregation, but with Hoover's support, new activities, like daily prayer groups and all night watch services every Saturday, were added to improve the spiritual

---

a product, however indirect, of the Azusa Street revival. The fact is, however, that Minnie Abrams—a Methodist missionary in India who worked for about 10 years at Pandita Ramabai's Mukti Mission—had received her Pentecostal experience during the revival started in 1905 at Mukti. The pamphlet that the Hoovers received from M. Abrams, *The Baptism in the Holy Ghost and Fire*, was her account and reflections on the mentioned revival. She only went back to the USA in 1909, and eventually visited Pentecostal churches in Los Angeles. In the background of the revival at Mukti was the participation of Pandita Ramabai in the Keswick Convention (July 1898), and her contacts through correspondence with the Welsh revival, as well as the personal participation of Minnie Abrams and Manorama (Ramabai's daughter) in a revival in Australia (1903). It is worth noting that Pandita Ramabai herself understood the movement of revival as a way of letting the Holy Spirit raise an indigenous (Indian) Christianity. On these issues see S.M. Adhav, *Pandita Ramabai* (Madras: The Christian Literature Society, 1979), pp. 216-36; P. Sengupta, *Pandita Ramabai Saraswati: Her Life and Work* (London: Asia Publishing House, 1970), pp. 305-308; S.M. Burgess, G.B. McGee and P.H. Alexander (eds.), *Dictionary of Pentecostal and Charismatic Movements* (Grand Rapids: Zondervan, 1988), article 'Abrams, Minnie F', p. 7.

18. Kessler, *Older Protestant Missions*, p. 110.
19. Kessler, *Older Protestant Missions*, p. 110.
20. Kessler, *Older Protestant Missions*, p. 116.

condition of the congregation. What happened then is described by Hoover himself:

> Laughing, weeping, shouting, singing, foreign tongues, visions and ecstasies during which the individual fell to the ground and felt himself caught up into another place, to heaven, to Paradise, in splendid fields, with various kinds of experience: conversations with God, the angels or the devil. Those who experienced these things profited greatly and generally were changed by them and filled with praises, the spirit of prayer and love.[21]
>
> When the Spirit fell upon us with power, the baptized persons, men, women and children, felt themselves compelled to rush into the street and to shout out loud (about their experience), to visit their friends and neighbours, to travel to other places, with the sole object of calling men to repentance and letting them know by their testimony that such a sublime experience was within the reach of every one of them today, as it was in the time of the Apostles.[22]

While the highly noisy meetings and the incursions into streets and other public spaces brought about the reaction of local authorities and the press,[23] the visits to other places, which of course included other Methodist churches, provoked increasing conflict with the national structure of that church and the mission Board. On 12 September 1909, Nellie Laidlaw, a new convert of Valparaiso, who was known for her gift of prophecy, while visiting the Sunday morning worship of the Second Methodist Church in Santiago asked for permission from the pastor to speak to the congregation. As Pastor Robinson, despite the plea of some members, refused, a group went out to the courtyard to hear Nellie Laidlaw's message, the whole situation ending in a bitter argument. The events were repeated at the evening service in the First Church, but as this time the police intervened, the situation ended with Nellie Laidlaw under arrest.[24]

21. Hoover, *Historia*, p. 33.

22. Hoover, *Historia*, p. 43.

23. Articles with sensational headlines were published by *El Chileno y El Mercurio*, suggesting that the authorities should intervene (cf. Lalive, *Haven of the Masses*, p. 8). In fact an investigation was carried out by the municipality after which Hoover had to agree to finish the services no later than 10.00 pm (Kessler, *Older Protestant Missions*, p. 123).

24. Hoover, *Historia*, p. 34. In a detailed description of these events, Kessler (*Older Protestant Missions*, pp. 116-22) makes Nellie Laidlaw (also known as the hermana Elena) the person directly responsible (Hoover would be the person

This date is generally regarded as the birth day of Chilean Pente-costalism, because from that time on the majority of the people in the congregations of the First and Second Methodist churches of Santiago started to hold separate services in private homes. Although Hoover had advised them not to organize a separate church before presenting their case at the next annual Methodist Conference to be held in February 1910,[25] already in December 1909 the quarterly Conference of Santiago decided to cut 'all official relations with all people who had withdrawn from the churches and continued to hold separate meetings in scan-dalous opposition'.[26] If the same did not happen in Valparaiso's church, it was simply because there the movement had not only the support but also the leadership of its pastor, that is to say, the missionary. But the way was being prepared for Hoover's doctrines and practices to be put on trial in the annual conference.

The Conference was held from 4 to 11 February 1910, in Valparaiso, that is to say, in Hoover's church. At the beginning a Disciplinary Commission under the chairmanship of Robert Elphick was designated to examine Hoover's situation. On 10 February the Commission sub-mitted its report to the Conference, making a detailed accusation against Hoover of 'teaching and publicly and privately disseminating false and anti-Methodist doctrines'.[27] Since Hoover was prepared to defend his point of view with quotations from Wesley's writings, and to recognize that in the first stages of the revival some excesses were tolerated but later eradicated,[28] the approval of the accusation by the Conference was

indirectly responsible for giving her freedom of action and letters of recommen-dation) for what he calls 'the wrong turning taken by the revival'. She is described as a woman of 'drunken and dissolute life', who practiced 'prostitution' before she was taken into the Hoovers' household and eventually professed conversion (p. 117). It is suggested that she suffered from schizophrenia, and that she died as an unre-pentant drug addict (p. 121). Although some of the basic information may well be accurate, one must bear in mind that many of Kessler's comments are based on recollections of witnesses from the other side of the conflict.

25. Hoover, *Historia*, pp. 38, 63.

26. Kessler, *Older Protestant Missions*, p. 122.

27. Lalive, *Haven of the Masses*, p. 10.

28. About the 'excesses' of the first stages of the revival, Hoover wrote: 'As in that time all those things were so new and strange, we found ourselves in the obli-gation to study them; and to do that, it was necessary to give some freedom. Seeing so much good fruits we could not condemn those things, simply because they were

not easy. Attempting an easier settlement, the Conference offered to withdraw the charges against Hoover if he would agree to take a holiday in his home country. Hoover agreed, hoping that he could find a better hearing of his case before the mission board at home.[29] However, a resolution theoretically addressed against Nellie Laidlaw was passed, which declared that the claims that the baptism of the Holy Spirit was accompanied by gift of tongues, visions, healings or other manifestations, were 'anti-Methodist, contrary to the Scriptures and irrational'.[30]

The two groups of Santiago, which had been virtually excommunicated, understood well that the Conference's resolution was not only against Nellie Laidlaw, but also against the revival movement as a whole. Consequently, their reaction was to organize themselves as a separate church with the name Iglesia Metodista Nacional (National Methodist Church). Hoover was at first determined to keep his promise of going on furlough, but the officers of Valparaiso's congregation pleaded with him not to leave them. After a quarterly Conference held in Valparaiso on 4 April with Pastor Rice as the new Superintendent, the officers of the Valparaiso church decided to withdraw from the Methodist Episcopal Church. This fact seems to have motivated the Hoovers to take their decision to resign from the Mission and to follow their Chilean brethren.[31] On 17 April, Hoover read out his letter of resignation to the congregation, stating that he was not separating himself from Wesley nor from Methodism, 'but only from the Church's government, by reason of conscience'.[32] Soon after, the groups of Santiago invited him to act as their Superintendent. Hoover agreed, but he suggested that the name of the new church should be Iglesia Metodista Pentecostal (Pentecostal Methodist Church, hereafter IMP) to make it clear that the division did not come out of nationalism.[33]

---

beyond our experience' (*Historia*, p. 35). 'It is better to leave untouched a bit of the work of the devil than to put wrongly our hands over God's work' (p. 30).

29. Lalive, *Haven of the Masses*, p. 11; Kessler, *Older Protestant Missions*, p. 126.

30. Hoover, *Historia*, pp. 62-63.

31. Kessler, *Older Protestant Missions*, pp. 128-30.

32. Hoover, *Historia*, p. 74.

33. Hoover, *Historia*, pp. 74, 98-99.

Looking at the Nature of the Conflict: Doctrinal or Cultural?

It is clear that all along in the events that broke the unity of the Methodist Church in Chile during the years 1909–1910, there were some doctrinal issues at stake.[34] As already indicated, the claim that the baptism of the Holy Spirit was a necessary complement to justification and sanctification, was a factor in the direction the revival took after 1907. There was also the question whether the 'signs and wonders' of the work of the Holy Spirit were something of the past, that is to say, restricted to the apostolic era,[35] or something available or even necessary for the churches of all ages. But, as Hoover himself kept saying, the division was not caused so much by doctrinal reasons as by conflicts over practices and church government.[36] Leaders of the IMP told Professor Hollenweger that 'the difference between the Methodists and us does not lie in a different doctrine. It is just that they merely have the Methodist doctrines whilst we experience them'.[37] In fact, Chilean Pentecostalism accepts the 25 faith articles of the Methodist Episcopal Church with no alteration, practises infant baptism, it continues with minor adaptations the Methodist system of church government and organization, and uses the old Methodist manual for worship and special ceremonies. This closeness to Methodism differentiates Chilean Pentecostalism from USA born Pentecostalism.

Some scholars have suggested that the conflict should rather be understood as a clash of 'mentalities'[38] or a 'cultural clash'.[39] In line with

34. Kessler, *Older Protestant Missions*, p. 124.

35. The opinion, generally accepted within the Western theological tradition since St John Chrysostom (fourth century), that the *charismata* were gifts temporarily given to the early church because of its weakness, was maintained by Luther and Calvin. See J.J. Comblin, *The Holy Spirit and Liberation* (New York: Orbis Books, 1987), p. 35. John Wesley seems to have separated himself from that tradition. See D. Dayton, *Raíces teológicas del pentecostalismo* (Buenos Aires: Nueva Creación; Grand Rapids: Eerdmans, 1991), pp. 25-26. However, one month after the conflict in his church, the pastor of the Second Methodist church of Santiago, Robinson, wrote an editorial article in *El Cristiano* (18 October 1909) defending the 'traditional' opinion, additionally stating that the work of the Spirit was always 'rational'.

36. Hoover, *Historia*, pp. 70-71, 74, 81-82.

37. Hollenweger, 'Methodist's Past', p. 176.

38. Lalive, *Haven of the Masses*, p. 10.

39. Hollenweger, *Pentecostals*, p. 198.

that interpretation, I have suggested elsewhere that the main aspects of the conflict were two, namely:

(1)   a conflict between a religiosity centred in the 'objectivity of dogma', in which faith consists of formal, conscious and rational acceptance of determined beliefs or doctrines, and a religiosity that gives primacy to the subjective experience of God, in which faith is a response to a kind of possession of one's being by the divine; and

(2)   a conflict between a religion mediated by specialists of the cultured classes (an illustrious clergy) and a religion in which the poor, simple people have direct access to God and in which that relationship can be communicated in the language of feelings and the indigenous culture.[40]

To validate this analysis, however, it would be necessary to show whether both cultures were already present within the Methodist church. Otherwise, it would be an anachronistic projection of a situation typical of late Pentecostalism back to the time of the Methodist revival. Furthermore, if we do find some evidence that simple people bearing a popular culture were indeed members of the Methodist church, then it should be explained how they made their way into an Anglo-Saxon religion embedded, as it seems to have been, in the rationalism of the late nineteenth century. Hoover, the main source for the descriptions of the pentecostal origins, despite some references about the social provenance of those converted when the revival was already in motion,[41] shows little interest in the social background of its protagonists. It has been pointed out, however, that the abundant correspondence of lay participants in the movement quoted by Hoover suggests that many of them had a level of formal education far beyond the reach of poor people.[42] To examine this matter in depth, the work of Kessler, despite being fairly criticized for mixing 'theology and church history' and for

40. J, Sepúlveda, 'Reflections on the Pentecostal Contribution to the Mission of the Church in Latin America', *Journal of Pentecostal Theology* 1 (1992), pp. 93-108 (95).
41. Hoover makes reference to the conversion of many humble people, some of them outlaws, but also to the attraction the movement had for some 'gentlemen of dignity and serious young men' (*Historia*, p. 43).
42. M. Canales, S. Palma and H. Villela, *En tierra extraña II* (Santiago: Amerinda-SEPADE, 1991), p. 24.

being 'full of moral and theological statements and judgements',[43] has proved to be very helpful. His thorough archival research, as well as his 'special reference to the problems of division, nationalism and native ministry',[44] provide many hints on the nature of the conflict.

A letter sent by Florence Smith, a Presbyterian missionary in charge of the school in Valparaiso, to Robert Speer, the Secretary of the Board in New York (22 January 1906), offers a good point of departure for the analysis:

> Undoubtedly the Chile mission (Presbyterian) *is far and away ahead of the M.E. church in education, culture, sound judgment and wordly wisdom*. Personally they are all charming gentlemen, but oh Mr Speer we do lack warmth of spiritual life and love, or it is that we do not know how to express the warmth and the love we feel. Mr Hoover, the M.E. missionary in charge of the work here, is a man of one idea. *He is not too cultured to call the Chileans brothers. He is narrow, even bigoted*, but I believe he can truly say: 'This one thing I do' and 'I count all but loss that I may win the Chileans to Christ.' He is inordinately proud of the remarkable success of their work—to us offensively so! There is a great deal of froth and bombast and other defects it is easy to point out, but the fact remains, *the poor have the Gospel preached to them*.[45]

It is clear from the date that this letter was written during the early stages of the revival. So, all the comments refer not to a 'pentecostal' church, but to the Chilean Methodist church. Hoover is presented as a good example of what appears to be typical of early Methodist work in Chile. In this portrait, two 'cultures' or 'mentalities' emerge, one (educated, cultured, rich in sound judgment and worldly wisdom, but lacking a bodily language to express feelings) represented by the Presbyterian mission; and another (poorly cultivated, narrow, 'bigoted', 'frothy and bombastic' to express feelings) represented not by the pentecostals, but by the Methodist church itself, its missionaries (at least some of them) included. The final statement makes it clear that through the latter, 'the poor have the Gospel preached to them'.

Kessler mentions a number of facts that support the impression that Hoover was not an isolated case, but something like the best example within a general tendency. For instance, the Presbyterian mission had

43. F. Kamsteeg, *Prophetic Pentecostalism in Chile* (Amsterdam: Vrije Universiteit, 1995), p. 56.
44. The subtitle of Kessler's book.
45. Kessler, *Older Protestant Missions*, p. 105, emphasis added.

taken great pains to raise and prepare a 'native ministry'. However, eventually the best of their national workers felt compelled to leave the Presbyterian mission and passed to the Methodist church. That was the case of Juan Canut (1846–1896, born in Spain but converted in Chile), whose fame and success as a Methodist preacher and founder of churches was such that even today the nickname given by the common people to the Protestants is *canutos*.[46] On September 1905 Robert Elphick, already mentioned, had decided to leave the Presbyterians to join the Methodist church. Although Elphick himself understood his problems with the Presbyterian church as 'doctrinal', Garvin, one of the missionaries, pointed out in a letter to Speer (2 October 1905) the problem of 'methods and manners':

> He [Elphick] is by temperament a Methodist and their methods and manners suit him better than ours. I am quite convinced that those methods and manners are quite adapted to many of the people; better perhaps than our own for the great majority of the Chilean people.[47]

Kessler also reflects on the fact that the Methodists' work in Spanish found considerably more opposition than that of the Presbyterians. This could be interpreted as an indication that both churches were trying to find their place in different sectors of Chilean society, the Presbyterians in the 'cultured' middle class, the Methodists among the poor and 'uncultured': 'The uneducated people in Chile were fanatical whereas the cultured class were liberal and seemed to be much more open.'[48] Leaving his derogatory language aside, Kessler seems to point in the right direction. To be sure, Protestant preaching was full of criticism against 'popular Catholicism'. While this kind of criticism might of course have been hurtful for the lower classes (thus their reaction), in liberal circles it might rather have produced sympathy. But despite the opposition the Methodists confronted, it seems that their 'methods and manners' allowed them to win some hearing among the poor.

We have then sufficient evidence to say that by the turn of the century a clash between two 'mentalities' or 'cultures' was developing within Chilean Protestantism. At first, this conflict expressed itself in the different missionary strategies of Presbyterians and Methodists. That the early Methodist work showed 'methods and manners' better

46. Kessler, *Older Protestant Missions*, pp. 49-50, 52-54, 101-102.
47. Quoted by Kessler, *Older Protestant Missions*, p. 63.
48. Kessler, *Older Protestant Missions*, p. 48.

suited to the Chilean people, is explained by the fact that it started as an independent and self-supporting missionary project of William Taylor. The first generation of Methodist missionaries 'tended to be drawn from the less cultured, revivalist fringe of the Methodist church in United States',[49] therefore most of them felt more comfortable working with simple people than with the 'cultured' middle class. The opinion of David Trumbull, the founder of the Presbyterian mission in Chile, that 'the Taylor mission as a Gospel agency in Chile is not worth a rap. It has rather brought missions in discredit',[50] certainly reflects the failures of the early beginnings, but also reveals a sort of cultural contempt.

However, after the Methodist Episcopal Mission Board had taken over the work, and specially after Taylor's death in 1902, the new generation of missionaries arriving in Chile was educated with 'the conviction that revivalism no longer adequately expressed Christianity in the modern world'.[51] The Methodist Episcopal Church had reached an established position in North American society, and its emissaries were now preachers of progress and modernization. As this new generation reached high positions in the local hierarchy, the 'official' self-understanding of the Methodist church came closer to that of the Presbyterians,[52] and the conflict of 'mentalities' became sharper *within* the Methodist church. Kessler's assertion that the 'wise action' of the General Conference of 1884, which marked the beginning of the take-over of

49. Kessler, *Older Protestant Missions*, p. 103.

50. Letter to Gillespie quoted by Kessler, *Older Protestant Missions*, p. 100. Kessler justifies Trumbull's criticism on the ground of what he considers Taylor's total lack of provision for those missionaries who could run into difficulties (pp. 99-100). He did not realize that this lack of provision was not the result of Taylor's improvization, but rather the expression of his conscious missionary theories and policies. See D. Bundy, 'The Legacy of William Taylor', *International Bulletin of Missionary Research* 18 (1994), pp. 172-76.

51. Kessler, *Older Protestant Missions*, p. 111.

52. This closeness between Methodists and Presbyterians is proved by that fact that soon after the division of 1910, a new style of cooperation developed among both churches. In 1914, a bookstore (El Sembrador), a union paper (*El Heraldo Cristiano*) and a union seminary were all started in Santiago (see Kessler, *Older Protestant Missions*, p. 75). Ecumenical cooperation only started once the 'uncultured' and 'bigoted' were excommunicated. No wonder that Hoover had dismissed inter-church cooperation as a waste of time and promoted within Pentecostalism a policy of 'intransigence and complete isolation from the other churches' (Hoover, *Historia*, p. 102).

the Chilean work, helped to overcome the old disagreements between
Taylor's mission and the North American church, and that in Chile 'led
to unity on a broadened basis',[53] can hardly be defended. On the contrary, the way in which the revival was handled by the Methodist hierarchy can be understood as a late outcome of the co-option of Taylor's
self-supporting mission by the North American church.[54] If some of
Taylor's missionaries did not follow their 'Chilean brethren', as Hoover
did, this is understandable because of the hardships of going independent from the mission.

What has been said so far indeed shows elements of a clash between
an 'official' (educated, rational, modern) culture and a 'popular' (uncul-
tivated, oral, traditional) culture. This conflict was already present in
the missionary 'home base', but it manifested itself more sharply in the
'mission field'. So far, the dividing line appears to be more determined
by differences of socio-cultural background than by nationality. Are
there besides, any elements of a tension between a 'foreign culture' and
the 'local culture'? In other words, could the conflict be understood as
an expression of the search for an 'indigenous church'?

Hoover himself was far from being an advocate of 'church indigenization'. When explaining the motives of his resignation to the Methodist church, he declared with emphasis: 'Nobody should think that
there is something of nationalism in this action. May God forgive us for
such a thought and free us from that wrong.'[55] Although in matters of
worship and spiritual life Hoover was always remarkably willing to put
himself at the same level or even under the guidance of his Chilean sisters and brothers, in matters of church government he had far less confidence in them. Actually, as he was getting older, he tried hard to find a
way of putting Chilean Pentecostalism under the authority of the North

53. Hoover, *Historia*, p. 103.

54. It may be argued that without the financial support of the North American
church, Taylor's mission would hardly have survived. That is possibly true, but it is
also true that the North American church was not prepared to support the Chilean
church as a self-governing one.

55. Hoover, *Historia*, p. 74. Hoover's position against 'church nationalism'
could well be the result of his own experience. In September 1895, when Hoover
returned to Iquique after his furlough in USA, he found that A. Vidaurre, the
Chilean worker in charge of the church during his absence, did not want to submit
himself to the authority of a foreign missionary. So Vidaurre left the Methodist
church with most of the congregation. Hoover had to start again from nothing,
which he did with success (see Kessler, *Older Protestant Missions*, p. 109).

American movement, or at least, to find a North American pentecostal leader as his successor.[56] He continued as Superintendent of the IMP until the struggle for power divided it between the years 1932–1934,[57] and in the same position in the Iglesia Evangélica Pentecostal (Evangelical Pentecostal Church, hereafter IEP), formed by those who supported him, until his death on 27 May 1936. To this day, the IEP is reluctant to accept in its temples musical instruments other than the sober organ, another sign of Hoover's legacy in matters of indigenization.

But Hoover's personal opinion does not necessarily deny that behind the Methodist division there was a move toward 'indigenization'. The 'self-supporting mission' that created the background for the revival and the further development of Chilean Pentecostalism, was in itself a sort of 'experimental model' for an indigenous mission. In his *Pauline Methods of Missionary Work*, published only two years after the beginning of his South American experience, Taylor argues 'that the goal of Pauline mission is independent churches that are self-supporting, entrusted with their own governance, and committed to an evangelistic style that enables them to grow according to their own cultural patterns'.[58] This small essay on missionary theory is amazing not only for having being written 33 years before Allen's *Missionary Methods: St. Paul's or Ours?*, but also because it was part of an ongoing missionary experiment designed in opposition to those who 'claimed that the mission board structure was *the* modern approach to mission'.[59]

We do not have evidence as to whether all of Taylor's missionaries in Chile knew much about his theories, but the spirit of his approach was indeed present in those working in Spanish. This spirit seems to have early permeated the Chilean workers of the Presbyterian church as well.

56. Kessler, *Older Protestant Missions*, pp. 281, 300. The 'doctrinal' differences that distinguished Chilean Pentecostalism from North American Pentecostalism (the question of infant baptism, the forms of baptism, in other words, the Methodist legacy) prevented Hoover from going further with his intentions. To be sure, he would have found a bigger 'stumbling block' in the opposition of the Chileans to that solution.

57. There was also an accusation of immorality against Hoover. However, Kessler shows clearly that although Hoover eventually 'confessed his guilt', this accusation was subservient to the struggle of power (pp. 303-307).

58. W. Taylor, *Pauline Methods of Missionary Work* (Philadelphia: National Association for the Promotion of Holiness, 1879), in Bundy, 'Legacy', p. 174.

59. Bundy, 'Legacy', p. 174.

One could well see the Methodist revival within the context of a wider search for reshaping the life of the churches into the local 'methods and manners.' The Presbyterian church of Concepción, for instance, which was in the charge of a 'national worker', Tulio Morán, was following a path quite different from that of the mission. A temporary illness of Morán in 1907 gave the mission the chance of sending a new missionary, James McLean, to put things in order. One of the first of McLean's reports reads:

> This congregation is nondescript in relation to any system of doctrine or policy. In government they are Congregationalist, as concerns baptism— ultra immersionists, in worship fiery Methodists. Hostility to the rich and educated extends its forbidding arms, an exaggerated type of communism repels the sane enquirer, and the relinquishment of voter's rights makes Christ appear in a false light to a liberty-loving citizen who prizes his blood-bought franchise. Can we not do something for the rich and polished sinners for whom Christ died?[60]

As the cause of such a development was thought to be the 'lack of supervision' by the mission, an experienced missionary, William Boomer, was moved to Concepción, and Tulio Morán became his 'associate' minister. The situation ended with Morán's resignation and the division of the church.[61] Morán and those who followed him later joined the pentecostal movement. In a different development, H. Weiss, the founder of the Christian Missionary Alliance's work in Chile, reported to Chile Evangélico (Concepción, 10 December 1909) how the revival reached their own churches in Valdivia. In his letter, Weiss tells the readers how humiliating it was at first for them, the foreign pastors, to see local laywomen interceding for them. 'Pastors are the first ones to resist the Holy Spirit and the last ones to humiliate themselves to the dust.' It seems that the fact that the 'foreign pastors' of the CMA humiliated themselves (as Hoover did in Valparaiso) into the 'methods and manners' of the national members of their congregations, prevented the

---

60. Quoted by Kessler, *Older Protestant Missions*, p. 66.

61. Kessler's comment on this incident is worth quoting: 'The basic trouble was not, however, a lack of supervision, but a surplus of United States nationalism. As soon as the missionaries discovered that the church practice in Concepçión was irregular, they reacted against what they felt was a failure to conform to the Gospel by asserting their Presbyterian law. The missionaries forgot that this law had arisen as a result of an attempt by European or Anglo-Saxon people to conform to the Gospel in their own environment' (p. 67).

division. In this case, the revival was welcomed within the church structure.

Therefore, the understanding of the conflict as a 'cultural clash' seems to have solid grounds, and the 'cultural factor' was to play a major role in the further development of Pentecostalism. Whatever Hoover's intentions and thoughts had been, the church he helped to found became the very first Chilean self-supporting, self-governing and self-propagating church.

'Cultural Adaptation' in the Evolution of Chilean Pentecostalism

If one century after the arrival of J. Thomson, the first missionary, Protestants comprised no more than the 1.4% of the total Chilean population (National Census 1920), the last census (1992) showed that Protestants (*Evangelicos* and *Protestantes* together) have reached 13.2% of the population 14 years or older.[62] Despite the fact that these figures comprise all the Protestant groups together, all observers agree that this rate of growth has to be seen as the result of the dynamic expansion of Chilean Pentecostalism.[63] The fact that the 'explosive' growth did not start until the 1930s,[64] that is, after the world-wide economic depression toward the end of the 1920s forced major structural changes in Chilean society, led sociologists to explain Pentecostal growth mostly by reference to external social factors. Starting from the paradigm of a transitional situation from a fundamentally agrarian, religious, traditional and authoritarian (feudal) society towards a society that is basically urban, secularized, modern and democratic, Pentecostalism was seen as one expression or symptom of change.[65] Although this line of Weberian

---

62. C. Parker, 'Radiografía a la religión de los chilenos', *Mensaje* 428 (1994), pp. 178-81.

63. Until the 1960 census, traditional Protestant churches seem to have grown at a rate hardly higher than the rate of growth of the Chilean population as a whole, and in some cases even lower than it (see Lalive, *Haven of the Masses*, p. 16).

64. The percentage of Protestants in the national censuses since 1907 are: 1907, 1%; 1920, 1.4%; 1930, 1.4%; 1940, 2.34%; 1952, 4.06%; 1960, 5.58%; 1970, 6.18%; 1992, 13.2%. The census of 1982 did not ask about religious affiliation. The census of 1992 asked only about the population 14 years or older.

65. The classics are the books already mentioned by E. Willems and C. Lalive d'Epinay. The famous formulation of the latter goes as follows: 'If Pentecostal preaching met such a response, it is because (in market terms) it supplied a demand

interpretation is still very fashionable,[66] the purpose of this section is to
address the importance of internal factors that could help us to understand Pentecostalism's appeal to the lower classes of Chilean society.[67]
In fact, the external social factors alone do not explain why Pentecostalism has succeeded in attracting poor people where and when traditional
Protestantism has not. The attention, then, needs to be focused on the
ability of Chilean Pentecostalism to translate the Protestant message
into the forms of expression of the local popular culture.[68]

Despite Hoover's rejection of 'nationalism' as a right motive for their
separation from the Methodist Episcopal Church, the division forced the
new movement to rely on national resources, both human and material,
for its future development. Except for Hoover, all the ministry and leadership of the new church had to come from the Chilean converts, most
of them reared in the context of popular Catholicism. Thus it was inevitable that an unconscious process of cultural adaptation of the Protestant message and the ways of church life had taken place. W Carter was
the first to notice that this adaptation had proceeded through a complex
relation of rejection and continuity:

> ... not only has Pentecostalism known how to meet a felt need; it has
> known how to fit its ritual into the culture, while yet maintaining its un-
> questionably unique identity. For example, its church buildings may be
> on deserted side streets. But it follows the traditional pattern of religion
> in the plaza, by constantly holding open air meetings there. It rejects the
> traditional saint's day processionals, but it preserves the basic idea that
> one should process in religion. One sees immense groups processing
> from the evening plaza rally to their Pentecostal temple, singing songs

which was caused by the slow transition from a traditional and seignorial type of
society towards a secularized, democratic society' (*Haven of the Masses*, p. 30).

66. Although with some variations, the more recent work of D. Martin (*Tongues
of Fire*) follows the same line.

67. All the literature agrees that Chilean Pentecostalism has grown mostly, and
almost exclusively, in the poorer sectors of society, especially between unskilled
workers with endemic instability of employment, house keepers, servants, and small
independent artisans and vendors. As a rule, they are *mestizo*, that is to say, of
mixed blood (Indian and Spanish).

68. It is fair to recognize that both Lalive and Willems were well aware of the
importance of this aspect. Willems speaks of the 'compatibilities and incompati-
bilities' with the basic structural aspects of the native society (*Followers of the New
Faith*, pp. 21-25). But they were mostly interested in the impact of the structural
changes going on in the society as a whole on Pentecostal growth, and vice versa.

that are accompanied by guitars and that come straight out of the popular music of the masses. It instructs its members to refrain from the frequent evening visits with friends in the neighbourhood bar. But it offers, in its place, nightly, informal services with one's friends at the local temple. It retains extended, private prayer, but it dictates that it should be done in a clearly audible voice. It rejects miraculous healing through the saints, but it claims that divine healing may be easily had by direct prayer to God.[69]

Because Carter's observations show very well how this dynamic of rejection and continuity works, further examples are not necessary. However, some aspects of his interpretation need some discussion and clarification. First, one gets the impression that there was a 'unique Pentecostal identity' already defined or finished before it entered into contact with the local culture, and that this identity has been maintained without essential change throughout the process of adaptation. Such an idea is dispelled by the simple fact that Pentecostalism did not arrive in Chile as a ready-made missionary product. One should rather see what Chilean Pentecostalism is, that is to say, its identity, as one result of the complex relation of continuity and discontinuity between the Protestant tradition received from the missionaries, popular Catholicism, and the local culture.

Secondly, one gets the impression that as a rule, Pentecostalism adopted *forms* but never *contents* from the local religious culture. This would mean that the doctrines received from the missionaries have always been maintained pure, and only dressed with local clothing. However, this theoretical clear-cut distinction between content and form proves to be more difficult in practice. A case in point is the last of Carter's examples, that of healing. The importance of healing could be seen as a sort of 'point of contact' between primitive Christianity,

---

69. Quoted by Lalive, *Haven of the Masses*, p. 63. Consistent with his interest in structural change, Lalive himself applies this paradigm of continuity and discontinuity (rejection) to the analysis of the relation between the Pentecostal community and what he sees as the basic institution of traditional society: the hacienda (the land estate). According to him, the structure of the Pentecostal community with its face-to-face relationships resembles the structure of the hacienda; while the pastor and the kind of authority he enjoys, resembles the figure of the patrón. The element of discontinuity is that the Pentecostal community does not reproduce the class structure of the hacienda: In the Pentecostal community, both the congregation and the pastor belong to the same social class (see pp. 32-33, 82-84, 129-32).

revivalist Protestantism, popular Catholicism and Amerindian religiosity. In Chilean popular Catholicism, religious healing operates through the institutionalized practice of the *manda*: when people plea to a local saint, virgin, or *animita* (a small shrine located in the place where somebody suddenly died by accident or murder), for curing of diseases suffered by themselves or by relatives, they promise to perform different kinds of religious duties or sacrifices (lighting of candles, pilgrimage, and so on) if the saint/virgin/*animita* actually responds to their plea. When healing is experienced, failure to comply with the promise means the danger of becoming ill again. Although Pentecostalism denies that saints, virgins or *animitas* have real power to heal (only God heals), one can recognize the structure of the *manda* in many testimonies of pentecostal conversions related to healing experiences: the faithful attendance at the church or the discharge of other pentecostal duties (like evangelization), as well as the abandonment of mundane vices, is presented as the fulfilment of a promise made before God when pleading for healing from a serious disease. New episodes of illness are actually interpreted as caused by the failure to comply with the promise, or by relapsing into old vices. Here, we do not have traditional religious forms only, but religious meanings surviving in Pentecostalism as well. Those meanings bear implications for the understanding of God's grace, which might look rather unorthodox from a classical Protestant perspective.

Finally, one gets the impression that the process of adaptation to the local culture has been quite smooth and homogeneous. Another of Carter's examples shows that the process has been much more problematic, and that some adaptations have been contested by other groups within Chilean Pentecostalism: the adoption of instruments and styles of popular music. The typical portrayal of Chilean Pentecostalism through the image of a group of poor and cheaply but well dressed *Mestizos* singing to the Lord accompanied by guitars, mandolins and tambourines, overlooks the fact that the second biggest pentecostal church, the IEP, regards the use of those instruments as an undue concession to 'the world'. Unlike others, this adaptation seems to have been the result of a conscious move toward 'Chilenization'. Manuel Umaña, the pastor of the First Church of Santiago, and later on the leader of the IMP, asked Genaro Ríos, a popular artist who had joined the church in 1930, to form a church band. Ríos, along with his two brothers, adapted existing hymns into the style of popular music, and introduced them with his instrumental accompaniments into the services in 1931.[70] At first, this innovation was not only rejected by those churches which a couple of years later followed W. Hoover to form the IEP, but also by some of those who supported Umaña during the struggle of power that led to the great division. In fact, the 1936 IMP's Conference (two years after the division) decided to expel the Ríos brothers from membership,[71] so they formed a separate church, the Ejercito Evangélico de Chile (Evangelical Army of Chile). However, as the innovation was readily accepted by lay people and soon proved to have great appeal to those outside the church, it gradually became a standard practice in the IMP and in many other younger pentecostal churches. The fact that the IEP until today rejected the use of popular intruments does not mean that the old imported Protestant style had been maintained. While the instrumental pentecostal music resembles the musical taste of the peasantry of central Chile, which is very much a Mexican import, the way of singing in many IEP congregations resembles the moanlike style of southern Chilean folklore, which often lacks instrumental accompaniment.

Conclusion

The foregoing discussion has shown that the explicit motives of the Chilean Pentecostal revival were very much the typical ones of all movements of religious reform or renewal: going back to the sources. In this case, the 'sources' meant both the primitive church as portrayed in Acts, and the early Wesleyan movement in England as portrayed in the journal of John Wesley. There was a demand for 'purity' of faith as opposed to the concessions North American Methodism had made to modern rationalism. However, underneath the surface, there was a much more implicit process going on, that towards the reshaping of the Christian experience and church life into the 'local customs', the local culture. Although the latter process seems to have already been active in the background of the early Methodist revival, it became dominant after 1910, when the pentecostal movement was severed from the Methodist Episcopal Mission Board, and therefore forced to rely on national resources for its further development. In fact, this forced secession converted the young Chilean Pentecostalism into becoming one of the

---

70. Kessler, *Older Protestant Missions*, p. 309.
71. Kessler, *Older Protestant Missions*, p. 309.

earlier self-supporting, self-governing and self-propagating Latin American Protestant churches.[72] Since then, a complex relation of continuity and discontinuity between the new movement and its surrounding popular culture developed. Chilean pentecostal identity (or identities) can be seen as a result of this dynamic of continuity and discontinuity. As the process of selection and/or substitution implied in this dynamic has been made from within instead of from without the local culture, Pentecostalism has effectively succeeded in incarnating the gospel into the *mestizo* culture of Chilean peasantry and lower class urban population. Chilean pentecostal identity is, then, the fruit of a process of syncretization[73] between the Protestant (Methodist) legacy and the religious culture of the *mestizo* lower classes of Chilean society.

This indigenous character of Chilean Pentecostalism may have indeed become a crucial factor in its growth among the Chilean lower classes. But let me now consider the relevance of this character for the understanding of the religious and theological significance of Pentecostalism. As already mentioned, in 1961 Eugene Nida suggested that Chilean Pentecostalism should be seen as a expression of an indigenous Christianity rather than fitting it within a general category of 'Pentecostal-

72. Despite the rejection of the Pentecostal revival by missionary Protestantism, it did not fail to recognize this aspect of Chilean Pentecostalism. In the Report on the Church on the Field of a Regional Conference held in Santiago after the 'Panama Congress on Christian Work in South America' (1916), we find the following comment: 'In the Chilean Protestant churches there have arisen three separatist independent movements. [...] The last case was that of the so-called Pentecostal movement, where the pastor of one of the largest churches, a missionary, allowed himself to become sadly unbalanced on religion and to be over-ruled by ignorant, some time malicious fanatics. [...] The Pentecostal movement carried with it a great number of sincere people and has spread throughout two thirds of the country. It has been entirely self-supporting and has kept up during the six years of its existence a burning enthusiasm which has kept it alive'. E. Bauman and P. Walker, *Committee on Cooperation in Latin America, Regional Conferences in Latin America* (New York: The Missionary Education Movement, 1917), pp. 99-110 (101). This contrasted with the failure of the missionary boards' attempts at promoting self-support in the 'younger churches' in Latin America (on this issue, see Kessler, *Older Protestant Missions*).

73. I use the word syncretism in a rather positive way. I have developed my understanding of the syncretistic processes as necessary mediations of the universality of the Gospel in my doctoral dissertation, particularly Chapter 14 (Sepúlveda, 'Syncretism').

ism'. But does this mean that Chilean Pentecostalism is not, strictly speaking, pentecostal?

Indeed, Chilean Pentecostalism differs from so-called 'classical Pentecostalism' in a number of aspects usually considered as central for the definition of pentecostal identity: infant baptism by sprinkling; strange tongues as a charismatic gift among others, but not as a necessary initial evidence; a rather unclear distinction between the 'works of grace', so that often the baptism of the Holy Spirit is identified with the experience of conversion, and so on. But I do not think that this means that Chilean Pentecostalism is not really 'pentecostal'. The New Testament Pentecost (Acts 2) was the central source and inspiration of the Chilean revival, and still is central for Chilean Pentecostalism's self-understanding.

Rather than disqualifying Chilean Pentecostalism from being 'truly pentecostal' because it does not fit within the 'classical' definition (which is mainly American), the Chilean experience suggests the necessity of a broader definition, and the same is probably true of other Pentecostalisms in Latin America and elsewhere.[74] In my interpretation, a broader definition should recognize that the rediscovery of pneumatology by modern Pentecostalism has to do mainly with the spiritual freedom to 'incarnate' the gospel anew into the diverse cultures: to believe in the power of the Holy Spirit is to believe that God can and wants to speak to peoples today through cultural mediations other than those of Western Christianity.[75] Being pentecostal would mean to affirm

74. I fully agree, for instance, with the broader definition adopted by Allan Anderson in his trilogy on South African Pentecostalism: *Moya: The Holy Spirit in an African Context* (Pretoria: University of South Africa, 1991); *Bazalwane*; and *Tumelo*. See also Anderson's contributions to this book in his Introduction and article.

75. It is well known that a number of African and black scholars have insisted on the 'Africanness' of Pentecostalism, highlighting William J. Seymour's role and the participation of black people in the revival of Azusa Street (see the relevant contributions to this book). I think that such interpretation is more or less in line with my approach. However, to understand better the theological significance of Pentecostal pneumatology, rather than emphasizing the 'Africanness' of Pentecostalism, I would prefer to emphasize the spiritual freedom of Africans, as well as Asians, native and *mestizo* Latin Americans, ethnic minorities within the 'first world', and so on to express their religious experiences, church life and worship, in terms of the own cultural patterns. Chilean Pentecostalism is again a case in point: because of the absence of African elements in Chilean popular culture, the ways of

such spiritual freedom. From such a perspective, the insistence on a fixed definition of pentecostal identity, especially notorious in white American Pentecostalism, would appear as a western attempt at domestication of the liberating power of Pentecost.

expression of Chilean pentecostals are rather different from the ways of black pentecostals elsewhere. To the latter, the ways of the former could appear rather cold. But does this mean that those ways are less Pentecostal? What both ways of being pentecostal have in common is the conviction (and the experience) that the Holy Spirit enables them to encounter God and worship him in terms of their own cultures.

RESPONSE

J. Andrew Kirk

If the coming of the 'Third Church' is the most important factor in
world Christianity during the twentieth century, the phenomenon of the
pentecostal movement within the Church of the South is the most explosive reality of the last 50 years of the second millennium. Few observers
of the world Church would want to dispute either of these two statements. However, the way in which Pentecostalism should be interpreted
and its present significance assessed is, as Juan Sepùlveda has carefully
demonstrated, much more open to controversy.

The last 15 years or so have witnessed a spate of literature on Pentecostalism that attempts a re-evaluation of its standing, not least in
Latin America. The earlier standard versions of the reasons for its phenomenal growth, which concentrated on the sociological components of
'social adaptation in a time of rapid and conflictive social changes'
(Sepùlveda) have been widened by the inclusion of cultural and genuinely theological explanations. This is particularly true of Sepùlveda's
paper, in which both cultural (namely, the ability to develop an authentically indigenous and fast growing Christian movement) and theological determinants (namely, the recovery of the personal and communitar-
ian freedom of the Spirit as a liberating power) are highlighted.

My own view is that this redressing of the balance is necessary if one
is to obtain a fair interpretation of Pentecostal reality in its undoubted
contemporary diversity. The Marxist insistence on the dependence of
religious superstructures on an all-encompassing socio-economic infrastructure reigned within a progressive socio-political and theological
analysis in Latin America, roughly between 1965–1985. In these years,
it was natural to view Pentecostalism (and traditional Catholicism) as
the epiphenomenon of social changes brought about by ubiquitous economic processes. However, as Sepùlveda has brought out clearly, such
an interpretation imposes on the life of the Church categories that do

not do justice to its own self-understanding. Even in Marxist terms, as long as the socio-economic remains the dominant interpretative perspective, it violates the integrity of the subject. So, theological, cultural and social factors (in that order) all have their place in understanding the recent history of these movements.

There is much more of a willingness today to question the reductionism of those observers who seek to bracket out both the importance of a supernatural reality manifesting itself in these communities and perhaps an over-literalistic adherence to certain elements of the life of the early Church. These observers often concentrate on the social dislocation of marginalized groups brought about by continuing failures to introduce substantial and permanent land reform in Latin America. The social realities may partially explain why the dispossessed would be open to beliefs and practices alien to the context of their early upbringing, and why they might find them such a compelling attraction that they are willing to change their religious allegiance. But they do not explain how these beliefs and practices arose in the first place. The 'alienation' theory of religious commitment confuses categories. It tends to a narrow, albeit universal explanation that can have no place for exceptions.

This debate is, I think, the general background against which Juan Sepùlveda undertakes his study of the birth of Pentecostalism in Chile. His first thesis is that Chilean Pentecostalism is the result of an independent development, contemporary to that of Los Angeles. Indeed, there is evidence of simultaneous manifestations of similar phenomena in other parts of the world—Mukti in India is mentioned as another example. Moreover, though twentieth century Pentecostalism may be distinguished from other revival movements of the middle and late nineteenth century, it is only due to the different nature of the extraordinary powers that accompanied them, not to the existence of such powers in themselves.

The second thesis is that the revival in Chile took place largely among people belonging to the poorer social strata of society. This began within the Methodist Church, which was founded by a generation of Methodist missionaries that Sepùlveda says 'tended to be drawn from the less cultured, revivalist fringe of the Methodist Church in the United States' and who, therefore, 'felt more comfortable working with "simple" people than with the "cultured" middle class'.

Sepùlveda's third thesis is that the clash, which led to the separation within the Chilean Methodist Church, could be understood as an expression of the search for an 'indigenous church'. The evidence for this is somewhat ambiguous; what is much clearer is that once the split had occurred, the new body became 'the very first Chilean self-supporting, self-governing and self-propagating church'.

The fourth thesis is that the reason for Pentecostalism's growth among the popular sectors of society is its ability to 'translate the Protestant message into the forms of expression of the local popular culture'. This, thinks Sepúlveda, meant that almost 'all the ministry and leadership of the new Church had to come from the Chilean converts, most of them reared in the context of popular Catholicism'. Certainly, many observers have remarked how a number of the popular practices of Latin American Pentecostals (processions, healings, multiple weddings) and some beliefs (the relationship between illness and faithfulness to one's vows) mirror those of popular Catholicism, though with a changed content.

It has been calculated that, on the basis of the present rate of growth, by 2010 there will be more non-Catholics worshipping each week than Catholics in Latin America—that within *the* Catholic continent! It is also reckoned that within Brazil (and maybe in other parts of Latin America as well) as much as 75% of all Catholics worshipping each week do so in the context of the Base Ecclesial Communities. These figures, even if somewhat exaggerated, point to the power of a grass-roots expression of Christian faith to attract ordinary people. As one who has lived on the outside of Pentecostalism, but who has seen something of its vitality and its direct and simple (some would say simplistic) adherence to 'the teaching of the apostles, to fellowship, to the breaking of bread and to prayer', I am impressed by the seemingly inverse relationship between its internal strength and its dependence on support from outside. It used to be said that there was a direct correlation between the early support given by Protestants (including Pentecostals) to the Sandinista movement in Nicaragua and the low number of foreign missionaries. There is probably more than a grain of truth in this observation, showing what may happen when national Christians are left to make their own decisions on their own. One of the characteristics of both the Pentecostal and the Base Ecclesial Communities is that ordinary Christians are made aware that the Word and the Spirit of God both 'belong' to them, and do not have to be mediated by a remote and alien, professional ecclesial class. The continuing story is pregnant with missiological implications.

Lee Hong Jung

Introduction

In this chapter I would like to interpret the relationship between the Korean *minjung*[1] and the pentecostal movements during the Korean church's historical development in mission. In spite of the 'minjung-ness' of its origins, Korean Pentecostalism of the early twentieth century was quickly dogmatized and spiritualized by theological fundamentalism and the policy of the US American missionaries of separating religion and politics. Especially after 1960, Korean Pentecostalism was materialistically distorted in the process of syncretization with Korean shamanism and North American capitalism. Consequently, the mainstream Korean churches, making a religio-social myth of the 'miraculous growth' of Pentecostalism, have been 'pentecostalized' into following this syncretized combination of capitalism, shamanism and religious fundamentalism. I will approach these missiological issues in three stages: (1) defining the *minjung* as the subjects of the pentecostal movement; (2) analysing the ecclesiological, ideological and religio-cultural reality of Korean Pentecostalism; and (3) suggesting a 'new Pentecost' based on a people-centred *missio Dei*, a liberation/salvation-centred syncretism, and a shared economy.

The Pentecostal Movement and its Minjungness

The twentieth-century Pentecostal/Charismatic Renewal in the Holy Spirit, with its goal of world evangelization, represents a third force in Christianity along with the Catholic/Eastern Orthodox and Protestant

---

1.   The Korean term *minjung* can be generally defined as those who are oppressed politically, exploited economically, alienated socially and kept uneducated in cultural and intellectual matters.

churches. This third force has swept through three interconnected waves—Pentecostalism, the Charismatic movement and mainstream church renewal—resulting in three distinctive groups: the 'Classical Pentecostal' denominations, the Charismatic movements within older churches, and a new type of emerging Christian church, that is 'indigenous non-white churches'.[2] Changing the geographical map of salvation, indigenous non-white churches in particular have shifted the numerical and spiritual centre of Christianity from the white West to the Third World.[3]

Pentecostal movements have occurred among the *minjung* and have been revitalized by the *minjung*-oriented, communal and liberative nature of the historical pentecostal events rising up from the bottom. Classic Pentecostalism, for instance, originated in the encounter of a specific Catholic spirituality with the black spirituality of the former slaves in the United States. William Joseph Seymour, spiritual hero of the 1906 Azusa Street Revival in Los Angeles, was a *minjung*—a son of former slaves, a victim of the racist policy of Charles Parham's Bible School where he 'was allowed only to listen outside the classroom through the half-open door'.[4] Seymour, while emphasizing the necessity of holiness or sanctification, 'affirmed his black heritage by introducing Negro spirituals and Negro music into his liturgy at a time when this music was considered inferior and unfit for Christian worship'.[5] In a racist society, the black pentecostal movement brought out the spiritual power and cultural heritage of the black people as the *minjung*, and had both religious and revolutionary dimensions quite different from the success-oriented white American way of life.

Without doctrinal unity or world-wide organization, the indigenous non-white pentecostal movement has grown rapidly, and the reason for this seems to lie also in its black roots, that is the *minjungness* of the Third World people. According to Hollenweger, this can be summarized as:

2.   D.B. Barrett, 'The Twentieth-Century Pentecostal/Charismatic Renewal in the Holy Spirit with its Goal of World Evangelization', *International Bulletin of Missionary Research* 12 (1988), pp. 119-29. See also W.J. Hollenweger, 'After Twenty Years' Research on Pentecostalism', *International Review of Mission* 75 (1985), pp. 3-12.

3.   Hollenweger, 'After Twenty Years', p. 3.

4.   Hollenweger, 'After Twenty Years', pp. 4-5.

5.   Hollenweger, 'After Twenty Years', p. 5.

orality of liturgy; narrativity of theology and witness; maximum participation at the levels of reflection, prayer and decision-making and therefore a form of community that is reconciliatory; inclusion of dreams and
visions into personal and public forms of worship; (they function as a
kind of icon for the individual and the community;) an understanding of
body/mind relationship that is informed by experience of correspondence
between body and mind; the most striking application of this insight is
the ministry of healing by prayer.[6]

Today many of the characteristics of strongly growing non-white indigenous churches are, according to Hollenweger, very close to those of
early Pentecostalism, and they cause tension with the churches that
were exported from Europe and America. The tensions are described by
Hollenweger as:

racism (or European/American superiority complex) versus an intercultural and inter-racial understanding of Christianity; literacy versus orality; abstract concepts versus narrativity; the anonymity of bureaucratic
organisations versus family and personal relationships; medical technol-
ogy versus a holistic understanding of health and sickness; western psy-
cho-analytical techniques versus a group and family therapy that centres
on the human touch, prayer and a daily informal education in dreams and
visions.[7]

In contrast to those pentecostal movements in the Third World, Pentecostalism in the West is fast developing into an evangelical middle-
class religion, losing the elements vital for its rise and expansion in the
Third World. Their socio-political pioneering work such as inviting
black and female students into their educational institutions and a plan
for world peace, was very quickly forgotten. They have been rapidly
replaced by 'efficient fund-raising structures, a streamlined ecclesiastical bureaucracy and a Pentecostal conceptual theology'.[8] In the North
Atlantic, this theology follows the evangelical traditions, to which is
added belief in the baptism of the Spirit, mostly but not always characterized by the initial sign of speaking in tongues.[9] It seems that early
Pentecostalism and the non-white indigenous churches were rooted in
an open, communal and liberative spirituality of the *minjung*, such as

6.   Hollenweger, 'After Twenty Years', p. 6.
7.   Hollenweger, 'After Twenty Years', p. 10.
8.   Hollenweger, 'After Twenty Years', p. 4.
9.   Hollenweger, 'After Twenty Years', p. 6.

the black people. The inner logic or rhetoric of their pentecostal affec-
tions has been continuously revitalized through an eschatological vision
of the *minjung* all over the world, in the words of pentecostal theologian Steven Land: 'God as Eschatological Presence', 'Salvation as
Eschatological Transformation' and 'the Church as Eschatological Mission'.[10] As compared with the institutionalized and materialistic pentecostals in the North Atlantic, this only proves in my view that the
minjung are the subjects of the pentecostal movement, and that minjungness is its vital life-giving force.

The Minjungness of Korean Pentecostalism and the Great Revival of 1907

Historically speaking, a dynamic dialectical interaction between the
pentecostal movement and the reality of the Korean *minjung* was bound
to exist. The Korean *minjung's* interaction with the pentecostal movement is in part shaped by and dependent upon the dynamic Korean
context in which they were immersed. The suffering, struggle and hope
of the Korean *minjung*, that is the socio-biography of the *minjung*, are
integral parts of the reality of Korea, and this is the real context in
which the pentecostal movement is to be understood. Aroused by an intense sense of national crisis and humiliation by the establishment of
a Japanese protectorate over Korea in 1905, the Korean people were
driven into churches for security and consolation. The Korean people
seemed to respond to the Christian message (particularly the biblical
event of Exodus) with a socio-political hope for national liberation.
Koreans saw in Christianity 'a training ground and a resource for national rejuvenation, reform, and national independence'.[11] Almost all of
the elements of the movement for national independence and patriotism,
such as former members of Tonghak[12] and the Independence Club, and
soldiers, came to the churches for guidance, organization and

10. S.J. Land, 'Pentecostal Spirituality: Living in the Spirit', L. Dupre and D.E.
Saliers (eds.), *Christian Spirituality: Post Reformation and Modern* (3 vols.; London:
SCM Press, 1990), III, pp. 490-93.
11. Suh Kwang-Sun, 'American Missionaries and a Hundred Years of Korean
Protestantism', *International Review of Mission* 74 (1985), pp. 5-18 (15).
12. The Eastern way of learning.

support, and the churches became centres for the nationalistic movement and the salvation of the nation. According to William Blair, a witness of the Great Revival of 1907, 'there were not lacking many hot-
heads in the Church itself who thought the Church ought to enter the
fight' because 'the country wanted a leader and the Christian church
was the strongest, most influential single organization in Korea'.[13]

It was the missionaries' concern, however, that 'had she departed
even a little from the strict principle of non-interference in politics,
thousands would have welcomed her leadership and flocked to her banner'.[14] There was every reason for the missionaries to want to avoid
such an occurrence. Missionaries had to protect the church from an anti-
Japanese uprising and the danger of making the young church a political agency, not only for security but also for the survival of their mission work in Korea. The missionaries therefore preached the 'doctrine
of love and forbearance, and forgiveness even of enemies',[15] almost
exclusively concentrating on the uneducated and deprived masses and
relying on the religious enthusiasm of a pentecostal revival movement.
Many massive revival meetings were held and designed as a search for
religious experience. Blair said:

> We [missionaries] felt that the Korean church needed not only to repent
> of hating the Japanese, but a clear vision of all sin against God, that
> many had come into the church sincerely believing in Jesus as their
> Saviour and anxious to do God's will without great sorrow for sin be-
> cause of its familiarity ... We felt ... that embittered souls needed to
> have their thoughts taken away from the national situation to their per-
> sonal relation with the master.[16]

Missionaries viewed the Great Revival of 1907 as an outpouring of
the Holy Spirit and emphasized the spiritual and religious dimension of
the mass experience. Missionary reports of the mass revival meetings
reveal positive impressions of the 'spirituality' of such a revival movement. However, as Suh Kwang-Sun points out, 'the public confession
of sin was ostensibly limited to immoral acts; there was no mention of
how people in the revival meetings felt about their national tragedy, or

---

13. W.N. Blair and B.F. Hunt, *The Korean Pentecost and the Suffering which
Followed* (Edinburgh: The Banner of Truth Trust, 1977), p. 63.
   14. Blair and Hunt, *Korean Pentecost*, p. 63.
   15. Blair and Hunt, *Korean Pentecost*, pp. 63-64.
   16. Quoted in Yoo Boo-Woong, *Korean Pentecostalism: Its History and Theology* (Frankfurt: Peter Lang, 1988), p. 78.

the collective sin of the people as nation'.[17] The missionaries made every effort to cleanse and purify the revolutionary dimension of the Korean church and to keep it free from political movements. They were successful in spiritualizing and depoliticizing the Korean church through the emotion-filled revival movement of 1907. The revival meetings were successful both in increasing membership and in setting the tone of Korean Protestantism: emotional, conservative, pentecostal, individualistic and other-worldly. Through such missionary efforts, Korean Pentecostalism put down deep roots in the infrastructure of the Korean religious consciousness, that is, shamanism.[18]

In the case of Korea, spiritualization and depoliticiszation went together with anti-intellectualism. In spite of numerous Bible classes, the Christian message had to be oversimplified to proselytize the Korean masses. Missionaries emphasized the memorizing of biblical passages following the letter of the Scripture. According to Suh Kwang-Sun, 'The common people of Korea, who were the first to learn the Korean spirit and the first to be awakened by Christian literature, became dogmatic literalists in their Christian belief'.[19] This non-intellectual and indeed almost anti-intellectual approach of the missionaries in missionizing the Korean masses became quite apparent when missionaries began to reflect on the question of theological education. W.D. Reynolds, in his 'ideals and principles' for the training of the Korean ministry, emphasized the restriction on 'higher education' for Protestant ministries. One of the 'don'ts' was 'don't send him to America to be educated, at any rate in the early stage of mission work'.[20] And a 'do' was 'seek to keep his education sufficiently in advance of the average education of his people to secure for him respect and prestige but not enough ahead to excite envy or a feeling of separation'.[21] At the earlier stage of evangelistic work by missionaries, it was too easy for them to impose on Korean Protestant churches the North American brand of religious fundamentalism along with its anti-intellectualism. These missionaries' ideologies quickly dogmatized and institutionalized both the spiritual

17. Suh, 'American Missionaries', pp. 10-11.
18. Suh, 'American Missionaries', p. 11.
19. Suh, 'American Missionaries', p. 11.
20. W.D. Reynolds, 'The Native Ministry', *The Korean Repository*, 3 (1896), pp. 200-201.
21. Reynolds, 'Native Ministry', p. 201.

and the revolutionary dimensions of Korean Pentecostalism, and the various schisms among the Protestant churches in Korea since the 1950s were also deeply rooted in them.[22] These missionary ideologies of Korean Protestantism have long been criticized in the eventful century of church growth and progress, as causing an identity crisis.

In my view, the crisis of present day Korean pentecostal movements, together with that of mainline churches, derives chiefly from two conflicting dimensions. One dimension is the cleavage and conflict between the present Korean reality and the conventional self-understanding of Korean Pentecostalism. While the pentecostal churches historically have identified themselves with doctrinal fundamentalism, political conservatism, self-righteous pietism and crusade-like evangelism, the present Korean reality reflects a combination of the desire to recover Korean historico-cultural identity, the conflict between neo-colonized capitalistic modernity and anti-imperialist nationalistic modernity, and the phenomenon of post-modern plurality. The second dimension is the cognitive disharmony between the North Americanized life and work of the Korean pentecostal movements—individualistic, dualistic, dogmatic and unecological—and the Korean people's peculiar way of thinking and lifestyle—empirical, communal, organic, holistic, ecological, flexible, critically transcendental and syncretistic. These two disharmonious dimensions have interacted with the socio-historical context of present Korean pentecostal movements. This in turn gives rise to the issue of how the Korean pentecostal movements and their rapid growth relate both to the ideological superstructure and to the pluralistic infrastructure of the society stemming from its mode of production. The most important task is to analyse critically the socio-historical context of one of the so-called 'marvels of modern history', that is, church growth in Korea and the ideological and religio-cultural realities of the Korean pentecostal movements.

The Ecclesiological Reality of the Korean Pentecostal Movement

Although the concepts of success and failure are relative, it is apparent that the Korean churches have been successful in terms of growth and social influence, and it is generally agreed that Korea has been one of the countries most receptive to Christianity in Asia. In the words of the

22. Suh, 'American Missionaries', p. 12.

missionaries, the Korean church has grown 'like wildfire'.[23] Moreover, Christians are preponderant in the cities rather than in rural areas, and particularly in the educated middle and upper classes. This means that Korean churches have expanded into the capitalistic system via the new middle/upper class social strata. Although it is true that the most explosive growth came about during the past 20 years when Korea was undergoing modernization, it is also necessary to observe the historical trends and background to the church growth that took place before the recent industrialization. According to Kim Byong-Suh, these can be classified into three time periods: first, growth with an emancipation motif (1884–1910); second, growth with a pioneering spirit (1906–1930); and third, growth with sectarian factionalism (1940–1960). These three stages of growth all prepared the way for the explosive growth of the Korean churches in the course of modernization.[24]

Students of the Church Growth school, missionaries and those Korean clergy who take a solidly church-centred perspective, usually account for the special characteristics of, and reasons for, Korean church growth with all or some of the following factors: (1) God's special providence and mercy; (2) a history of martyrdom; (3) the religious nature of the Korean people; (4) suffering under Japanese colonialism; (5) the 'Three-Self' mission policy; (6) migration from north to south and the situation of division; (7) Holy Spirit movements; (8) prayer movements; (9) enthusiastic faith with the expectation of the return of Christ; (10) popular mass Gospel proclamation; (11) work of the 'house of prayer' in member training; (12) evangelism by local area worship services; (13) Bible studies in the early morning prayer meetings and various study groups; (14) frequent revival meetings; (15) joyful participation in many seminars and training programmes; (16) Gospel-centred messages which appeal to the masses; (17) respect and obedience to the clergy.[25] In my view, most of these factors can be found in the historical development of Korean Pentecostalism.

23. R.E. Shearer, *Wildfire: Church Growth in Korea* (Grand Rapids: Eerdmans, 1966)

24. Kim Byong-Suh, 'The Explosive Growth of the Korean Church Today: A Sociological Analysis', *IRM* 74 (1985), pp. 60-64.

25. M.L. Nelson, 'An Evaluation of Korean Church Growth seen from a Foreigner's Perspective', *Mokhoe-wa Sinhak (Ministry and Theology)* (1993), pp. 114-20; S.H. Moffett, *Asia and Missions* (Seoul: Presbyterian Theological Seminary, 1976), pp. 83-89.

The factors that contributed to stimulating the pentecostal movement before the national liberation, according to Yoo Boo-Woong, generally have been agreed upon by Korean scholars to include the following: (1) the Korean people's innate religiosity and the contemporary religious environment; (2) the syncretization of Korean religions such as Confucianism, Buddhism and Taoism in a 'shamanistic' religious environment; (3) a religious and spiritual 'vacuum' among the Korean people; (4) social crises caused by tremendous national turmoil and social upheaval resulting in this 'new religious movement'; (5) the 'positive' mission policies and strategies based on the Nevius method, self-propagation, self-government and self-support of the Korean churches.[26] Another important factor stimulating the rapid growth of Korean Pentecostalism after the Korean War was the new mission strategy known as 'Global Conquest' of the North American Assemblies of God, the largest of the 'Classical' pentecostal denominations to work in Korea. This programme represented a shift in focus from rural and remote areas to rapidly growing urban centres.[27] In practice, the first thrusts of Global Conquest were in the areas of literature and the creation of urban evangelistic centres. Gradually, the Boys and Girls Missionary Crusade and the Light-for-the-Lost programmes formally became the literary agency of Global Conquest. In the meantime, urban evangelistic centres were developed in several major cities, Seoul becoming the pilot project. Seoul was not only the first, but also the most successful of the evangelistic centres, having 7,000 adherents by 1967. In 1983, it celebrated its twenty-fifth anniversary, by which time it had 615 full-time staff members and 280,000 members.[28]

Probably the best-known and most 'successful' pentecostal preacher in Korea is Reverend Cho Yong-Gi (known in the West as Dr Paul Yonggi Cho), whose philosophy of ministry is 'find need and meet need'. For him, the important question is how the Korean church can meet what the majority of Korean people need. Why do the Korean working class and particularly the women go to the shaman? Because they need health, wealth, fertility and success in their life ventures. Cho

26. Yoo, *Korean Pentecostalism*, pp. 71-74.

27. E.L. Blumhofer, *The Assemblies of God: A Chapter in the Story of American Pentecostalism*. II. *Since 1941* (2 vols.; Springfield, MI: Gospel Publishing House, 1989), pp. 146-47.

28. Blumhofer, *Assemblies of God*, p. 147.

Yong-Gi's preaching meets those needs exactly: 'Anything is possible if you have faith.' He often claims that the Christian faith is positive thinking and that Jesus Christ is a positive thinker.[29] His preaching formula, the 'Threefold Blessings of God', is based on 3 John 2: 'Beloved, I pray that all may go well with you and that you may be in health; I know that it is well with your soul.' The 'Threefold Blessings of God' are popularly interpreted by him as first, 'that all may go well with you' means business or material prosperity; secondly, 'that you may be in health' means good health or longevity; and thirdly, 'that it is well with your soul' means protection from evil spirits. According to Yoo Boo-Woong, shamanistic belief is also concerned with these three 'blessings' and Cho Yong-Gi's preaching is seen to satisfy the needs of the majority of Korean people. His healing ministry is based on the baptism of the Holy Spirit, speaking in tongues and driving away evil spirits from sick persons using the name of Jesus. His role in Sunday morning worship looks exactly like that of a shaman or *mudang*. The only difference is that a shaman performs his wonders in the name of the spirits, while Cho Yong-Gi exorcizes evil spirits and heals the sick in the name of Jesus.[30]

Perhaps it is true that the rapid growth of the Korean pentecostal movement is a true myth or miracle caused by the moving force of the Spirit in the history of Christian mission in a post-Christian era. I do not wish to minimize God's economy in church growth. Church growth in Korea, however, cannot merely be explained as the result of the passionate efforts of the Korean church to evangelize their own people. Church growth cannot always be seen as authentic evidence of the success of the church-in-mission, and be unconditionally justified and universalized as the unique sign of God's salvation in a secular, religiously pluralistic society, because it does not happen in a social vacuum and is not ideologically and ethically neutral. To illustrate this, I will consider three facts. The first is that the most remarkable quantitative church growth took place during the 1970s and 1980s, when there was a rapid increase in the rate of economic growth and when social mobility was most dynamic. The second fact is that in the 1970s and 1980s adherents of the other main religions and the new religions also increased relatively quickly, although less so than did the Christians. The third is that

29. See Yoo, *Korean Pentecostalism.*
30. Yoo, *Korean Pentecostalism.*

since the late 1980s, the rate of church growth has gradually declined, and in Korean society critical attitudes toward the church have recently increased.

In order to reveal the socio-historical factors and influences behind a religio-social myth such as church growth, other factors in the Korean social context must be taken into account. First, the political factor that has caused the Korean people to seek substantial psychological stability and support through religion has been the long-lived, centralized, anti-communist military dictatorship of the last 30 years. Secondly, from the 1960s onward successful government-directed economic growth has caused inequalities of distribution, Mammonism and a blind drive for success and growth. In this crisis, many Koreans have sought a religious way to compensate for their deprivation, under the influence of the specifically Korean religio-cultural desire for blessedness in this world. Thirdly, the industrialization and urbanization of Korean society have caused the destruction of community and the forfeiture of social and cultural identity. In this situation, many Koreans have sought communality and identity through involvement in religion. Thus membership in institutional religions has grown as well as the number of new religions, in particular the conservative, charismatic, pentecostal churches which stress well-being in this world. I suggest that the present church growth in Korea may be a religio-social myth that has arisen from the collaboration between fundamentalist religious conservatives, a dictatorial ruling ideology, monopolistic capitalism, and the neo-colonial, pro-American, anti-communist Cold War system in a divided Korea, particularly since the 1960s. In the myth-making process of Korean church growth, there has been a syncretistic relationship between three ecclesiological ideologies: (1) church-growth-for-church-growth's-sake; (2) schism, individual church-centrism and denominationalism; and (3) ecclesiastical authoritarianism.

The Ideological Reality of the Korean Pentecostal Movement

Since no religion exists in a vacuum, all activities of religion are limited by and orientated to the social context. That is, the social structure and the conflicts inherent in it have exerted a profound influence on the religious field in general. It is, however, also true that institutional religion is sufficiently autonomous to be able to realize two potentialities:

a potentially conservative and a potentially revolutionary function.[31] Although there are many different criticisms to be made of the characteristics of Korean society, some factors can be premised by a common recognition among Korean social scientists since the 1980s, namely that Korean society is to a certain extent still a neo-colonized society dominated by imperialistic countries, in particular the USA and Japan. The modern history of Korea is a history of the making of a capitalist nation and at the same time, a history that has unfolded in a deep relationship with imperialism: first, it is a history of the invasion of imperialism; second, it is a history of the rapid development of a neo-colonized capitalism; and third, it is a history of intense political changes—interventionist wars of imperialism, revolutions and counter-revolutions and the enhancement of people movements.[32] As a result of this process, Korean society today is in confusion due to the unsolved state of all these contradictions: the national contradiction, the class contradiction and the contradiction of division. In this process, the Christian communities and their missions, especially after the Korean War, were deeply connected with the neo-colonial powers and civilizations; in many cases the biblical message and Christianity as a whole identified with neo-colonial values and interests. In spite of the *minjung*ness of its origin, it is undeniable that in many cases the Korean pentecostal movements and mainline Korean churches obscure the real societal and structural relationship and, especially in the period of division, they have identified ideologically more or less completely with the ruling power, being criticized by some as a 'factory' for that ruling power.[33]

The resources for the ideological reproduction of Korean Protestantism, according to Kang Won-Don, can be classified into five factors. The first is the fundamentalist theological thought that was inherited initially from the missionaries. The second is a political theology based on the separation of religion and politics, which has blocked the praxis of the church public so that it has supported the existing system. It has remained politically and ideologically indifferent to, or has

31. O. Maduro, *Religion and Social Conflicts* (Maryknoll, NY: Orbis Books, 1982), p. xxii.

32. Chang Sang-Wan *et al.*, *Imperialism and Korean Society* (Seoul: Han Ul, 1991), pp. 17-19.

33. Kang Won-Don, 'Reproduction of the Ruling Ideology in the Korean Church', Korean Industrial Society Study Institute (ed.), *Economy and Society* 10 (1991), pp. 101-103.

even approved of, various activities supporting the ruling power. The third is an apolitical, ahistorical and other-world-oriented form of faith, which has to a certain degree prescribed the character of the Korean church since the Revival of 1907. This has resulted in the programmatic ideology of so-called success and blessing. The fourth is a doctrinalized anti-communism that is derived from the negative response of the Korean church to the appearance of socialism in the 1920s, the historical process of the formation of a pro-American, anti-communist divisive system in the southern part of Korea after 1945, and the historical experience of the People's Democratic Revolution in the northern part of Korea and the resulting Korean War. The fifth is an extreme cultural imperialism based on the absoluteness of Christianity and the superiority of North American culture. This has resulted in the identification of the Christian gospel with imperialistic North American culture and the characterization of Korean traditional culture as heresy.[34]

During the development of Korean capitalism with its concomitant anti-communist ideology, Korean Pentecostalism alongside the mainline churches has formulated its own basic politics. According to Hong Kun-Su, this can be stated as follows: (1) capitalism is democratic, but communism is dictatorial; (2) capitalism is humanitarian and moral, but communism is inhumane and immoral; (3) capitalism produces freedom, love and peace, but communism produces destruction, violence, genocide and revolution; (4) capitalism is religious and Christian, but communism is anti-religious and anti-Christian; and (5) the USA is a good Christian nation that has enjoyed God's blessing as the chosen people of today and is a great benefactor and saviour to Korea, whereas North Korea is the Evil Empire which should be destroyed.[35] These ideologies as reproduced by the mainline Korean churches in general and by Korean Pentecostalism in particular have had a number of results in Korean society, as outlined by Kang Won-Don. First, the Korean church has provided a theological justification for Korea's inferior brand of capitalism and has mobilized the church masses ideologically through the reproduction of capitalistic principles in the making of theology and the management of the church. Secondly, the Korean

34. Kang, 'Reproduction', pp. 96-100.
35. Hong Kun-Su, 'The Common Task of the Mission of the South-North Korean Churches', The Reunification Committee of KNCCC (ed.), *The Encounter between the South and North Churches and Theology of Peace-Reunification* (Seoul: Minjung-sa, 1990), p. 157.

church has institutionalized the divided situation and has integrated it into the church public, providing a religious justification for the ruling elite which has continuously advocated an ideology of anti-communism through its division-oriented theology. The Korean churches have thus become centres of anti-communist agitation. Thirdly, the Korean church has reproduced religious ideologies that cover up the essence of the national contradiction and serve the material interests of imperialism. Fourthly, the Korean church has reproduced an ahistorical, apolitical and other-world-centred form of faith, that is, religious goods that implicitly express material interests, and it has finally cut off the raising to conscience and systematization of a political opposition, and has supported the material interests of the ruling class of Korean society. Fifthly, this reproduction, distribution and consumption have ensured the unique quantitative growth of the Korean church and the emergence of a religious elite.[36]

The Religio-Cultural Reality of the Korean Pentecostal Movement

The ideology of the Korean pentecostal movement has also given rise to serious problems in the religio-cultural realm. The Christocentrism of Korean Pentecostalism, characterized by exclusive and superior attitudes towards other religions and cultures, has created a serious conflict with traditional Korean religion and culture. Korea has a religiously pluralistic society, where there coexist Buddhism with 18 sects, Confucianism, Protestantism with 94 denominations, Catholicism, Ch'ondo-gyo (Heavenly-Way-Religion), Won (Circle) Buddhism, and recently Islam; so far 393 described or non-described new religions or sects, as well as many folk faiths. Article 19 of the Constitution guarantees freedom of religion, no national religion, and a policy of the separation of politics and religion, so that the religious situation is competitive and flexible. The friction and conflict between religions in Korean society derive basically from the general character of any religious belief system that is able to validate itself even without any external support or authentication. Because of the absoluteness of the belief system, other thoughts and realities become objects of salvation. The more religious identity grows, the more self-pride and superiority also grow. The stronger the solidarity with one's own religion, the stronger the exclu-

36. Kang, 'Reproduction', p. 104.

sive attitude towards other religions. The more aggressively any religion is attached to the expansion of its power, the more it emphasizes faithfulness to the in-group and bolsters rejection and hostility towards the out-group. This exclusivism easily combines with superiorism or ethnocentrism and gives rise to three negative attitudes: (1) particularism, which identifies one's own group as the chosen people and harbours prejudice and discrimination against other religions, uncritically condemning them all as cursed; (2) religio-cultural imperialism, which usually collaborates with political and economic power ideologies, aiming at the conquest and domination of other religio-cultural territories; and (3) the adoption of a patronising attitude which takes pity on and tries to enlighten other religions by offering them one's own religion's world view, civilization and path to salvation. These three negative attitudes represent the typically exclusive and superioristic characteristic of Korean Protestantism, and in particular Korean Pentecostalism.

According to a 1993 survey, 'Religious Life and Social Consciousness of Urban Christian Church Members',[37] the typical Korean urban Protestant's attitude towards other religions is exclusivist. To the question 'What do you think of other religions?' urban church members answered: (1) 'The Christian truth is the one and only truth' (exclusivism: 44.3%); (2) 'Although other religions have truths, the Christian truth is superior to others' (inclusivism: 33.1%); (3) 'All other religions have the same truth as Christianity after all' (pluralism: 22.6%). An exclusivist attitude was manifested more strongly by women than men, by the middle aged more than others, by the less educated and the married. The higher the ecclesiastical position and the more conservative the denomination, the more exclusive the attitude towards other religions. Moreover, the stronger the religiousness, the more exclusive the attitude towards other religions. The survey shows that the more enthusiastic the personal religious life, religious experience and church attendance, the more faithful, doctrinally orthodox and convinced of salvation, the deeper one thinks one's faith is, the more exclusive is one's attitude towards other religions. That is, deep religiousness reinforces religious exclusivism in the Korean Protestant. Similarly, according to another 1993 survey, 'Religion and Religious Consciousness of

37. KNCCC Survey, 'Religious Life and Social Consciousness of Urban Christian Church Members' (1993).

the Koreans', Protestants have proved to be the most exclusivist.[38] Moreover, data presented in 'A survey of Korean Religious Leaders' Consciousness' show sharply how exclusive Protestant pastors are. While Buddhist monks and Catholic priests have an attitude of coexistence with and a desire for the mutual prosperity of other religions, the Protestant pastors take a position of rejection and exclusion. Protestantism, because of its exclusive attitude towards other religions, is seen as the most undesirable religion by both Buddhist monks and Catholic priests. The exclusiveness of Korean Protestants has also caused a rejection of the rituals of other religions, especially the ancestor veneration of Confucianism, which is typically indigenized in Korean traditional culture.[39] It seems obvious that for the majority of Korean Protestants, including pentecostals, Christianity is the only true religion and all others are false, and therefore to become a Christian means to reject all other religious and philosophical traditions. Eastern spirituality and Christian faith are incompatible and irreconcilable, and absolute exclusivism is upheld as a prerequisite for a faithful Christian.

The above-mentioned negative aspects of the Korean church in general and Korean Pentecostalism in particular in the ecclesiological, ideological and religio-cultural realms have caused an extreme identity crisis in spite of its much-celebrated rapid growth. The more one questions how a conventional theology of mission has related to and engaged directly and transparently with church expansionism, the suffering and struggling people, and other religio-cultural realities in the history of Korea, the more acutely does one feel its limitations. It is, therefore, an urgent task for the Korean pentecostal movement to reconstruct a new identity and a paradigm of mission that responds better to both the present Korean mission context and to the Korean people's effective history.

Towards a New Pentecost: An Open Conclusion

Desiring a new Pentecost in the midst of the Korean reality outlined in this article, I would like to suggest three alternative missiological reformulations as open questions in the dialogue with Korean *minjung*

38. Korean Gallup Research Institute, *Religion and Religious Consciousness of the Koreans* (1994), pp. 128-29.
39. Institute for the Study of Modern Society, 'A Survey of Korean Religious Leaders' Consciousness' (1990).

religious thought. First, a conversion to the people's reality as a third baptism in the Holy Spirit is needed in the search for a Korean ecumenical Pentecostalism. In western theological hermeneutics, humanity is open-ended to the world, and the world is open-ended to God, the Ground of Being. Thus the people are open-ended to God. God is the ontological power of the world-experience, the ontological ground of the linguistics of existence, and the hermeneutical foundation for inter-religious dialogue.[40] In the theology of the Korean *minjung* religions such as *Tonghak* and *Chungsan*, however, this order is reversed: God and the world are open-ended to the people. The people are the centre of God's encounter with the world and of inter-ideological and interreligious dialogue, which seeks the common ground for God-praxis.

The final result of a fusion of horizons in *Tonghak*,[41] a liberation-centred syncretism in a mutually critical correlation between the given context of *Tonghak* and the great religious traditions of the East, was *Innaech'on*, literally meaning 'the people are Heaven'. For *Tonghak* the resolution of *han* (a historically accumulated resentment and bitterness of Korean people) only becomes possible when Heaven is united with the people. The people and Heaven (God) are identical. Justice and equality as essential to the nature of God reveal one of the central notions of *Tonghak*, *Minsim ch'onsim* (the people's mind and Heaven's mind are identical). Heaven's mind is in the collectively integrated mind of the people, and therefore the people's mind is the channel for the Heavenly Mandate, *Ch'onmyong*. As a result, all people should be treated as God is treated *(Sainnoch'on)*. The people are the locus in which *Innaech'on* is realized and where the apocalyptic transformation of the world, *Huch'on'gaebyok*, springs up. The logic of *Innaech'on* therefore rightly implies that it is the people who are the direct medium through which the Heavenly Mandate is revealed. The people see or find God face to face. The messianic vision and praxis of *Huch'on'gaebyok* is realized in this concrete world by the people with the people, realising the true meaning of the *oikoumene* as the household of life, the whole inhabited earth.

40. Kim Kyoung-Jae, *Christianity and the Encounter of Asian Religions* (Zoetermeer: Uitgeverij Boekencentrum, 1994), p. 44.

41. *Tonghak* is a Korean national religion established by Cho Che-wu at the end of the nineteenth century.

In the *Chungsan* tradition,[42] a people-centred *missio Dei* is addressed by a key notion, *Chohwajongbu*, the government realizing the harmony between the way of Heaven and the affairs of human beings. The subjects of the building of *Chohwajongbu* are the *Namjoson*, a collective symbolic image of the *minjung* and *minjok*. Therefore the strategy and method that will save all nations will come from *Namjoson*, and the locus of salvation—the salvation of the whole society, of the whole of humankind, and of the whole universe—will be the locus of *Namjoson*, the locus of the *minjung*, where the spirit world and human beings are unified in a concrete term.

In Korean Buddhism, Wonhyo understands the *oikoumene* from the people-centred perspective. The common ground of Wonhyo's ecumenism is the people. His Buddhist ecumenism, *T'ong Pulgyo* (One Unified Buddhism) or *Ilsung Pulgyo* (One Vehicle Buddhism), was concretized in the praxis of *minjung* Buddhism. Wonhyo experienced a conversion from church-ecumenism to people-centred ecumenism. He embodied a Bodhisattva through working for the liberation/salvation of the *minjung* because the people themselves are Bodhisattva. The people are the centre that integrates the sacred and the secular. For the people, the mutual, interpenetrating, living life of here and now is the beginning of religion, the centre of faith-praxis, and core of a web of mission.

Therefore the spirituality of Korean Pentecostalism must be clearly characterised by constant basic reference to actual conditions, that is a passion for reality. Starting from and returning to the reality, this passion for reality can become a touchstone for avoiding sterile abstraction and getting to grips with actual reality, for moving quickly from theory to practice, for moving beyond mere interpretation to transformation, for abandoning all idealism and spiritualism and putting our feet on the ground in commitment and organized action. The people's reality is the locus in which God's indignation is revealed: 'God listened to the cry of his people and took a stance in relation to it; God decided to enter the struggle for historical liberation.'[43]

The second missiological reformulation suggested here is that the Korean pentecostal movement should rediscover *minjung* languages and 'reshamanize' itself from the perspective of liberation/salvation-

42. *Chungsan* is a Korean national religion established by Kang Il-Sun at the end of the nineteenth century.

43. P. Casaldaliga and J.M. Vigil, *The Spirituality of Liberation* (Kent: Burns & Oates, 1994), pp. 26, 17-20.

centred syncretism. The authentic memories of God's people were not completed two thousand years ago, and they cannot be imprisoned within the Christian canon. The text of God's revelation was, is, and will be written in the people's life in their everyday struggle for survival and liberation. The locus of God's ever-growing truth in history is the people's life itself. The Holy Spirit as *ruach Yahweh*, the life-giving and life-sustaining *spiritus creator* works in the fundamental context for doing theology, and the Bible and church tradition are horizons of that context which at some time become the reference for the people's own ongoing search for God. Korean Pentecostalism as the latest participant in God's liberation/salvation in Korean history has first of all to search carefully for God's salvific, liberative ways in Korean tradition, including *missio Dei* vis-à-vis the Korean people's rich religio-cultural heritage. As the *minjung* are recognized as the core of God's liberation/salvation, the history, religion and culture of the *minjung* should be taken account of as the most important points of reference of God's liberating and salvific ways in Korea. Based on the hermeneutical principle of mutually critical correlation, Korean Pentecostalism has to realize a creative religious fusion—a true or fine syncretism, that is liberation/salvation syncretism—between the horizons of Christian tradition and Korean tradition.

It is therefore imperative for Korean Pentecostalism to rediscover *minjung* language from all religious and revolutionary resources in Korea (especially from their oral books) in order to tune in to these socio-psychological information systems and to communicate with the 'theologians' of this oral culture. As Hollenweger describes it, 'the medium of communication [of the minjung] is ... not the doctrine but the testimony, not the book but the parable, not a systematic theology but a song, not the treatise but the television programme, not the articulation of concepts but the celebration of banquets'.[44] Speaking in tongues in this sense should not therefore be dogmatized as the only initial sign language in Pentecostalism. Speaking in tongues can be better understood as 'a means of communicating without grammatical sentences, a kind of atmospheric communication' and as 'a natural gift that many human beings possess'.[45] It is a human ability that may not necessarily be used in Christian spirituality; it is not abnormal, it also occurs outside Christianity, and it is not a primitive but a primal and

44. Hollenweger, 'After Twenty Years', p. 10.
45. Hollenweger, 'After Twenty Years', p. 7.

highly complex mode of communication. Hollenweger says that 'all the elements of oral theology function as a logic system for passing on theological and social value and information in oral societies... The individual memories can be plugged into the communal memory in such a way that ... everybody has access to the total information of the community'.[46] The oral, narrative and enthusiastic form of *minjung* spirituality is an unexplored potential medium of a Korean ecumenical Pentecostalism.

Given the shamanized nature of this Pentecostalism, a mature fusion of the Christian horizon with Korean shamanism should be more seriously considered in the light of liberation/salvation-centred syncretism. Despite the missionaries' efforts to reject shamanism and to guard Christianity against it, the Korean church has been shamanized and has taken deep root in indigenous Korean religiosity. The vitality of the Korean church, a success story of Christian mission in the non-Christian world, raises the risky question as to whether or not the shamanized Korean church is compatible with the gospel of Jesus as liberator, that is, whether we can find a liberating spirituality in the shamanized church. Confronted with this critical dilemma, Korean *minjung* theologians have discovered anew that Korean shamanism is the religion of the *minjung*. The shaman rituals are performed to cure the sick, to comfort the bereaved and to reconcile broken families. Shamans even feed and make happy the unhappy wandering spirits of the deceased which have no place to settle. The *minjung* are *han*-ridden people. The *han* of the *minjung* is not only a psychological state, but also arises out of the political and economic realities interacting and bringing themselves to bear on the mind and body of the *minjung*. Thus the *minjung* live with *han*, accumulate *han* and die with *han*. If shamanism performs what Suh Nam-Dong describes as the 'priestly function of comforting the han-ridden minjung',[47] it should be the role of a shamanized Korean *minjung* Christianity like Pentecostalism to comfort the *han*-ridden people and release their *han*. This leads to forgiveness of sin, a liberative act. In this sense the dichotomy between the pentecostal *minjung* and the socio-political *minjung* can only undermine the holistic sense of the liberating spirituality of the *minjung*. The spirituality of the *minjung* has risen out of deep feelings of *han*; its role is to overcome

46. Hollenweger, 'After Twenty Years', pp. 10-11.
47. Suh Nam-Dong 1983, *Minjung Sinhak-ui Tamgu* [Research of Minjung Theology] (Seoul: Hangil-sa, 1983), p. 44.

not only individual *han* but also the collective *han* of the people; it is the crying and moaning of the *han*-ridden spirits of the people to God, a liberating spirituality, a crying out for liberation and a struggle for liberation from the *han*-creating socio-political and economic structures. This *minjung* spirituality, deeply embedded in Korean shamanism, is a struggling spirituality which will not give in to the oppressive feelings of *han* but will fight against the oppressive structures of *han*.[48]

This liberating *minjung* spirituality has been clearly seen in the collective nature of the village community's shaman rituals, *Taedong Kut*, and its lively festival. The *Kut* is the place where the people become a community, whole and united, and recreate their energy to labour and love. *Taedong Kut* is not constrained by individual greed, nor is it merely a religious affair, but is rather open to the world and to the community for the sake of peace, justice, and well-being. This is the true liberating spirituality of shamanism. What moves the *Kut* and what is at the same time created by the *Kut* is its life-giving force, the *Sinmyong*, the spirituality that the *minjung* in the village *Kut* experience, participate and share in. It is not necessarily a religious feeling, but rather a 'highly spirited feeling', a 'creative dynamism flowing out of one's viscera', a 'Kut-level feeling of strength for life', a feeling of the body as a whole.[49] The *Sinmyong* is in the very life of the minjung, and the *Kut* is the event of *Sinmyong*, and this is arguably a Korean way of Pentecost. The shamanized Korean church should therefore revive and revitalise the liberating spirituality of the *minjung*. We do not have to deshamanize Korean Christianity but reshamanize it. That is, the liberating gospel of Jesus Christ should be fused into the *minjung* spirituality of the Korean shaman tradition: in this way, the liberating tradition of *minjung* spirituality in Korean shamanism could transform the shamanized Korean church, and at the same time, the liberating spirituality of Jesus Christ could transform the shamanized church.[50]

The third reformulation suggested is that Korean Pentecostalism should consider a theology of Sharing Economy rather than of Property.

48. Suh Kwang-Sun, 'Shamanism and Minjung Liberation', in V. Fabella, P.K.H. Lee and D.K.S. Suh (eds.), *Asian Christian Spirituality: Reclaiming Traditions* (Maryknoll, NY: Orbis Books, 1992), pp. 31-35 (33-34).

49. Lee Chung-Hee 1992, 'Liberation Spirituality in Dae-dong Gut [Taedong Kut]', in Fabella, Lee and Suh (eds.), *Asian Christian Spirituality*, pp. 36-43 (41-42).

50. Suh, 'Shamanism', pp. 35-36.

The domination of capital in the global market is causing a multidimensional victimization of the *minjung* in Korea as well as in the world. Through the vehicle of the transnational corporate power entities, capital victimizes the Korean *minjung* as subjects of their 'household' (*oikonomia*) in their homes and communities as well as in the market. A drastic and radical geopolitical change will bring about the opening, erosion and breakdown of the traditional current boundaries of peoples and communities. There is a close connection between the dynamic of the global market and local communities. The relationships between human beings, among groups and communities, and between humanity and nature, will be governed by the complex conflicts resulting from rapidly shifting contradictions in the global market.[51] The identity, values, life-style and perceptual sensibility of the people and communities will be under severe attack from innovations of the hi-tech multimedia in their life and communities and the impact of the global information process and its network. This information and multi-media gap will cause an imbalance of power among the people between the Haves and the Have-nots, which will be much more serious than it is in terms of economics. Globalization will also accelerate the deterioration of the life environment that already is in a serious situation due to the last two centuries of the drive towards industrialization. Its factors and causes are very much interconnected with the multidimensional nature of modern civilization.[52]

In view of contemporary global economic realities, the teaching of Prosperity Theology seems to be simply nonsense. Not only are the majority of the people living on this planet poor, but the majority of Christians living in the world are also poor. If it is God's will that all his children should be financially prosperous, if it is not his will for any of his children to be poor, who are the poor? Thanks to the religious enthusiasm based on Prosperity Theology, many of the poor are being offered false economic hopes, just as many invalids and physically handicapped people are offered the false hope of perfect health by some of those very same preachers. Prosperity Theology is fundamentally anthropocentric and is a product of the highly individualistic and self-centred culture of late-twentieth-century western capitalism.[53]

51. Kim Yong-Bock, 'Asian Reality as the Context for Reading of the Bible' (unpublished paper presented at Nanjing Theological Seminary, March 1996).
52. Kim, 'Asian Reality'.
53. W.W. Gasque, 'Prosperity Theology and the New Testament', *Evangelical*

In the critical situation of globalization, the locus of the people should be the locus where the principle of *Sangguk*, 'being mutually destructive', (i.e. distortion, confrontation and struggle between individuals, ethnic groups, nations, humans and the gods of religions) shifts to the principle of *Sangsaeng*, 'being mutually constructive or living mutually', through *Haewon'gongsa* and *Ch'onjigongsa*, a total *han-puri* (solving *han*). This transformation, the core of *missio Dei*, is in my opinion a chaotic event, a Pentecost that happens in the midst of the people. The people arouse God's compassion, the people know God's will through compassion, and the people realize God's will with God's compassion. The biblical event of Pentecost broke down the walls of nation, colour, language, sex and social class. The true sign of Pentecost was not Prosperity Theology but a Sharing Economy. 'Food is Heaven. As we eat, God enters us. Food is Heaven. Oh, food should be shared and eaten by all.'[54]

Through the poem 'Food is Heaven', Kim Chi-Ha expresses his conviction of the sanctity of life. The poet experiences the mysterious body of the deity within the food that people share in common. The human body is heaven and heaven is the human body, and there is neither the upper nor the lower, neither the oppressor nor the oppressed, neither the body nor the spirit. This word picture corresponds to a symbol of the dwelling of God in the *oikoumene* in the form of the Eucharistic meal, that is the central image of the life of the world.[55] In reality, the lack of daily bread for which Christ taught us to pray, brings hunger, starvation and death to a world that is now unjustly divided between rich and poor. Here is the meeting of 'ecumenics' and 'economics'. The Eucharist calls for a daily sharing of bread and material and spiritual resources with the millions of hungry people in this world, because through them God, the Trinity, comes on a pilgrimage to us at every moment.

Review of Theology (1996), pp. 44-45.

54. Kim Chi-Ha, *The Gold-Crowned Jesus and Other Writings* (trans. Kim Chung-Sun and Shelly Killen; New York: Orbis Books, 1978), p. xv.

55. K. Raiser, *Ecumenism in Transition: A Paradigm Shift in the Ecumenical Movement?* (Geneva: WCC, 1991), p. 111.

RESPONSE

Bae Hyoen Sung

Dr Lee's article on 'Minjung and Pentecostalism' is a stimulating one, in that it seems to deal with both socio-political and spiritual issues for the Korean church. In this sense, his research is a creative attempt to provide Christians with a balanced perception of the gospel. Moreover, at least on the face of it, I agree with his view that the nature of the entire Korean church has been greatly affected by Pentecostalism. It is true to say that many denominational churches in Korea share Pentecostal faith, experience and worship such as the baptism of the Spirit, speaking in tongues, signs and wonders. However, this fact does not mean that Pentecostalism has lost its own particular identity in Korea.

In spite of Dr Lee's concern for an integrative endeavour, his view on Korean Pentecostalism appears limited by a subjective and partial interpretation. He seems to confuse the specific forms of Korean Pentecostalism with the more general Korean revival movement. As far as Korean Pentecostalism is concerned, we have to define the difference between the earlier evangelical revival movement and the later Pentecostal Movement. It is possible to analyse the nature of Pentecostalism from three perspectives. One is from the perspective of classical Pentecostalism, which focuses on the ministry of the Holy Spirit with speaking in tongues and receiving the baptism of the Holy Spirit. This is closely related to the denominational characteristics of churches like the Church of God, the Church of God in Christ and the Assemblies of God (or in Korea, the Full Gospel churches).[1] The other perspective is the Charismatic movement, whose background is based on Catholic and other mainline churches. Finally, there is also the 'Third Wave' group

---

1. These denominations are related to the Holiness Movement. See V. Synan, *The Holiness Pentecostal Tradition: Charismatic Movements in the Twentieth Century* (Grand Rapids: Eerdmans, 1997), pp. 68-156.

of evangelicals.[2] Dr Lee does not distinguish between the Korean churches generally and the Pentecostal churches in particular. In short, his article has a tendency to generalize about all the Korean churches and to miss the specific meanings and history of Pentecostalism. According to his argument, all Korean Churches are Pentecostal churches. In other words, his view of Pentecostalism is based on a standardization of the Korean Church, and his article is not concerned with classical Pentecostalism at all.

In addition, by giving priority to *minjung*, Lee's understanding of Pentecostalism is primarily a socio-political one. In actuality, he uses *minjung* as the central theological theme by which he interprets the movement. Minjung is something, but not everything—but according to Lee, *minjung* is the subject of human history, the term that encompasses everything. By focusing on *minjung*, he fails to understand the essence of Korean Pentecostalism, which goes beyond the boundaries of *minjung*. In particular, his understanding of *minjung* is not as much concerned with personal and spiritual issues within Pentecostalism as with collective and socio-political ones. Moreover, I suspect that in Lee's understanding, Pentecostalism is often regarded as a manifestation of a 'problematic' religious symptom. For him, Pentecostalism is regarded as non-intellectual, fundamentalist and shamanistic. He identifies Korean Pentecostalism as a shamanistic-centred religion. Here there is inconsistency in the development of his ideas. Although he understands the shamanistic tendency negatively, nevertheless he suggests that Korean churches should learn from shamanism. On the contrary, the Korean Pentecostal churches challenge the worldwide church by sending all over the world people who have experienced the Holy Spirit. Therefore, this positive aspect of Korean Pentecostalism should be acknowledged also.

Korean Pentecostals are those who base their convictions on their experience of the baptism in the Holy Spirit. They have their distinctive Pentecostal characteristics, which have greatly influenced the Korean Church. The rapid growth of Pentecostal churches in Korea today may be attributed to their strong pneumatological position. Seen from a wider perspective, they are 'conservative evangelical' churches, in that their faith is based on the biblical tradition. However, their understand-

2.   This group does not want to be called pentecostal but the 'Third Wave'. Vinson Synan puts it as 'a successor to the first two, i.e. the classical Pentecostals and the charismatics', *Holiness Pentecostal Tradition*, p. 271.

ing of the Holy Spirit goes further than mere doctrinal formulations, which often hinders Evangelicals from experiencing the pneumatological presence. In their view of the book of Acts, Pentecostals regard the baptism of the Holy Spirit as an endowment of power for evangelism. At the same time, they see the Holy Spirit as a motivator of social activity. Therefore, both these significant aspects of the work of the Holy Spirit must operate together in order to bring wholeness to people. Nevertheless, the priority in these two major Christian themes is to seek the kingdom of God and his will first. Pentecostals give prime importance to searching for the fullness of the Holy Spirit. Seen from this perspective, it is true to say that Pentecostals in Korea are in general those who pay more attention to 'spiritual' matters. From this point of view, Dr Lee's understanding of Korean Pentecostalism is, in a sense, too centred on a socio-political perspective.

The twentieth-century Pentecostal Movement started almost simultaneously all over the world in a spectacular way. However, as Robert Menzies puts it, its theological foundations are 'firmly planted in the nineteenth century Holiness movement and American revivalism'.[3] In order to understand Korean Pentecostalism in an integrative way, it is therefore necessary to consider the Pentecostal movement not only from inside the Korean-specific context, but also from outside that context as well. The former stimulates us to dig out interdisciplinary research on Korean Pentecostalism, including socio-political and religio-cultural studies. On the other hand, the latter leads us to focus on the pan-Pentecostal connection through which Pentecostals throughout the world find their common identity. The broad nature of the movement that followed the Pentecost event in the book of Acts was not restricted to a narrow doctrinal and denominational level, but was open to all people by the acknowledgment of the transforming power of the Holy Spirit.

3.   R.P. Menzies, 'Evidential Tongues: An Essay on Theological Method', *Asian Journal of Pentecostal Studies* 1 (1998), pp. 111-23 (111).

RETHINKING SPIRIT BAPTISM:
THE NATURAL AND THE SUPERNATURAL

Walter J. Hollenweger

Introduction

Evangelicalism was passed on to Pentecostalism via the North American Holiness Movement of the nineteenth century, but the Evangelicalism of that time was something very different from Evangelicalism today. The great evangelicals of the last century, like Finney, Mahan, Upham, Torrey and others, understood by the term 'Spirit baptism' or 'holiness' (for them identical terms), that this was not only a religious commitment but also a social and a political one. Following their understanding of the Holy Spirit, they helped the black slaves to flee slavery at a time when this was illegal; they provided education for them at their schools and universities; they had women pastors (the beginning of the feminist movement can be traced to this period in Evangelicalism); they suggested a world organization for peace not unlike the United Nations; many of them were pacifists; they also fought capitalism which they considered to be at the root of war, providing alternative means of production from the capitalist system. Frank Bartleman and other early pentecostals saw clearly that the reason for wars was not the fight for democracy or justice but the need to gain influence for economic expansion and to have control over markets. That is why early pentecostals in many countries, especially in the USA, officially enrolled as conscientious objectors—in contrast, today pentecostals have military chaplains. The writings of these conscientious objectors were later deleted from evangelical and Holiness literature; one has to have the original copies or reprints of the originals to discover this. It is astonishing how the ideas of these people were mutilated—without ever indicating that large chunks were left out of this early literature. In fact pentecostals and evangelicals should understand modern biblical criticism much better than they do, as they have changed their founding documents more than any biblical copyist has done!

However, my topic is 'Rethinking Spirit Baptism', and not the evangelical roots of Pentecostalism, which I have written on elsewhere.[1] Spirit Baptism is one of the many Catholic influences in Pentecostalism. Any observer of Pentecostalism will see that it is particularly successful in Catholic cultures, and this has its reasons. One reason is that Pentecostalism has not only oral black and evangelical roots, but also Catholic roots. To these roots belong especially its strict Arminianism (the doctrine of free will)—the bone of contention between the reformers and the Catholics—the reformers believed in the unconditional election of God, the Catholics in free will. The Catholic doctrine of free will passed from Anglicanism via John Wesley to Methodism, and from North American Methodism and the Holiness Movement to Pentecostalism. The Catholic roots influenced other aspects of Pentecostalism, which are also differences from Reformed Protestantism. To the Catholic roots can be attributed Pentecostalism's belief in two worlds, a supernatural and a natural, its hierarchical church structure (bishops or pastors with episcopal authority, the most common form of pentecostal church government), and its doctrine of two (or sometimes) three stages in the *ordo salutis*, the decisive element being a second or (sometimes) a third religious crisis experience in the life of a believer which is different from salvation.

These Catholic elements were mediated to Pentecostalism by John Wesley, whose theology had such a profound effect upon the nineteenth-century Holiness movement, the precursor of Pentecostalism. Wesley was a linguist who read numerous Catholic books in several languages,[2] and translated them for his lay preachers. The central idea was called 'perfection' which was attainable during one's lifetime. Wesley's Swiss assistant William Fletcher of Madeley called this experience 'baptism of the Spirit' (as a noun this term is not in the Bible), for the first time in church history. These ideas were taken up by North American Methodism (which later gave them up), but they worked their way through the Holiness Movement into Pentecostalism. This is one reason why Pentecostalism has conducted an official dialogue with the

1.   Documentation and discussion on this subject is to be found in W.J. Hollenweger, *Pentecostalism: Origins and Development Worldwide* (Peabody, MA: Hendrickson, 1997), chapters 12–15, 17 .

2.   Detailed in Hollenweger, *Pentecostalism*, chapter 12.

Vatican for over 20 years. The central concept in these Catholic ideas is
'Spirit baptism', which in pre-Vatican Catholicism provides no problem—hence the relative ease with which the Catholic hierarchy deals
with the Catholic Pentecostal movement, resulting in relatively few
splits from Catholicism by Catholic Pentecostals. This movement for
them is quite rightly just a revived Catholicism. In short, one could say
that Pentecostalism is a way of being Catholic without accepting the juridical structures of the Catholic Church.

However, these Catholic ideas are being rethought in some pentecostal quarters. To begin with, only a minority of pentecostals accepted
the original pentecostal doctrine of 'initial evidence'—the view that
speaking in tongues was the 'initial evidence' of Spirit baptism. 'Initial
evidence' was not in the first pentecostal declaration of faith, that of
William Joseph Seymour at Azusa Street. The old German pentecostal
movement never accepted it—there, only the newer pentecostal churches, supported by the North American Assemblies of God in Germany,
accepted this doctrine. Many Third World pentecostal churches, like the
important Chilean pentecostal churches, never accepted this doctrine
either. That may be the reason for the North American Assemblies of
God and the Church of God founding a 'real' pentecostal movement in
Chile. As pentecostal scholars learned Greek and became New Testament professors in reputable universities and colleges, they realized that
the doctrine of the initial evidence was difficult to defend. This is part
of the critical heritage of Pentecostalism. There is a critical awakening
among pentecostal scholars, who fight the notion that Pentecostalism is
Evangelicalism plus something; Evangelicalism plus fire, or dedication,
missionary success, speaking in tongues or gifts of healing. They realize, for instance, that the heavy dispensationalism which one finds in
Evangelicalism gets into conflict with pentecostal hermeneutics, such as
the long held belief of Evangelicals that the gifts of the Spirit were
confined to the time of the early church. Pentecostals are not prepared
to relegate the gifts of the Spirit to the formative period of Christianity.
Therefore, Pentecostalism is a denomination *sui generis*, and not just
another variation of Protestantism or Evangelicalism. Its roots in the
oral traditions of African American slaves or the oral *mestizo* tradition
of Latin America, in the Catholic tradition of Wesley, in the Evangelical tradition of the North American Holiness movement (with its far-
reaching political, social and ecumenical programmes), in the critical
tradition of both the Holiness movement and critical western theology,

and in the ecumenical tradition—all this qualifies Pentecostalism as a movement which is not just a sub-division of Evangelicalism, even if the official statements of Pentecostalism mostly use out-dated concepts of the turn of the century and sometimes give the impression of a form of Evangelicalism.

For the time being, critical pentecostal theologians find it difficult to get a hearing. They publish at least four scholarly periodicals and hold regular scholarly conferences, whose minutes are good trend indicators of what is happening in Pentecostalism. And yet these men and women deserve to be taken seriously by both pentecostals and non-pentecostals alike. Many of them have done theology in the context of memories of suffering and defamation, of being ridiculed and persecuted (sometimes by their own brothers and sisters in the faith who have 'gone over' to the right-wing money aristocracy of this world under pretext of being 'faithful' to the gospel). These scholars use standard methods of historical and exegetical research. Because of their specific religious socialization they refuse to drive a wedge between 'the spiritual' and 'the material', thus they take seriously the praxis of early Pentecostalism, although perhaps not its ideology. The trouble is that these publications are not read by many pentecostal leaders, let alone the rank and file. In most cases the pentecostal popular periodicals do not report the critical yet deeply spiritual and helpful essays and dissertations of their own scholars—all the more reason for the mainline theological journals and Selly Oak Colleges to take these topics up. However, it is my own experience that most mainline publishers want either sensational (for instance, 'The Toronto Blessing') or simply 'uplifting' manuscripts from pentecostals. They do not often seem to be interested in specialized analyses like Pentecostalism and Ecumenism, Pentecostalism and Social Ethics, Pentecostalism and Pacifism, Pentecostalism and Feminism, Pentecostalism and critical exegesis, and so on. Yet, on these issues pentecostals have original contributions to make which are based on their grass roots experience.

Baptism of the Spirit, 'subsequent and different from conversion'

An issue widely discussed among pentecostal scholars today is the question of the subsequence and difference of the baptism of the Spirit to salvation and conversion. For a long time, Classical pentecostals taught that a person can be 'saved' but not be baptized in the Spirit, and in many pentecostal denominations the 'initial evidence' of the baptism in

168 Pentecostals after a Century

the Spirit is speaking tongues. This doctrine has already been questioned by the Chilean pentecostals (who have a strictly Methodist doctrine),[3] by the old German pentecostal movement[4] and by Leonhard Steiner from Switzerland, who in 1939 asked: 'Is it right to base our conception of the baptism of the Spirit on the Acts of the Apostles, and the experience of the twelve apostles? Can this experience be deduced from the epistles written by them?'[5]

These pentecostals agree with Brick Bradford, long time general secretary of the Presbyterian Charismatic Communion who identified Spirit baptism with regeneration or baptism in water in one.[6] For Russ Spittler (an Assemblies of God theologian in the USA) subsequence is a 'non issue', for 'the early pentecostals did not intend to frame a new *ordo salutis*, an algorithm for piety'.[7]

Pentecostal New Testament scholar Gordon Fee, who wrote a commentary on Corinthians for the International Critical Commentary suggests 'that there is in fact very little biblical support for the traditional pentecostal position' of the baptism in the Spirit, but he argues further that this is of little real consequence to the doctrine of Spirit baptism. He gives a number of historical and cultural reasons for the rise of the doctrine of 'separate and subsequent experience'. He writes that we now have churches where:

> people can be in the church, but evidence little or nothing of the work of the Spirit in their lives... It is precisely out of such a background that one is to understand the Pentecostal movement with its deep dissatisfaction with life in Christ without life in the Spirit ... The fact that this experience was for them usually a separate experience in the Holy Spirit and subsequent to their conversion is in itself probably irrelevant. Given their place in the history of the church, how else might it have happened?

3.   In the Introduction to the hymnbook: Ignacio Vergara, 'The Iglesia Metodista Pentecostal grew out of the Methodist Episcopal Church', *El Protestantismo en el Chile hoy* (Estudio socio-religoso, 1; Concepción, Chile: Cemuir, 1986), p. 123; see also Hollenweger, *Pentecostalism*, chapter 10.

4.   W.J. Hollenweger, *Pentecostals* (Peabody, MA: Hendrickson, 3rd edn, 1988), pp. 231-43.

5.   L. Steiner, *Europeiska Pingstkonferensen i Stockholm* (Stockholm: Förlaget Filadelfia, 1939); see also Hollenweger, *Pentecostals*, pp. 67-68, 325, 335.

6.   Hollenweger, *Pentecostals*, chapter 27.

7.   R. Spittler, 'Suggested Areas for Further Research in Pentecostal Studies', *Pneuma* 5 (1983), pp. 39-57 (43).

Thus the Pentecostals should probably not make a virtue out of a necessity. On the other hand, neither should others deny the validity of such experience on biblical grounds...[8]

In other words, Fee and others want to stress the fact that pentecostals, charismatics and others have had a valid experience that is important for their lives and that they call baptism in the Spirit. But they should not make a dogmatic statement on the basis of their experience, nor should they make it normative for all other Christians. This leads other pentecostal scholars to ask for a more critical interpretation of the doctrine of the Holy Spirit. In biblical tradition there are at least three pneumatologies: Luke (which has in three passages a kind of subsequential experience with the Spirit), Paul (for whom water baptism and Spirit baptism are identical) and the Old Testament testimony, according to which all people have the 'Spirit of Life'—otherwise they would not live. If we find such a variety of doctrines of the Spirit in the Bible, it is also understandable that today's churches also have different doctrines—it is not only understandable but it is also legitimate and necessary. We will never have a unity in the Christian church on the basis of theological statements and doctrines. This is neither necessary nor possible, because the Bible is an example of unity through and by these different approaches to the Spirit and to Christ. Unity is more to be found in the liturgy of the church, such as in the Lord's Supper, prayer and the offering—Paul took up a collection for his theological enemies in Jerusalem! Furthermore, one has to know that in many pentecostal churches a great proportion of the members have never spoken in tongues, and the same applies for a number of pastors.

Natural and Supernatural

The Pentecostal theologian Russ Spittler says that 'glossolalia is a human phenomenon, not limited to Christianity nor even to religious behaviour ... It cannot be the essence of Pentecostalism'. I think that Spittler is right. The notion that glossolalia (or in fact any other of the gifts of the Spirit like healing or precognition or prophecy) is something 'supernatural' is in my view biblically and scientifically untenable.

---

8.   G.D. Fee, 'Baptism in the Holy Spirit: The Issue of Separability and Subsequence', *Pneuma* 7 (1985), pp. 87-99 (88, 96-98).

Biblically, it is untenable because the list of charismata in the New Testament includes so-called 'extraordinary' gifts (healing, prophecy, glossolalia) and so-called 'ordinary' gifts (management, teaching, giving money to the poor, even being married or unmarried). So, the mark of 'supernaturality' is not a concept of the New Testament. Paul's criterion for a charisma is not determined ontologically but functionally. For instance, *pneumatikos* ('spiritual') and *sarkikos* ('natural') are not ontological but functional terms, that is to say, they serve to do something. A charisma is a natural gift which serves *pros to sympheron* ('for the common good'), it operates in an ecclesiological and christological context (nobody can say *anathema Iesous*—Jesus is cursed—in the Spirit) and it is open to judgment by the ecumenical community.

Scientifically, speaking in tongues has been demonstrated to be a human ability that may or may not be used in Christian spirituality. It appears quite frequently outside Christianity and is not abnormal, only uncommon in certain cultures. Just as music, normal speech and the bread in the Eucharist are common gifts of creation and may be transformed in the liturgical context, so speaking in tongues is a natural gift that many human beings possess. As they live in societies in which speaking in tongues is considered eccentric or even insane, they do not have a chance to discover this natural ability. The same is true for the gift of healing, which many have but do not get the opportunity to develop. In a society in which singing or dancing were ostracized, few people would dare to discover their gifts in these fields. The function of speaking in tongues is similar to that of dreaming, singing or dancing— or being silent. It is, as Spittler says 'a form of right-hemisphere speech'.[9] Speaking in tongues is non-cognitive, but meaningful nevertheless. It is a means of communicating without grammatical sentences, a kind of atmospheric communication. When a whole congregation sings in tongues in many harmonies without following a set piece of music, these pentecostals are building a cathedral of sounds, a socioacoustic sanctuary, which is particularly important for people who have no cathedral or have left it. Just as a cathedral is built of ordinary stones, so glossolalia is made of ordinary sounds. And just as, when put together in a masterpiece, the stones in a cathedral do not change onto-

---

9.   Spittler, 'Suggested Areas', p. 52. See also Spittler's article 'Glossolalia', in S.M. Burgess *et al.*, *Dictionary of the Pentecostal and Charismatic Movements* (Grand Rapids: Zondervan, 1988), pp. 335-41.

logically but change functionally, so speaking in tongues can become a piece of art which, like the cathedral, proclaims: *God is here.*

In this connection one might consider a comparison between Dadaism and Pentecostalism, where I have observed the following points of contact. Dadaism emerged during World War I in Zurich in a multi-lingual and international milieu of immigrants, similar to the context of the beginning of Pentecostalism in Los Angeles. Not far away from the Cabaret Voltaire, the meeting point of the Dadaists, one also found the first Swiss Pentecostal church. That church also grew in a milieu of uprooted people. The poems of the Dadaists, which were simultaneous in several languages, appeal directly to the senses. There is a lack of semantic meaning of the vocals and sounds as they are in themselves the message. Every listener makes his or her own interpretation, similar to what happens with speaking in tongues. Thus Dadaism (and speaking in tongues) creates a community that cuts across languages and definitions. Furthermore, it is no coincidence that after Dadaism and Pentecostalism a new expression of art, Cubism, emerged. Cubism created multi-perspective images, images that present an object simul-taneously from different viewpoints, just as the Dadaistic poem com-bines several languages, or singing in tongues creates a piece of art simultaneously in several languages. Whether there are social parallels between the aforementioned expressions of art and Pentecostalism I do not know. However, the similarity of the phenomena and their appear-ance at the same time and at the same place cannot be an accident. A researcher who understands more about these art forms might take up this issue. Perhaps the fact that Hugo Ball presented a Christmas Play very early in the Cabaret Voltaire without words (only sounds) might be of significance for this research.

The New Testament does not know the word *hyperphysikos* and it is quite impossible to translate 'supernatural' into Hebrew. The concept simply does not exist. God is a God of the natural and the 'supernat-ural', and there is no distinction between the two. Both realms of real-ity, the one which we think we understand (the so-called 'natural') and the one which we do not or do not yet understand (the so-called 'super-natural') are God's creation and the realm of his reign. He even reigns in Sheol, which some Bible translations translate somewhat inexactly as 'hell' (Ps. 139.8).

This reinterpretation of pentecostal theology has been clearly seen by the pentecostal Miroslav Volf from Croatia, who did his doctoral dissertation with Jurgen Moltmann on 'Human Work, Divine Work and New Creation'.[10] By 'work' Volf does not mean 'work in the church' but work in general. 'Charisma should not be defined so narrowly as to include only ecclesial activities.'[11] The Spirit of God is not only active *in* the fellowship of the church but is also active in the world.

> The Spirit ... Who is poured out upon all flesh (Acts 2.17ff) imparts also charisms to all flesh: they are gifts given to the community irrespective of the existing distinctions or conditions within the community ... Very frequently charismatic is taken to mean extraordinary. Ecclesiologically this restricted undertaking of charisma can be found in some Pentecostal (or 'charismatic') churches which identify charismatic with spectacular. A secularized form of this 'supernaturalistic reduction' is found in the commonly accepted Weberian understanding of charism as an extraordinary quality of a personality. One of the main points of the Pauline theology of charisms is to overcome this restrictive concentration on the miraculous or extraordinary.[12]

Volf is supported in this view by the charismatic theologian J. Veenhof, who does not want to use the terms 'natural/supernatural' in connection with the charismata.[13] All these reflections make one thing abundantly clear: it is the end of the dichotomy between the natural and the supernatural.

10. M. Volf, 'Human Work, Divine Spirit and New Creation: Towards a Pneumatological Understanding of Work', Abstract of German original, *Pneuma* 9 (1987), pp. 173-93.

11. Volf, 'Human Work', p. 184.

12. Volf, 'Human Work', p. 185.

13. J. Veenhof, 'Charisma: bovennatuurlijk of natuurlijk?', in *Ervaren Waarheid: Festschrift voor Prof Dr H Jonke* (1984), pp. 130-33.

RESPONSE

Richard Massey

Professor Hollenweger has helpfully highlighted two aspects within
Pentecostalism that are of ongoing significance in the continuing debate
both within and without the movement. They are the issues of the
specific nature of Pentecostal experience in the areas of whether an initial baptism in the Spirit is a distinct and subsequent experience after
conversion and secondly, whether the gifts of the Spirit are supernatural
or natural.

Baptism in the Spirit: A Subsequent Experience?

Some valuable discussion has gone on recently in several publications,
notably those of James Dunn, Menzies, Shelton, Stibbe and Pawson,[1]
and I have recently had personal correspondence with David Pawson on
this subject. Also of interest is that this topic was the main discussion
issue in the British Charismatic Leaders Conference in January 1997, a
restricted annual conference of leaders from both the Pentecostal and
Charismatic groups. In July 1998 the issue was again debated at the
European Pentecostal Theological Association conference at Mattersey
Hall, Yorkshire. Most scholars recognize a general pattern that has

---

1.   J.D.G. Dunn, 'Baptism in the Spirit: A Response to Pentecostal Scholarship
in Luke–Acts', *Journal of Pentecostal Theology* 3 (1993), pp. 3-27; R.P. Menzies,
'Luke and the Spirit: A Reply to James D.G. Dunn', *Journal of Pentecostal Theology* 4 (1994), pp. 115-38; J.B. Shelton, 'A Reply to James D.G. Dunn's Baptism
in the Spirit: A Response to Pentecostal Scholarship on Luke-Acts', *Journal of Pentecostal Theology* 4 (1994), pp. 139-43; M. Stibbe, *Baptism in the Holy Spirit* (Ton-
bridge, Kent: Sovereign World, 1995); D. Pawson, *Fourth Wave—Charismatics
and Evangelicals: Are We Ready to Come Together?* (London: Hodder, 1992).

emerged in terms of identifying Spirit Baptism within the Christian experience, summarized as follows :

- Classical Pentecostals hold to either a second stage experience (Assemblies of God and most 'Oneness' groups) or a third stage experience (Holiness Pentecostals).
- Neo-Pentecostals and early Charismatics usually promote a second stage experience.
- Charismatics today have various viewpoints. Some hold to Spirit baptism as an initiation/ conversion continuum, but definite and accompanied by some evidence. Others speak of it as a release or renewal (not so distinctive). These views are also found among Catholic Charismatics, and especially among the 'Third Wave' movement associated with John Wimber.

The debate centring on Dunn's approach (conversion/ initiation) is not simply that of where the baptism in the Spirit fits into the order of experience, but whether it is distinctive and discernible. Hence Menzies and Shelton seek to maintain the Classical Pentecostal approach that Luke–Acts is about a baptism in the Spirit as power for service to be experienced after conversion. Similarly, aspects of this were maintained in the earlier Charismatic approaches. However, the more recent release/renewal/Third Wave types tend to lessen the idea of distinctiveness. It is about this latter position that Pawson and elements of the Charismatic Leaders Conference group are becoming increasingly concerned. Possibly an emphasis on the distinctive nature of Spirit Baptism is better than a debate about subsequence.

Gifts of the Spirit: Natural or Supernatural?

The Classical view expressed in Harold Horton is still widely held by mainline Pentecostals.[2] This sees spiritual gifts as being wholly supernatural. British Pentecostal leader Donald Gee encouraged a modified position. He stated: 'The purely natural abilities and characteristics of the believer may provide a background upon which the Holy Spirit works with His supernatural gift.' However, Gee admitted that it was difficult 'to try and discover the exact point where the supernatural is added' and that 'there are ministries that on the surface appear to have

---

2.   H. Horton, *The Gifts of the Spirit* (Nottingham: Assemblies of God Publishing House, 10th edn, 1971).

less of the supernatural about them than others'.[3] More recent Charismatics tend to be prepared to see a development of Gee's position even
to include the eccentric view of Bishop David Pytches, who in an Ap-
pendix, 'Revelation and the Human Brain' suggests that the 'right hemisphere [of the brain] is the operations room of the gifts of the Holy
Spirit'![4] My own concern is with the whole problem of reductionism
within any area of Christian faith and experience. Professor Hollenweger may well have to explain more clearly, for most Pentecostals,
how he avoids this charge. Perhaps a neglected approach, which is
being revived at the moment, is that of Edward Irving's emphasis on
Christ's reliance on spiritual gifts within the context of his truly human
life.[5]

3. See R. Massey, *Another Springtime: Donald Gee, Pentecostal Pioneer*
(Guildford: Highland Books, 1992), Chapters 8, 9.
4. *Prophecy in the Local Church* (London: Hodder & Stoughton, 1993).
5. See G. McFarlane, *Christ and the Spirit: The Doctrine of the Incarnation
According to Edward Irving* (Carlisle: Paternoster Press, 1996).

CRUCIAL ISSUES FOR PENTECOSTALS

Walter J. Hollenweger

Missiological Issues

At the beginning of its missionary reflection, pentecostal mission has resolutely taken the line of Roland Allen's *Missionary Methods: St Paul's or Ours?*[1] It is astonishing that this high Anglican missionary to China 'unwittingly exerted a profound influence on pentecostal mission through his writings'.[2] So deep was his influence that he not only shaped the thinking of pentecostal missionaries but also the activities of pentecostal mission. This can best be demonstrated in the life and work of Melvin Hodges, leading pentecostal missiologist. In 1950 he asked a simple question: why the weakness of many mission churches in the Third World? His answer: because missionaries have treated people like irresponsible children. They have mistaken the scaffolding for the building. Missionaries, said Hodges, are not intended to be a permanent factor; they must work themselves out of a job. Mission work has been centred too long on the mission station rather than on the local church. Too many missionaries have been sent, and in Hodges' opinion all this amounts to a lack of faith. His book *The Indigenous Church* has proved to be the most significant work on mission the pentecostal movement has yet produced. Hodges asserted that:

> the faith which pentecostal people have in the ability of the Holy Spirit to give spiritual gifts to the common people ... has raised up a host of lay preachers and leaders of unusual spiritual ability—not unlike the rugged fishermen who first followed the Lord. This played a major role in the spectacular spread of Pentecostalism.[3]

1.   R. Allen, *Missionary Methods: St Paul's or Ours?* (London: Robert Scott, 1912).
2.   G. McGee, 'Missions, Overseas (North American)', S.M. Burgess *et al.* (eds.), *Dictionary of the Pentecostal and Charismatic Movements* (Grand Rapids, MI: Zondervan, 1988), p. 626.
3.   G. McGee, 'Hodges, Melvin Lyle (1909–1988)', Burgess *et al.* (eds.), *Dic-*

His statements were meant in the first instance as a criticism of the mainline mission societies, at a time when pentecostals were poor and could not rival them. In the meantime pentecostal churches in the West have become rich, and while the original missiology and praxis are still upheld, there are some grave departures from this strategy. The devastating critique of Peruvian pentecostal Zavalo Hidalgo on the Assemblies of God missionaries in Peru who detached the local churches from the values and needs of the local culture in favour of an Assemblies of God orthodoxy is proof of these departures.[4]

These problems are recognized by some pentecostal missiologists who isolate the following issues. First, the emergence of Third World pentecostal churches with their own theology is a threat and a promise at the same time to western pentecostal orthodoxy—like the Chilean pentecostals who reject the 'initial evidence' doctrine and practise infant baptism, and the African pentecostals who allow polygamy. Secondly, pentecostal missionaries, says Larry D. Pate, are prisoners of their own western culture due to their monocultural education.[5] Furthermore and thirdly, western pentecostals have not realized that in the global mission movement many Third World churches send more missionaries out than the former missionary churches do. Third World missionaries are in many cases more cost-effective and better equipped than North Americans or Europeans—*that* western pentecostals have still to learn. We do not need to find more labourers for the harvest. We need a more effective management of the global missionary task, which also means an intercultural and global education of missionaries. This is not just a technical point; it means that western pentecostals must learn that many theological insights which they have forgotten will emerge from their Third World sister churches.

To take as an example the *Dictionary of Pentecostal and Charismatic Movements*, now a standard reference book for pentecostals in the West.[6] In the statistical sections of this book, the compilers sing the hal-

tionary, p. 403; see also D.D. Smeeton, 'Towards a Pentecostal Missiology: A Review Article', *EPTA Bulletin* 5 (1986), pp. 128-36.

4.   Review of R.Z. Hidalgo, *Historia de las Asambleas de Dios del Peru* (Lima: Ediciones Dios ed Amor, 1989), by D. Bundy, *Pneuma* 13 (1991), pp. 94-96.

5.   L.D. Pate, 'Pentecostal Missions from the Two-Thirds World', M.A. Dempster *et al.* (eds.), *Called and Empowered: Global Mission in Pentecostal Perspective* (Peabody: Hendrickson, 1991), pp. 242-58.

6.   G. McGee, 'Missions'.

lelujahs of the truly amazing growth of Pentecostalism, but in the theological and biblical section not a thread of the theological insights of Third World Pentecostalism is mentioned. In other words, pentecostal missiology will have to address the question of how to cope theologically with the bewildering pluralism within Pentecostalism, Charismaticism and Independentism world wide. Apart from human pride and weakness (from which Pentecostalism is not exempt), there are very real reasons for ignoring this research question. To begin with, many documents are not in English and are difficult to get hold of. A further difficulty is that more often than not the theology of pentecostals in the Third World is not contained in their confessions of faith but in their songs, prayers, liturgies and testimonies—in other words, in their oral theology. A type of research is required therefore that can deal with these forms of theology, which are in any case nearer to biblical forms of theology than to western theologizing. Furthermore, the *overt* meaning of their documents often hides the *hidden* but true meaning. At first glance it looks like straightforward evangelical theology, but one has to find out the meaning of the words. It would be helpful to discover— as they are starting to do in some pentecostal colleges—that the first Christians were not theologically homogeneous. There are many different theologies in the New Testament with differences greater than those between Catholics and Protestants, all celebrating the vast, colourful pluralism of early Christianity. For this, one needs to use the tools of modern exegesis, which are slowly but surely coming into pentecostal educational institutions. All these developments have to be seen in the context of missiological reorientation within Evangelicalism, particularly in the Lausanne movement. The Lausanne report is a mine of information for both Evangelicals and their antagonists.[7]

I shall now concentrate on particular areas where these missiological issues become glaringly visible in Pentecostalism.

Signs and Wonders

The first area of my concern relates to healing and 'miracles'. Pentecostals have always had a praxis of prayer for the sick—their books and

---

7.   J.D. Douglas (ed.), *Let the Earth Hear his Voice: International Congress on World Evangelization, Lausanne, Switzerland, 1974* (Minneapolis: World Wide Publications, 1975). See an analysis in Walter J. Hollenweger, *Pentecostalism: Origins and Development Worldwide* (Peabody, MA: Hendrickson, 1997), chapter 22.

periodicals are full of testimonies of healings. The key figure in the emergence of a special kind of healing ministry was the evangelist William Marrion Branham (1909–65), for whom I was a personal translator in Switzerland. Branham possessed an extraordinary diagnostic gift and was able to diagnose illnesses and sometimes even the names of persons he had never seen. Unfortunately, although his diagnosis was mostly correct, his healing prognosis was accurate only in rare cases. The excuse of the healing evangelists in such cases has always been that the patient did not really believe—a cruel indictment. For the healing evangelists were convinced that faith leads automatically to health. The Bible often shows, however, that healing and forgiveness of sins also occur through the faith of *other* people. Some pentecostal individuals immediately criticized the healing evangelists, as did Leonhard Steiner in Switzerland, who repeated his critique at a Pentecostal World Conference but was at that time ignored and removed from the international scene.[8] It was only when the healing evangelists started to organize their own financial basis that there was strong criticism from the pentecostal churches themselves. The lifestyle of many of the healing evangelists with their luxurious villas, air-conditioned dog kennels, highly priced cars and clothes from the most expensive fashion houses —in some cases, also their sexual extravagances—made their glory pale.

It seems that the charismatic leaders of European mainline churches have learned nothing from the debacles of the past. They continue to invite these evangelists—now selling the same product under the new trading label of 'The Third Wave'—and this in spite of the severe criticism by the great majority of North American pentecostals and the Fuller Theological Seminary in Pasadena, like the pentecostal Mac-Donald, who describes the healing evangelists as follows:

> Single women, especially widows, are the preferred diet of this species of religious wolf. The evangelist weeps and melts the heart of the women. He declares that the kingdom of God is about to collapse and his own stronghold is in danger unless substantial financial resources are sent to him immediately. But Paul never collects money to build up his organisation... The greatest threat to the Pentecostal/ Charismatic movement

---

8.   L. Steiner, 'Divine Healing in God's Redemption', D. Gee (ed.), *Fifth World Pentecostal Conference: Pentecostal World Conference Messages, Toronto, Canada 14–21 September 1958* (Toronto: Testimony Press, 1958), pp. 137-48.

in the last two decades of this century will be the rise and fall of *personal* kingdoms, because when they fall, as inevitably they must, the faith of those who do not have their eyes on Jesus, will fall with them'.[9]

Some new pentecostal preachers pretend they will live to the age of one hundred and ten and then die of old age—not of sickness. Others believe that they will not die at all. They exploit their fans without mercy. If one of them goes bankrupt, they say: 'Sorry, you did not really believe. Your own fault.' Some people have given the evangelist thousands of dollars and then have gone bankrupt. Others drive out demons by the hundreds, and provide plastic buckets into which patients can vomit the demons. To this Robeck says: 'The suffering of Paul spoke louder than his miracles.'[10] Many of these evangelists do not call themselves pentecostals but—as already mentioned—'Third Wavers'. They see the world as a cosmic and moral duality. There is no room for the natural. Everything is either divine or demonic. They reject historical critical research in favour of their own experience. We are successful, they say, so what is the need to ask the truth questions? This is of course a syncretism that is no longer theologically acceptable. They replace the biblical principle of truth for the North American yardstick of success, and argue that if you are successful your success must be good. Against this, many critical pentecostals argue that Jesus did not ever make a fuss about demons. Robert A. Guelich, who is not a pentecostal but whose article appears in the pentecostal journal *Pneuma*, refers to the New Testament scholar Gerd Theissen and says:

> Exorcism is not a sign of faith. There is no spiritual war in Scripture between the faithful and the demons. The exorcism of these evangelists resembles more the doings of pagan exorcists than New Testament exorcism. The battle was won already (Barth). *That* is what we confess.[11]

That, however, may not be quite true (Mk 16.17). Allan Anderson also implicitly criticizes the 'power concept' of these evangelists: 'there are not always instant solutions to life's vicissitudes'.[12] Boasting about their financial and building successes does not show the spirit of Jesus.

9.   W. MacDonald, 'The Cross Versus Personal Kingdom', *Pneuma* 3 (1982), pp. 26-37.

10.   C.M. Robeck, 'Signs, Wonders and Witness', *Pneuma* 3 (1982), pp. 1-5.

11.   R.A. Guelich, 'Spiritual Warfare: Jesus, Paul, Peretti', *Pneuma* 13 (1991), pp. 33-64.

12.   A. Anderson, *Moya: The Holy Spirit from an African Perspective* (Pretoria: University of South Africa Press), p. 72.

Recently, I read about a charismatic church that boasts it has more
square footage than any other church building. So what? Pentecostals
discovered that the 'faith message' (namely, the conviction that those
who believe will be healed) does not have its origins in the Charismatic
renewal, but was taken from E.W. Kenyon, as a dissertation submitted
to (of all places!) Oral Roberts University in Tulsa, Oklahoma revealed.[13] They read again carefully Jas 5.13-18 and discover that the
order of events there is very different from what most churches teach.
Confession comes after healing and forgiveness. We have distorted the
generous gospel of Jesus Christ. He is much more generous than his
interpreters make him out to be. Hispanic North American pentecostal
Eldin Villafañe takes up John Wimber's *Power Evangelism* and comments:

> The tendency of many, including Wimber, is to see this struggle [against
> demonic powers] as too individualistic and not to see that spiritual war-
> fare must correspond to the geography of evil—the sinful and evil struc-
> tures of society ... They must see that the texture of social living makes
> no easy distinctions between the personal and the social.[14]

What is astonishing in this short overview is not so much the eccen-
tricities of these money evangelists, but the decisive, exegetically and
theologically clear critique by pentecostal theologians. All the sadder
that of all people, some charismatics with a decent theological education still try to give a platform to the apostles of signs and wonders. It is
clear that this critique does not solve the problem of how to have a
liturgically and theologically sober healing ministry in our local churches, pentecostal and non-pentecostal alike. Here as elsewhere it is true
that the best critique of the false is the praxis of the true.

That is why I now turn to what I consider the 'praxis of the true'.
That which our universities and our mainline churches produce on this
topic is generally shallow. They excel in their critique of the flamboyant
healing evangelists, and they turn the biblical texts on physical healing
into inner psychological events. But what is their alternative? Why

---

13. Review of D.R. McConnell, *A Different Gospel: A Historical and Biblical
Analysis of the Modern Faith Movement* (Peabody, MA: Hendrickson, 1988), by
D. Smeeton, *EPTA Bulletin* 8 (1989), pp. 93-94. See also Reviews of A. Brandon,
Health and Wealth (Eastbourne: Kingsway Publications, 1987), by D. Petts, *EPTA
Bulletin* 8 (1989), pp. 93-94.

14. E. Villafañe, *The Liberating Spirit: Towards an Hispanic American Social
Ethic* (Grand Rapids: Eerdmans, 1993), p. 201.

should the biblical texts not really mean what they say? That is, that the proclamation of the gospel, the community of Jesus Christ has something to do with ministry to the sick; that in the Christian church we believe that God is interested not only in our souls but also in our bodies. So too the church should be interested in our bodies and provide a proper ministry for those who are depressive, who suffer, and who do not find the kind of help they are looking for in the medical profession. For Christians from the Third World this is a matter of course. For them illness is always also an expression of a disturbed relationship, either to oneself, to other people, to the dead, to the ancestors, to the clan or tribe, or to nature.

The catastrophic consequences of exporting our medical industry has also been noticed by the World Health Organisation in Geneva.[15] If we trample down the convictions of our patients—because we cannot share them—we can at best treat these patients but not heal them. Can we imagine what it means for an African, who understands illness to be the result of a broken relationship, when in the hour of crisis in sickness, he or she is separated from friends and family, is touched by foreign people and is obliged to swallow foreign food and medicine? Such disrespect for a sick person makes him or her feel like a car put into the garage for repair. This approach had led—not only in Africa but also in the West—to wrong diagnoses and to illnesses that have actually been *caused* by the medical profession. It has been known for a long time in medical literature that about 30% of our illnesses are caused by doctors and hospitals.[16] That is why many mainline churches in Europe have introduced services in which those who wish it are anointed by lay people. Healing is a natural gift and many lay people have this gift. It is the duty of ministers to help them discover and develop this natural gift and to exercise it in public in a form which is theologically and liturgi-

15. D.J. Djukanovic and E.P. Mach (eds.), *Alternative Approaches to Meeting Basic Health Needs in Developing Countries* (Geneva: World Health Organisation, 1975). Detailed literature and discussion in Hollenweger, *Pentecostalism*, chapter 18.

16. H. Gerlach, 'Magische Heilkraft des Vertrauens: Von der Vernunft des Irrationalen in der Medizin', in G.K. Katenbrunner (ed.), *Die Pillenpest selbsvergiftung aus Angst vor dem Schmerz?* (Herderbücherei Initiative, 26; 1978), p. 64. See also Robert Eagle, *Alternative Medicine: A Guide to the Medical Underground* (London: Future Publications, 1978), p. 10.

cally acceptable, an issue taken up by the World Council of Churches.[17] There is no time to go into details of the plight of the medical industry. It will surely collapse for financial reasons—that is why British hospitals have engaged Christian and non-Christian healers to help them as part of the medical team—it is cheaper.[18] Of course, this is done in public and in cooperation with medical people. This raises the question of healers who are not Christians, which question ironically is never asked in relation to the much more dangerous pharmaceutical industry. We do not ask the dentist: are you saved? All we want to know is whether he or she is responsible. The same applies to healers outside Christianity, be they traditional healers in Africa or shamanistic healers in Korea. This topic has only been discussed a little by pentecostals but in praxis, cooperation is necessary. A Christian theology of healing must start with creation.

Ecclesiology: Who Belongs to the Church?

The second area concerns how pentecostals conceive of the church, and who belongs to the church. In the past pentecostals understood the church as the company of the 'saved', who had to fulfil certain minimal ethical and religious conditions. But that too is changing. Observes Miroslav Volf:

> A church is a community of people who congregate in order to call on, to testify and to confess Christ the liberator ... They do not need to be characterized by a certain grade of personal or social holiness in order to be called the church ... The real sinner is not the outcast but the one who casts the other out ... Sin is not so much a defilement but a certain form of purity: the exclusion of the other from one's heart and one's world.[19]

That ethical standards are changing according to context and surrounding culture is very visible. This is true in relation to divorce, for

17. See the report 'Auf der Suche nach einer christlichen Antwort auf die heutigen Gesundheitsprobleme', *Informationen 80 des Evangelischen Missionswerkes* (Hamburg, 1988) (with a report of the Christian Medical Commission of the WCC).

18. Hollenweger, *Pentecostalism*, pp. 237-43.

19. Miroslav Volf, 'Kirche als Gemeinschaft. Ekklesiologische Überlegungen aus freikirchlicher Perspektive', *Evangelische Theologie* 49 (1989), pp. 52-76 (64); *idem*, 'Exclusion and Embrace: Theological Reflections in the Wake of "Ethnic Cleansing" ', *Journal of Ecumenical Studies* 29 (1992), pp. 232-33, 264.

instance. In the past cohabitation was condemned. Now, the British Assemblies of God find it biblical, proving that ethics is culturally conditioned. In the past the North American missionaries prohibited polygamy. Now, the Assembliées de Dieu in Burkina Faso and Togo allow polygamists to be baptized with all their wives and admit them to the Eucharist—in North America they even have a special periodical for pentecostal homosexuals and lesbians; in the Dutch Charismatic Movement active homosexual pastors officiate the Eucharist. This shows that there is a pluralism in Pentecostalism and that ethical norms are changing.

One of the crucial issues in this development is the understanding of the church, or in charismatic/pentecostal terminology: who is a church member? One has to distinguish between the expressed soteriology and the lived soteriology. When a black laborer who is a pentecostal pastor in Birmingham says 'Hallelujah, I am saved', he means that he has literally been saved (like *sozein* in the New Testament). He owes his physical, psychological, cultural and spiritual existence to the saving power of Jesus Christ and his saving community. Without him, he would be lost, literally he would be dead. Nobody would care for him and he would be crushed in the machinery of a modern city. But when an insurance agent in Holland who has been converted in a charismatic prayer group says: 'Hallelujah, I am saved', he means something very different. He would not be dead without Christ. He could still live on with his weekend house, his sport and his leisure activities. But he has now found a direction and a religious meaning for his life, sometimes also a spiritual family and a shift in priorities, which is certainly not to be despised. But it is very different from the salvation experience of the black pastor in Birmingham who actually cannot live without the saving communion. 'Salvation' means something different to different charismatics and pentecostals. The concept that only the 'born again' (people whose conversion can be checked outwardly) belong to the church, is now being eroded. Volf says that 'a Church is a community of people who congregate in order to call on, to testify and to confess Christ the liberator'. They do not need to be characterized by a certain grade of personal or social holiness or religious experience in order to be called the church. The church 'lives solely on the sanctifying presence of Christ, who promised to be wherever people congregate in His name'.[20]

---

20. Volf, 'Kirche als Gemeinschaft', pp. 64, 66.

That this understanding of the church is changing in some pentecostal circles is shown in the softening of the formerly rigid rules on divorce, on 'cohabitation'—and in some quarters even on homosexuality. If one were to go to any long established pentecostal church one would see for oneself what has changed in the last 20 years concerning dress, cosmetics, lifestyle and sexual ethics. Together with this softening of ethical standards goes the deplorable waning of the role of women. Women were important at the beginning of both Pentecostalism and the Charismatic movement and many pentecostal churches were founded by women, but today they are pushed into the background.

Hermeneutics: Who Interprets Scripture Correctly?

The third issue relates to hermeneutics. Most pentecostal believers would answer the above question by stating that every believer decides the correct interpretation, because Scripture is clear in itself. This also was the understanding of the reformers. But this leaves an important question open as to why pentecostals (together with other Christians) come to very many different interpretations of Scripture if Scripture is very clear. Furthermore, these very different interpretations are given on almost every issue, from the understanding of the church to the understanding of Spirit baptism (about 12 different opinions), to ethics and glossalalia, to name just a few. One is left wondering why on many issues (for instance on burial) Christians have invented their own extra-biblical traditions, together with the sermon, the church building and youth work—none of which is in the New Testament. Why do some pentecostals take literally the command by Jesus in the Gospel of John to wash each others' feet, and others do not? Why are black pentecostals uneasy about Paul's obvious hesitation to attack the institution of slavery, but take literally his condemnation of homosexuality? Why do many pentecostals reject infant baptism, yet they appoint army chaplains, organize Bible schools and celebrate 25 December as birthday of our Lord—all of which are not mentioned in the New Testament?

My answer to these questions is that Christianity is a syncretism *par excellence*, and all churches are syncretistic. But each syncretistic church thinks it has the 'pure gospel'. We have taken on board many customs and ideas from our pagan past. We think that what we believe is the pure gospel and sell this Eurosyncretism to the Third World, when they want to invent their own Third World syncretism. The truth

of the matter is that the Bible is not a systematic and coherent system—
in fact it was not written for us but for the specific addressees mentioned in the text. That it has something to say to us speaks for its quality. We do not have one gospel but four (or five, if we count Paul). All
Bible readers read the Bible selectively. They emphasize one idea or
experience and neglect another. That is why we come to different forms
of Pentecostalisms. This is inevitable, but it makes an ecumenical dialogue necessary between the different opinions.[21]

A Lost Ecumenical Vision

The Charismatic Renewal has lost both its ecumenical vision and its
critical roots. At the beginning it was an ecumenical grass roots movement. Catholics and Protestant Charismatics worshipped together in Ire-
land, for example. Simon Tugwell, a Dominican theologian, went with
Charismatic nuns to the BBC for a prayer meeting with spontaneous
singing in tongues. Arnold Bittlinger was a former Lutheran Charismatic. At first there was a significant number of women in the leadership of the movement, but they have all been silenced and marginalized. Instead of a movement with an ecumenical vision, the Charismatic
Renewal has become either the hot-bed for all kinds of new churches
or—in the case of the Catholic Church and perhaps also the Anglican
Church—it has become a section of the evangelical or even funda-
mentalistic part of their churches. This is astonishing, because there is
hardly anything in common between Evangelicals and charismatics.
Evangelicals and fundamentalists are and were the bitterest enemies of
Pentecostalism, who have written more books against them than anyone
else. They have even called Pentecostalism 'the last vomit of Satan'.[22]
Speaking in tongues was considered demonic or at least insane, and so
it is very strange that Charismatics have taken over all of the evangelical language. My prediction is—in spite of all that is said – that the
Charismatic Renewal will develop into new denominations, with the
exception of the Charismatics in the Roman Catholic Church where

21. See my chapter on 'Syncretism' (chapter 11) in Hollenweger, *Pentecostalism*.
22. G. Campbell Morgan, quoted without primary documentation by R. Spittler,
'Are Pentecostals and Charismatics Fundamentalists? A Review of American Uses
of these Categories', in K. Poewe (ed.), *Charismatic Christianity as a Global Culture* (Columbia: University of South Carolina Press, 1994), pp. 103-16 (110).

Charismatics become the most faithful followers of the pope and admirers of the virgin Mary.

I base such a statement about the loss of the ecumenical vision on my knowledge of the charismatic movements. Almost all pentecostal churches started as ecumenical revival movements whose leaders remained in their churches. Jonathan Paul, founder of Pentecostalism in Germany, remained a Lutheran pastor baptizing infants. Louis Dallière was leader in France, a Reformed minister. Anglican vicar Alexander A. Boddy spearheaded the pentecostal movement in Sunderland, England, in a mining community. He joined the miners on strike and in demonstrations, and organized food for them during these times, remaining an Anglican vicar until the end of his life. The Chilean pentecostal movement was an ecumenical revival movement that did not want to form a new church, but was forced to do so by Methodist missionaries from the USA. With few exceptions, all these pentecostal churches developed into evangelical middle-class churches. The development can be traced in four phases, as follows:

First phase: An ecumenical renewal movement breaks through racial, social, educational and denominational barriers. It sees in the experience of the Holy Spirit the one and important force that sweeps away all denominational, racial, educational and social divides.

Second phase: Local congregations are set up, usually buying a building and establishing an identity as an independent church. The process of evangelicalization starts as they seek a theology.

Third phase: National and international denominations are organized (pension funds for the pastors, Bible Colleges, catechisms, confessions of faith, church buildings). Pentecostalism is no longer an ecumenical renewal movement but becomes visible as one of the denominations.

Fourth phase: The denomination returns to the original ecumenical root by starting a dialogue with the Roman Catholic Church, the theological faculties and organized ecumenism. This, however, leads in certain cases to splits from the denomination. The separated group starts the process again at phase one, saying for example, 'We are not pentecostal; we are Third Wave'.

In general each phase takes a generation, 25 years. What is important for this discussion is the fact that the older Classical pentecostal denominations and the African initiated churches are now somewhere between the third and the fourth phases. Twelve pentecostal churches are already member churches of the World Council, Latin American and black churches leading the way, whilst the Charismatic Renewal in the main-line churches has to be placed between phases one and two. All indicators point in the direction of the creation of neo-pentecostal churches, although this is officially denied and the new organizations take on new names ('Third Wave', 'Charismatic Centre', 'Christian Centre', and so on). It is almost an unwritten law that further fragmentation will take place in the name of 'planting new churches', and these new churches consider themselves the 'biblical', 'spiritual' churches, unlike the 'dead' and stubborn churches they have come out of. I do not think that the setting up of so many new churches is really what the Spirit wants us to do. It is a good thing to have many different local churches with different cultures, traditions and intake—as long as these churches really work together. That would be a case for a 'council of churches' on a local basis, who really help each other financially, theologically, accepting each other's ordination, baptism and Eucharist. This would be a new kind of grass roots ecumenicity, not organized from above but from below.

The Emerging Pentecostal Middle Class

Pentecostalism has become a respectable middle-class denomination, not just in the West but also in many Third World countries. Many years ago, when I went to the headquarters of a certain North American classical Pentecostal denomination, I asked why it was that they lived in the better part of the city. They told me that it was because they were saved, born again and baptized in the Spirit. That was why they had a motor boat in the lake and three cars in the garage. If the blacks in the poorer part of the city would get converted and saved they would not have any economic problem. Conversion is the key to all difficulties.

Of course, if a person is poor the pentecostal experience is often an incentive to give a better education to one's children and to be more economical with one's money, resulting in a better lifestyle. But it is a gross oversimplification to say that the pentecostal experience solves all these kinds of problems. That philosophy was also espoused by Pat Robertson, a serious contender for the presidency of the United States and a leader of the 'religious right' behind the Reagan presidency. This is a political stance also found in Europe. In Switzerland there are right wing reactionary and old fashioned parties that are very religious, in which Charismatics and pentecostals are involved. Anti-abortion measures resulting in the criminalizing of women (which is an issue of individual conscience) become almost the top priority of this political programme, while replacing the work force with capital to produce another half million unemployed or supporting a war effort (matters of great political and economic consequence) are encouraged. This I could never understand. Why is it, I ask myself, that the Holy Spirit is only interested in what happens in the bedroom and not in what happens in the boardroom?

In Guatemala the German researcher Heinrich Schäfer[23] speaks of the 'money aristocracy' of charismatic renewal centres and prayer groups which meet once a week for an expensive meal in a fashionable hotel, inviting high profile speakers. While they do this the majority of the indigenous Amerindian pentecostals are in abject poverty and unemployed. During the recent civil war many of these Amerindians organized trade unions and were suppressed by the police and imprisoned with the assistance of the US government at the time. The one who tortured one of these indigenous people was a charismatic police officer, who goes to the Hilton Hotel and says 'Hallelujah, I am saved' on Tuesday morning. Then he goes to the police station and tortures his own brother in the Lord in the afternoon. This is not an isolated incident, but represents what is happening all over the world, where Pentecostalism is divided along social lines. Former General Secretary of the South African Council of Churches, Frank Chikane, who was involved in helping the black people of Soweto and organizing lawyers in the time of apartheid, was also imprisoned several times and tortured by a white deacon in his own pentecostal church, the Apostolic Faith Mission.[24] It is *not true* that when one gets 'right with God' and is 'born again' that all problems are solved. Some of the most cruel things happening in the world are happening among 'born again' Christian capitalists, even though some are protesting about these things. The reason for this attitude is the necessity to defend a newly acquired social and economic status. When I was in South Africa I met some of the white leaders of the Apostolic Faith Mission. One of their leaders was in the government defending apartheid. They told me: 'Give us time—in a

23. H. Schäfer, '...und erlöse uns von dem Bösen', in Uwe Birnstein (ed.), *Gottes einzige Antwort: Christlicher Fundamentalismus als Herausforderung in Kirche und Gesellschaft* (Wuppertal: Peter Hammerst, 1990), pp. 118-39.

24. A. Anderson, *Bazalwane: African Pentecostals in South Africa* (Pretoria: Unisa Press, 1992), p. 51.

hundred years we will bring the blacks up to our standard', as they discussed which of three luxury cars should take me to the airport.

We have invented a capitalistic system we call 'free market' which is neither 'free' nor 'market'. This system only functions under the following conditions: (1) by producing millions of unemployed; (2) by producing enormous amounts of arms and ammunition; (3) by creating human-made famines throughout the world; and (4) by destroying the environment, using up the air, water and other resources. If we do not change, then Karl Marx will be right predicting that the capitalists are their own gravediggers.[25] The competition between the races, the sexes, between the poor and the rich, between peoples in the Third World—this competition thought to be a blessing of God by Margaret Thatcher —has economic root causes and results in people making war with each other. The church is not generally developing alternatives to the capitalistic system; the only ones who made a beginning at this were Mennonites and Quakers, who in times past created alternative means of production, democracy in industry and co-ownership of capital and work-force.

A Biblical Model for Evangelism

Pentecostals are so convinced of the power of their experience that they want to pass it on to everybody. That makes them efficient evangelists. Sometimes, however, they realize that evangelism is a dialogical process in which the evangelists also learn something of the gospel from the ones they want to evangelize. The classical example of this is the so-called conversion of Cornelius, which could just as well be called the conversion of Peter, because Peter learned in the process of his evangelism that Cornelius had not to become a copy of Peter's own Jewish Christianity. Peter realized that Cornelius had discovered a different brand of Christianity, Hellenistic Christianity. Therefore many of the age-long rules given by God, which were a matter of course for Peter, did not apply to Cornelius, like circumcision, temple, Sabbath, food taboos, and so on. That Peter got into conflict with his mission committee in Jerusalem because of his 'liberalism' was the price he had to pay for his dialogical evangelism. According to the report of Luke,

---

25.   Karl Marx and Frederick Engels, *Manifesto of the Communist Party* (ET 1888; Moscow, 1952), p. 60; see W.J. Hollenweger, 'Karl Marx (1818–1873) and his Confession of Faith', *Expository Times* 84 (1973), pp. 132-37.

this mission committee accepted that in the case of Hellenistic believers their own convictions were rightly overruled: 'When they heard this they were silenced. And they glorified God ...' (Acts 11.18). An amazing story!

As a Christian I am interested in the translation of the Cornelius experience into present-day evangelistic practice.[26] There are many 'Cornelius's' in our society. They can be invited to evangelize *with* us, like a bank director at the shore of Lake Zurich who was willing to play Pontius Pilate in a passion play. Naturally, he did not usually go to church, but since he had been invited to actively participate in this service, he was there. When he went on the stage to utter his lines—'I am Pontius Pilate, procurator of the *Iustitia Romana*. I believe this Jesus is innocent, but I cannot help him because he talks when he should be silent, and he is silent when he should answer my questions'—he suddenly began to stammer. Why? Because he realized that he was not just *playing* Pilate; he *was* Pilate. Of course, the entire bank staff and all the bank director's neighbours and friends were there in church, and they realized that they were also in the same boat with him. Evangelistically speaking, this is called 'conviction of sin'—but in this instance it was not produced by a sermon of hell and brimstone; it came from inside, through the Holy Spirit.

Then, the woman playing Pilate's wife came to the stage. 'I told him', she said, 'to leave this Jesus alone. After all, I had a dream, but he never listened. Why is it that the dream of a woman has no power over the *realpolitik* of a man? Why is this?' Two hundred women in the church nodded their heads: 'What a good thing that someone tells these men what we suffer'. One can imagine the discussions that took place afterwards in the schools, in the pubs, in the bank, in the families. Evangelism means—according to the biblical model—to work *with* the 'sinners', not *at* them. Thus we learn something about the gospel from the unchurched, just as Peter had learned from Cornelius. The next article will give another example of 'dialogical evangelism'.

26. More examples and discussion on 'dialogical evangelism' in W.J. Hollenweger, 'Evangelism: A Non-Colonial Model', *Journal of Pentecostal Theology* 7 (1995), pp. 1-22; *idem*, 'Theology and the Future of the Church', in P. Byrne and L. Houlden (eds.), *Companion Encyclopedia of Theology* (London: Routledge, 1995), pp. 1017-35; *idem*, 'Music in the Service of Reconciliation', *Theology* 92 (1989), pp. 276-86.

Martin Robinson

Without question, I agree with Walter Hollenweger's suggestion that Pentecostals have put into practice the missionary ideas associated with Roland Allen. In most cases this application has been entirely unconscious, since few would have been acquainted with Allen's name, work or writings. But it is precisely this unconscious praxis that is important because it reflects a distinctively Pentecostal ecclesiology. The gifts of the Holy Spirit empower the individual believer to be a witness for Christ. Even though Pentecostals have a strong emphasis on the role of clergy, the participation of lay people is sufficiently important that the Pentecostal movement is in many ways a lay movement. To quote the Pentecostal leader David du Plessis, Pentecostals care more about Apostolic success than Apostolic succession. The success alluded to by du Plessis is not in the first instance a numerical measure; rather it is related to the successful manifestation of power in ministry. That success is exemplified by the diverse manifestation of the gifts of the Holy Spirit among the believers.

Missiologists such as David Barratt have attempted to document the dramatic growth of the Pentecostal movement around the world. The overall numbers cited by Barratt are often the main focus of attention. But the total number of Pentecostals does not convey the extent to which this growth has taken place on the frontiers of mission. Pentecostals are still numerically relatively weak in the traditional areas of Christianity's strength in the western world. It is in Latin America, Africa and Asia that their percentage growth is most evident. Barratt claims that 80% of all Christians in East Asia can be categorized as part of the Pentecostal/ Charismatic movement. This participation in mission has helped to dramatically shift the development of Christian missions during the second half of the twentieth century. At the beginning of the twentieth century, before the Pentecostal movement had begun, Christian mission was dominated by those churches that have sometimes been described as the 'mainline' denominations. The goal of these missions, as expressed by such conferences as the Edinburgh Missionary Conference held in 1910, was to evangelize the world in a single generation and so to complete the Great Commission. Edinburgh was designed to herald a new impetus in the marshalling of resources for such a task. But, as scholars such as Andrew Walls have documented, this early twentieth century, largely Anglo-Saxon missionary enterprise, was soon in difficulty. To some extent the work of Roland Allen recognized some of these problems and attempted to offer alternative remedies.

By the middle of the twentieth century, a coming crisis within western missions was evident to many observers. Writing in 1968, one demographic expert employed by the World Council of Churches expressed the depth of the problem in numerical terms:

> Towards the end of this century, Christians will comprise no more than eight per cent of the world's population æ assuming that present demographic growth will not be arrested in some unforeseen manner ... Even the best missionary strategy with a conventional approach to the field of church planting and church growth will have no material effect upon this prognosis.[1]

This gloomy prognosis has not been fulfilled. Instead, the percentage of Christians in the world stands remarkably close to the percentage at the beginning of the century at 34%. The difference between the prognosis and the reality reflects the astonishing growth of Christianity in those parts of the world where Christianity has not been historically strong. These are precisely the areas where Pentecostal witness is at its strongest. As David Bosch has noted, the crisis that has afflicted many of the western mainline denominations in relation to mission was to some degree a herald of a much wider crisis within western culture as a whole.[2] The old certainties have gone to be replaced by a series of questions and power assertions. I also agree with Walter Hollenweger that Pentecostals in the west have to some degree made many of the same mistakes as western missions in general. There have been some exceptions, but individuals who have not been sponsored by the major

1.   International Review of Mission, 1968.
2.   D. Bosch, *Believing in the Future: Toward a Missiology of Western Culture* (Valley Forge, PA: Trinity Press International, 1995), p. 1.

Pentecostal denominations have almost always pioneered these. Equally, their progress has usually been viewed with the same kind of suspicion that the Pentecostals have applied to the Latter Rain movement and the African Independent churches. I share Hollenweger's contention that the riches of the Pentecostal movement in the Third World have not been appreciated by Pentecostals in the West. But I want to suggest that recent developments in world missions have produced a new opportunity for a rich exchange of thought and praxis. Briefly these changes are:

- The reality is that mission is no longer 'from the West to the rest' but 'from everywhere to everywhere'. Third World Christians are sending missionaries to the west in increasing numbers.
- The challenge of the West as a major mission field has caused some humility amongst western Christians and a degree of bewilderment among Third World Christians.
- Population movements mean that major ethnic Christian movements are present in all the capitals of Europe in substantial numbers. It is claimed that London will be composed of a 'majority of minorities' within 20 years.

I frankly do not share Hollenweger's confidence in the potential benefits of 'the tools of modern exegesis', unless that exegesis is itself willing to shaped and influenced by a careful listening to the insights of Third World Christians. This kind of listening begins with the assumption that theology begins with mission.[3] I therefore want to highlight four potential areas around which some listening might take place.

1. *Signs and Wimbers*
The activities of some notorious healing evangelists are sufficiently publicized that there is a danger of missing the significance of power encounter as a means of re-establishing a legitimate encounter with the world as mystery and with God as transcendent, as has been suggested by John Wimber.[4] Consider the following conflict. A student from Ghana wishes to study the faith movement in Ghana. He approaches a

---

3.   W. Shenk, *Write the Vision: The Church Renewed* (Valley Forge, PA: Trinity Press International, 1995), pp. 42-43.
4.   J. Wimber, *Power Evangelism: Signs and Wonders Today* (London: Hodder & Stoughton, 1985).

professor in a western academic institution who sees great potential
for using this case study as an illustration of the power domination of
African culture by western missions. The student's African professor,
whose permission he also requires, will not agree to such a study. The
African academic knows only too well the game of his western colleague. He sees what his western colleague will not consider, namely,
that in African theological constructs the 'power' ingredient of the faith
movement has come to have an entirely different meaning than the one
which western eyes normally see using 'the tools of modern exegesis'.

2. *Pentecostalism as Spirituality*

Hollenweger rightly points to the bewildering pluralism within the Pentecostal movement. This issue was tackled directly by David du Plessis
following the period when he acted as the General Secretary to the
Pentecostal World Conference. He used the phrase 'Pentecost outside
of Pentecost' by which he meant that there was a Pentecostal movement
outside of the Pentecostal denominations. Du Plessis looked for an
inclusive description for these various phenomena. He spoke of Pentecostalism as a spiritual experience. Seen in this way, Third World
Pentecostals have much to offer a postmodern western world that is
currently in the process of throwing off a secular worldview in favour
of a religious encounter that is essentially neo-pagan. It might be a
shocking experience for western Christians using modern exegetical
tools to discover that there is a personal and individual encounter with
the structures of evil, which also needs to be taken seriously.

3. *Ecumenical Promise*

It is ironic that the Pentecostals, whose forefathers had a clear ecumenical vision for their new enterprise, should have been so often identified
with the most vehemently anti-ecumenical stance. Yet the ecumenical
promise contained in the creative genesis of the movement has not disappeared. It has more often reasserted itself as a means of creating an
informal ecumenism centred on the Great Commission. One Pentecostal periodical has recently described such a movement in this way:

> Strategic alliances—even between groups historically suspicious of
> one another—are making possible the wise use of both funds and per-
> sonnel in missions. A strong 'threefold cord' of traditional evangelicals,
> charismatics and members of mainline denominations has been woven

by the Holy Spirit. Massive co-operative efforts among ministries great
and small could produce a harvest of at least 1 billion souls in the next
five years.[5]

Creative listening between formal and informal ecumenical structures
might help to sharpen exegetical tools.

4. *A Missionary Church*

Missions, especially but not exclusively in the West, do not require yet
more Pentecostal denominations, but they do require new ways of being
the church. The syncretism spoken of by Walter Hollenweger needs to
be the response of lay people reclaiming the church as a lay movement.
Strangely, when this happens, the response of ordinary believers to the
meaning of Scripture is more astonishing for its agreement than its dis-
agreement. Can the creativity of Pentecostals, guided by prophecy and
spiritual intuition lead to a new Peter and Cornelius encounter?

Some of the most encouraging examples of new forms of the church
currently being witnessed throughout Europe suggest that this may indeed by a possibility. One example is that of a Wimber church plant in
a major Swiss city. Instead of establishing a new denomination, the
leaders of this group gave up their clerical status to be lay people in the
State Church. Their new group has become a fast growing lay movement within the State Church, one that stresses spirituality and dynamic
encounter with God. To misquote a famous advertisement, might it be
the case that only Pentecostalism can do this?

5.   D. Shibley, 'The Holy Spirit Around the World', *Charisma* (May 1996),
pp. 30-33 (32).

SCHOLARSHIP AND EVANGELISM: OIL AND WATER?

Lynne Price

Introduction

'I haven't had such a well-spent Saturday morning for ages; it was so stimulating and set off all kinds of thoughts', commented an enthusiastic non-church-goer after the first reading of Act 1 of *The Adventure of Faith*.[1] Sporting a red baseball cap, she was later to lead the noisy group who burst into a first century church meeting, disturbing the measured singing of the opening hymn and changing the tempo to reflect the enthusiasm of black seamen temporarily in the port of Synope. Faced with a growing and diverse church, Luke, auxiliary bishop, researched the council meetings of the early church in Jerusalem to find out how they had responded to change. His biblical narratives are the subject of the drama.

The Adventure of Faith, a missiological play with music, song and dance by Walter Hollenweger, was presented on Saturday 29 June 1996 at the end of the consultation on Pentecostalism. 'Presented' does not adequately convey the atmosphere of the occasion; with only three rehearsals (not all with the same people at the same time!) and the involvement of the audience in song and dance as participants in the drama, the event was more of a 'happening'. Though few of the experts, students or church officials at the consultation took part in the event, it in fact dealt with many of the conceptual issues addressed to Pentecostalism's past and present by formal papers and responses during the week: to whom does God give the gift of the Spirit and under what

---

1.   Not available in published form in English; a manuscript copy was kindly made available by Walter Hollenweger and photocopied for use. *The Adventure of Faith* and 21 other biblical plays have been published in German by Metanoia-Verlag, Kindhausen, Germany and are currently available, including *Requiem für Bonhoeffer* and *Hommage an Maria von Wedemeyer, Bonhoeffers Braut* (jointly authored with Estella Korthaus).

conditions? Which rules, norms and customs apply to Christians in different geographical, political and social contexts? How can a group maintain its identity without being exclusive? How does present experience of God and life relate to the Bible and tradition?

Walter Hollenweger's innovative combination of art forms with biblical scholarship moves reflection from the solely academic to the arena of evangelism, where non-experts, non-formally theologically educated, non-church leaders and non-Christians are involved in the process using a variety of talents and senses. What happens when the fruits of scholarship are incorporated in efforts to evangelize in such a participatory, dramatic form is the subject of this paper. I offer this retrospective account as an insider: a Methodist layperson and missiologist who, together with Werner Ustorf, the present Professor of Mission at the University of Birmingham and Selly Oak Colleges, and my husband, a chartered accountant and amateur musician, agreed to facilitate the production of one of Walter Hollenweger's biblical musicals.

Walter Hollenweger's Method

Readers of Hollenweger's chapters in this volume (especially the preceding one) will be familiar with the thinking that underlies the creation of these dramas. Hollenweger acknowledges the diversity of biblical texts and he asserts that evangelism in the New Testament is always dialogical and situational. The plurality of churches today (including the variety within Pentecostalism) and in particular the growth of Asian, African and Latin American churches, indicates a shift from the dominance of western mission and conceptual theology to an intercultural theology that takes seriously intuitive, affective, and physical (bodily and environmental) expressions of faith and life. He declares a pneumatology that holds that God's Spirit is given to all people, and not just to Christians.

Two recent papers by Hollenweger apply these insights specifically to the methodology of the musical drama.[2] The medium is seen as a dialogical method of producing a 'body-of-Christ theology'; historical-

2.   'Evangelism: A Non-Colonial Model', *Journal of Pentecostal Theology* 7 (1995), pp. 107-28; and 'Theology and the Future of the Church', in P. Byrne and L. Houlden (eds.), *Companion Encyclopedia of Theology* (London: Routledge, 1995), pp. 1017-35.

crit-ical exegesis, which has demonstrated the diversity of biblical approaches to religion and ethics, is made available to non-experts and thereby encourages them to think for themselves. The Bible, as a text of common humanity, offers examples of responsible syncretism by the authors and is a model for contemporary people in working out the expression of their faith and experience. The narratives presented in dramatic form invite participants to examine themselves and their own social, political and religious context. At the same time, the play is a vehicle for communication of good news: the stories are told, the Name is named, hopes are articulated, statements of faith are made. The written script is given, but can be modified, while artistic, dramatic, musical and dance interpretation is in the hands—and feet, minds, hearts and souls—of those taking part. Is this a recipe for chaos or the ingredients for a creative moment, an inspirational opportunity? Can oil and water mix?

Implementation

1. *The Preliminary Meetings*
Armed with Hollenweger's writing on the subject and a few telephone calls to Switzerland, we began the process of organizing the event to coincide with his visit, not only for the Consultation, but also the conferring of Honorary Fellowship of the Selly Oak Colleges on 1 July 1996. The choice of *The Adventure of Faith* from the many scripts available was made. As an evangelistic enterprise, Hollenweger considered it would be of interest to students and staff of the missionary colleges, theological students and those training for ministry, and local Christians. All these constituencies were given an invitation for everyone who wished to take part to attend a Saturday morning meeting one month before the event.

Meanwhile, following Hollenweger's approach, the core group was formed by the addition of a person with expertise in drama, David Hart, (a poet and arts administrator, formerly playwright and theatre critic) and a choreographer, Wendy McClay. The script was studied, reviewed and discussed, each member seeing different possibilities or obstacles from the perspective of their own disciplines. Was it dramatically effective, an act of worship or a public debate? Were scholarly research findings accurately conveyed and conversely, was the imaginative dialogue ascribed to biblical characters supported in any way by historical or anthropological data? The music in the script had to be supplemented by hymns and accompaniment for the dances with an unknown combination of instrumentalists and minimal rehearsal time. The person with the most equable response was the choreographer, who was not at all worried by the paucity of guidance for her area of responsibility—mostly one-line instructions such as 'Dance of the outcast, the unfit'. Those of us bound to words rather than music or movement were more anxious!

The musical director became the focus of the next phase by gathering together anyone who played an instrument who was willing to be involved. A clarinettist (a neighbour, middle aged, non-church going), a flautist (a friend in her twenties, church-going), a music graduate, a guitar player and composer (friend of a friend in his twenties, non-church going), and a guitar player (Allan Anderson, coordinator of the Consultation—who later switched to portraying Luke). Two other young adults attended one meeting on behalf of another who was later to play guitar; none had any church contacts. All read the script and found it exciting and thought-provoking. No one knew more than one other person in the group when they met; all enjoyed the opportunity to explore ideas, make music, eat and laugh together.

Attendance at the initial general meeting was disappointing, but the occasion was fascinating. An introduction was given to Walter Hollenweger's interests as a theologian and evangelist, and the purpose of the biblical drama was explained before a reading of Act 1, 'The Case of Philip Gladfellow', in which Philip is called to account for his rash baptism of a black, foreign, sexually irregular financier employed by a 'pagan Queen' without, in addition, a period of catechetical instruction or integration into a Christian community. One particular issue provoked polarized responses: there was objection to the expression of racist sentiments and questioning of whether there was evidence for this in the early church, while others accepted the script as a piece of drama articulating contemporary realities which needed to be thought and talked about. It was the non-church-going, academically theologically uneducated members who voiced the second perspective. Two church people with strong reservations about parts of the script were not seen again.

2. *The Rehearsals*

On Wednesday 26 June we had musicians and music, adult and child dancers, and Walter Hollenweger present to facilitate proceedings; what we didn't have was enough actors. Many people that evening were captivated, so we heard, by the influence of a mass, nationalistic ritual—an England/Germany football match, apparently of some importance. The arrival from Nottingham of Matthew Price and a friend saved the project from an early demise. The modest group, recovering from the pain of disappointment articulated by Walter Hollenweger (who has had as many as 600 participants in performances on the continent), set to work. Being faced with these testing circumstances cemented the group. Everyone was mutually supportive and co-operative. Some went the extra mile, like my son's Jewish friend who came to lend a hand backstage and temporarily stepped into the part of the evangelist, Philip. A generous gesture.

Friday saw an influx of four adults—a Czech and three Germans—and four children—one more Chilean and three Africans. Praise be! Newcomers were welcomed and quickly integrated through immediately being invited to participate. People re-sorted themselves into appropriate roles and tasks, focused on the united objective. There was no evidence of possessiveness, self-importance or jealousy. The drama director gently advised individuals on their delivery by building on positive attributes and viewing the action as a whole, and introduced movement and dynamic. The matter of racist attitudes arose again when rehearsing lines. Walter Hollenweger felt that the script, as a piece of drama, not a theological treatise, required the provocative edge of words like 'Negro'. Some participants agreed. Others were not comfortable with the choice of character to vocalize the attitude and another view was that the sentiments should be expressed, but the words in the script gave the wrong resonance. The problem was resolved through discussion, and changes were made without neutralizing the dilemma posed by the text, in the opinion of David Hart. The choreographer was working wonders through sensitive and apposite interpretations with three women and six children, none of whom were trained dancers. One of the women commented about how easily the children grasped the meaning of what they were engaged in and what to do. When we moved to Act 2, 'The Case of Simon Peter', their arms and legs, emerging from the edges of the curtains to the staccato rhythms of Poulenc, became the threatening crawling creatures of Peter's vision. Philip had a rough ride before the Council and Peter fared rather worse. Firm traditions had been broken in his encounter with Captain Cornelius, who was a Gentile and an enemy, and privileged experience—speaking in tongues—had been gifted before the evangelist had said all he intended. Cries of 'fanatic', 'lunatic', 'heretic' from James, Joseph Barnabas, Philip, Matthew and Mary the mother of Jesus thundered on him with punishing drumbeats.

It was only at the final rehearsal, completed an hour before the event, that all the elements were combined in a straight run-through and we glimpsed the whole.

3. *The Event*
About 50 additional people attended the public event. Seating was arranged so that everyone was part of the drama, and the characters emerged from the audience to take their places at the table set for the church meetings. The community as a body sang the great affirmations of Christian faith with hymns from different countries and the refrains written for *The Adventure of Faith* by Hans Jürgen Hufeisen, weaving a thread of assurance, thankfulness, hope and commitment through the sensual and intellectual tapestry of the biblical-exegetical drama. Two church-going members of the audience, who considered themselves non-singers, expressed surprise that they had been drawn into full-voiced participation and enjoyed the experience. Another felt it had been a useful teaching medium, relating the Bible to the present day, whilst one man informed me a few weeks later that as a result of the critical approach to the narratives he now engaged with the Bible in a questioning way instead of simply reading it. A college tutor thought the production was rather amateurish but effective in raising issues. A church-attending laywoman was of the opinion that ordinary people assuming the roles of biblical characters made the narrative live, while being intellectually stimulating. The accuracy of biblical material in the script was noted by a member of the Church of God of Prophecy, who pointed out how familiar members of his community were with the Bible and would appreciate this. 'Marvellous' and 'very interesting' were comments frequently made during the informal session at the end of the event—those not so enthusiastic perhaps kept their own counsel. 'These college people should do more of this sort of thing', observed one woman.

Towards an Appraisal

There are a number of ways in which the enterprise could be assessed. Approached on the one hand as a piece of scholarly work, and on the

other as an artistic drama, it is open to criticism by academics and specialists in the performing arts respectively. These are not our concerns
here (although that is not to say that they are not legitimate concerns).
Our focus is on the combination of these disciplines for the purpose of
evangelism. Hollenweger claims that this 'non-colonial' model of evangelism—participatory, collaborative, dialogical and artistic as well as
scientific—is an example of the way ahead for theology and the church.[3]

Having briefly noted responses of attenders, it is on the comments of
those who prepared and produced the event that I concentrate my attention. The unanimous opinion of the participants—African, Latin American and European, Protestant and Catholic church-goers, those of other
religious affiliation and none, employed and unemployed, of all ages—
was that taking part had been a worthwhile experience. A very mixed
group of people enjoyed working together, made friends and learnt
something about the Bible. The dispersal of responsibility for different
dimensions of the musical drama and the fact that few people knew
more than any other person in the group beforehand, enabled a truly
cooperative way of approaching the task. There were no insiders and
outsiders in this exegetical undertaking, but people with various expertise, knowledge and life experience combining efforts for the accom-
plishment of a task.

In attempting to assess the strengths, weaknesses and potential of the
enterprise I have consulted with participants. The responses reflected
the many levels on which this approach functions. As might be antici-
pated from the openness of the methodology, the experience meant different things to different people. With their permission, I record some
of their observations.

Pete Bailey (played guitar): 'I'm not a particularly religious person
and I'm not interested in church activities, but I thought *The Adventure
of Faith* was a good thing. I got involved and the way it was performed
was exciting. It covered areas I was not familiar with and put them in a
way interesting to anyone. People usually see things are to do with the
church and switch off, but in fact this was okay, I didn't feel uncom-
fortable with it.'

He read the script beforehand, discussed it at length with a friend,
and invited others to the event.

---

3.   Hollenweger, 'Evangelism', p. 127.

Mary Beasley (took the part of Mary, mother of Jesus): 'It brought Bible study alive by engaging so much more than the intellect—instead of academics discussing a question in isolation, other people who could contribute through their life experience were incorporated into the action. The question of communication with people who are not skilled verbally is particularly significant to me in my work with homeless alcohol and drug abusers and I am exploring how the method could be used.'

Because of Mary's area of work (and the fact that she is a wheelchair user), she was especially moved by the dance interpretation of the outcasts and unfit being barred from access to a church. '*The Adventure of Faith* opened up the possibility of a more united vision of "church".'

Werner Ustorf (core group member): 'In the first meetings the weaknesses of the play were seen, but when it was put together it worked—surprisingly! It is a way of discovering the courage of the early Christians; they had to find answers to problems and provided the kind of theology they needed to live together. That means you also discover how human the whole thing is, which is encouraging for ourselves. Faith is always our own construct, attempting to respond to something that encounters us in life. We ought to take the risk of having confidence in what we believe to be true. If evangelism in a western context is reconnecting people with the origins of traditional faith, raising questions and reforming the tradition, then the drama is very evangelistic. It makes you think, it does not make you believe.'

Matthew Price (played the part of Philip): 'It's the first form of group evangelism I've felt comfortable taking part in for a long time; it was not patronising, arrogant or smug evangelism, but a receptive, open, warm sharing of faith. As a student it was so nice to be welcomed and spoken to as an adult and a privilege to be in a position to encourage and be encouraged. People revealed admirable talents.'

Margaret Breiner (helped with all aspects of the production): 'The interaction of imagination and faith was very helpful and broke down the secular/religious divide in a creative way. I thought it had the same dynamic as *Ignatian Spiritual Exercises* but with a different dimension through doing it as a group. It is a good way of feeding people who are otherwise extremely put off by normal church for one reason or another. Having 'dropped off' church, I found this a good experience: I met a lot of interesting people and there was a real sense of common purpose through doing something together.'

David Hart (core group member, drama): 'I found the preliminary meetings and discussions pertinent, but there is nothing like doing the thing! The period in which we had the meetings coincided with my decision to stop going to church; I felt I didn't belong there, saying the Creeds did not seem intellectually or emotionally 'right'. I came to the rehearsals with very mixed feelings but as it turned out it was very important and very good for me. It was such a pleasure working with diverse people and I had lovely conversations in those few days. I was so impressed with what people were putting into the play. It helped me to feel more confident about other things I had been planning to do. I couldn't join in the credal bits of the script, but had to join in the 'Hallelujah', it was such an affirmation of life.' [*Hallelujah. Hallelujah. Songs are in every person living on the earth. They form a dream of peace and hope and love. Sing out this new song and breathe in the love. Share your life and joy. God is with us all.*] [4]

Allan Anderson (played the part of Luke): 'It was for me an interesting experiment and different from anything I had experienced in approaching evangelism. It made people aware of prejudices and the things that get in the way of evangelism and was a very graphic way of demonstrating how early Christians dealt with the subject. I was impressed with the way the music went and the participation of people who were not church attenders. This could be replicated; people were involved without a sense of being marginalized.'

Cathy Gurney (dancer—see opening quote): 'It was good to do something 'whole-bodied'; I had just retired from work [management, Social Services], and taking part in *The Adventure of Faith* coincided with a time of transition.'

Comparing memories of church attendance in her youth with the different impression of Christianity offered through grappling with contemporary dilemmas posed by the Bible and the script, Cathy would have liked more time to get to know the other participants and an opportunity to continue the discussion on racism. Her own engagement with this issue arising from considerable professional experience gave rise to some amused consternation about the responses of academics and ecclesiastics concerned about 'proper research' and the dramatic portrayal of questionable Christian attitudes. From the event as a whole,

---

4. Item no. 29 in Act 2, 'The Case of Simon Peter'. Canon by Hans-Jürgen Hufeisen.

Cathy felt the 'lesson' had been 'Carry on, even if things don't look hopeful'!

Dick Price (core group member—music, and pianist): 'The prospect of being responsible for musical direction was initially nerve-wracking but when we started trying things out, the atmosphere in the musicians' group was really positive. People came up with ideas and everyone tried to make them work. I was pleased that taking part in the event got people enthusiastic about playing their instruments.'

Dan Bloom (drummer and guitarist): 'I've never been involved with a project like that before. It was spectacular. I loved getting involved and there was a real community feeling: everyone was so valuable and I enjoyed everyone's participation, especially with the international flavour and people from different walks of life. I was glad I could contribute as a Jew and did not feel I was going against my own religion by participating because the presentation was more educational than evangelical. I think we should participate in each others' cultures and religion and would have liked more opportunity to talk about the event afterwards. Taking part in *The Adventure of Faith* has helped to get me back on track for thinking about my own faith.'

Stimulated by the concept of narrative exegesis, he borrowed my copy of Hollenweger's *Conflict in Corinth and Memoirs of an Old Man.*[5]

Can Oil and Water Mix?

Oil is chemically neutral and insoluble in water. When oil and water are stirred vigorously together the particles temporarily disperse; for an interlude they hang in the aerated water before floating to the surface. This offers, it seems to me, a helpful analogy of scholarship and evangelism in Hollenweger's biblical drama: the elements retain their identity, but in the ferment generated by activity and fresh air they are brought into a new and creative juxtaposition.

The responses of participants testify to the community-building value of the participatory, collaborative, dialogical and artistic methodology. All were accepted on an equal basis and supported each other; their talents were affirmed and in some cases blossomed; differences of opinion

---

5 . W.J. Hollenweger, *Conflict in Corinth and Memoirs of an Old Man* (New York: Pauline Press, 1982).

were talked through to a satisfactory solution for the immediate situation; words, music and dance were complementary, each expressing at different times harsh realities and questions, poignant emotions or statements of faith. The very mixed group of adherents and non-adherents demonstrated aspects of what a Christian community could be at its best. It is also evident that the experience resonated in individual lives. Through cognitive, affective and physical participation in the drama several participants indicated that they were drawn to reassessing their own life-situations—their faith, their priorities, their work, their potential.

It is difficult to envisage the possibility of these outcomes without the incorporation of historical-critical insights about the biblical narratives into the dramatic script. The very process of raising contextual questions, particularly clearly articulated in *The Adventure of Faith*, invites engagement and exploration. That is what makes the plays more than entertainment with a message, and it helps to render them 'user-friendly' to the unchurched, those disaffected by the institutional church and even those of other faith, as well as to church-goers. The step to asking questions about contemporary contexts becomes a natural one because the connection is persons (as participants in the drama and in 'real' life), not dogma or tradition.

The outcome of the method was not chaos—a danger of participatory ventures voiced in the consultation session on 'The Problem and the Promise of Pentecostalism' on the day before the performance. The 'givenness' of the script and short rehearsal time effectively provided limits and control. Much of the music was chosen and rehearsed by the musicians' group in advance; it would have been difficult to make changes at full rehearsal stage. I personally objected to the lack of representation of women characters and rather than have men's parts played by women, would have had an 'alternative' women's council meeting as part of the drama—perhaps gagged and silenced, but present!

I have noted that the central controversy on this occasion was racial prejudice; two white church people withdrew after the first reading of the script and one black church person expressed dissatisfaction with terminology, and only attended the first rehearsal. There is concern about these withdrawals. It was interesting to learn from Werner Ustorf that *The Adventure of Faith* had been produced in Munich two weeks before, and in that group the discussion centred around inequality, injustice and world trade; racism wasn't an issue. This is a clear indication that even though the script is a 'given', it provides ample scope for participants to bring to it their own contemporary agendas.

Concluding Reflection

Scholarship and evangelism *can* be effectively combined. The question that remains is whether we, the professed Christians, can cope with the challenges and uncertainties of the consequences. Hollenweger suggests that it may not even be desirable for non-Christian participants to become members of a church because 'the churches might destroy their emerging faith',[6] and indeed, none of these in our group, to my knowledge, has expressed a wish to become affiliated to an institution. Of the non-church going participants still resident in Birmingham, several have said they would appreciate more discussion sessions; others want further opportunities to make music and some of them would be happy to contribute to worship services; a reunion seems called for. I am asking myself, as a participant, church member and theologian, 'How should I respond?'

6 . Hollenweger, 'Theology', p. 1033.

GLOBAL PENTECOSTALISM IN THE NEW MILLENNIUM

Allan Anderson

Pentecostals and Social Transformation

According to the more inclusive use of the term outlined in the Introduction, I identify myself as a 'Pentecostal'. If there are any lingering doubts about this publication, they might be that some Pentecostals might consider parts of it to be too 'radical' and provocative, while 'ordinary' Pentecostal voices are not given sufficient expression. This final article is written partly in response to those concerns and partly to affirm this book's essential message. The 'problem' that Hollenweger has identified in Pentecostalism seems to lie largely in its ideology in the West, and particularly in white North America, where it has been identified with the 'success ethic' of capitalism. One notorious manifestation of this is the 'prosperity gospel', often an overt display of human greed in danger of corrupting the Christian gospel beyond recognition. Some western pentecostals, particularly in North America, have succumbed to its solicitation. Many other pentecostals have a spirituality which very often withdraws from 'worldly' issues like politics and the struggle for liberation and justice, which is true not only in North America but also in other parts of the world. This includes those black British pentecostals of whom Robert Beckford speaks in his article, tempered, as his evaluation is, by Gerloff's observations in the following article. There has also been criticism of the 'Americanization' of African pentecostals, where it is claimed that 'the Bible was being used to further economic and political ends',[1] and pentecostals have been accused of being 'agents of colonialism and barriers to liberation'.[2]

---

1.   P. Gifford, *Christianity and Politics in Doe's Liberia* (Cambridge: Cambridge University Press, 1993), pp. 210, 185.
2.   D. Martin, *Tongues of Fire: The Explosion of Protestantism in Latin America* (Oxford: Basil Blackwell, 1990), p. 233.

These are indeed problems for pentecostals to overcome; but the pentecostal approach to socio-political issues, especially in the non-western world, is ambiguous. In Chile, some pentecostals actively supported the oppressive regime of military dictator Augusto Pinochet, while others were followers of communist leader Salvador Allende.[3] In South Africa, most white pentecostals were tacitly promoting apartheid, while many black pentecostals sympathized with the liberation movements.[4] But even when obvious support for oppressive structures is absent, pentecostals generally have been regarded as having 'an apolitical stance often skewed in a conservative direction' and have lacked in effective socio-political involvement.[5] Political structures are often seen as evil, and pentecostals are exhorted by their preachers to have nothing to do with them. For the same reasons, early pentecostals were also pacifists. The danger with some forms of Christianity, Pentecostalism included, is that an emphasis on personal piety can become a sop for a lack of social conscience.

All this shows the importance of Walter Hollenweger's observations in this book. Pentecostals must rediscover their roots, for these forms of Pentecostalism betray the origins of the movement in the Azusa Street revival, which defied so many social mores of the time. Robert Mapes Anderson says that early Pentecostalism was 'an oblique expression of social protest', and he points out that it was 'born of radical social discontent'. But as it became institutionalized in its later history, it withdrew from the social struggle. A movement designed to protest against a social system that marginalized and oppressed its members 'functioned in a way that perpetuated that very system'.[6]

The stereotype of Pentecostalism in the West of a middle class 'prosperity gospel' with 'get rich quick' schemes for its members is to some extent justified, particularly since the advent of the Charismatic movement and the Full Gospel Businessman's Fellowship. Hollenweger has astutely observed its proclamation of success theology and the alliance

3. C.B. Johns, *Pentecostal Formation: A Pedagogy among the Oppressed* (JPTSup, 2; Sheffield: Sheffield Academic Press, 1993), p. 75; Martin, *Tongues of Fire*, p. 236.

4. A. Anderson, *Bazalwane: African Pentecostals in South Africa* (Pretoria: University of South Africa Press, 1992), p. 32.

5. Martin, *Tongues of Fire*, p. 265.

6. R.M. Anderson, *Vision of the Disinherited: The Making of American Pentecostalism* (Peabody: Hendrickson, 1979), pp. 222, 229.

between Pentecostalism and fundamentalism in the US New Right. The result has been, as Cheryl Johns points out, 'little emphasis on the social critique of Pentecostalism as a voice for the poor and oppressed', and US pentecostals have to some extent 'become one with ultra-conservative Republican politics'.[7] But there are enough concerned Pentecostal voices to mitigate this assessment. Pentecostalism is not a white middle class phenomenon in most of the world, but predominantly a grassroots movement among the poor. Although pentecostals have not been involved in much overt socio-political activity (with notable exceptions in several countries), in their own communities there is abundant evidence of social concern in structures created for the welfare of their members.[8] Douglas Petersen's *Not by Might nor by Power: A Pentecostal Theology of Social Concern in Latin America* (1996) is a comprehensive analysis of a pentecostal social theology. He states that it is precisely because of Pentecostalism's strength among 'the most disadvantaged or dissatisfied sectors' that it is 'deeply involved in its own kind of here-and-now social struggle' with 'far-reaching implications for social transformation'. He castigates those pentecostals who 'use their divine empowering and faith building message for self-serving purposes' and 'neglect the social responsibilities that should accompany this phenomenon'. He warns against a sense of triumphalism and isolation, which will result in pentecostals forfeiting 'the opportunity to participate in radical change or structural transformation.[9]

The commonly held idea that pentecostals are 'apolitical' or even 'anti-political' was not born out by our research among African pentecostals in South Africa, where there was a political involvement which did not differ perceptibly from that of the overall population.[10] Pentecostals in various parts of the world have various programmes of social action, and as José Míguez Bonino observes, in Latin America they have 'developed a social conscience not just at a personal and occasional level but in an institutionalized form', including social, medical and juridical assistance, and educational institutions. He draws attention to a 'new awareness of the place of social responsibility in the

7.   Johns, *Pentecostal Formation*, pp. 79-80.

8.   D. Petersen, *Not by Might nor by Power: A Pentecostal Theology of Social Concern in Latin America* (Oxford: Regnum Books, 1996), p. 115.

9.   Petersen, *Not by Might*, pp. 227-31.

10.   A. Anderson and S. Otwang, *Tumelo: The Faith of African Pentecostals in South Africa* (Pretoria: University of South Africa Press, 1993), pp. 58-60.

Pentecostal movement' which indicates 'a vision of a society that takes account of the structural aspects of human life (oppression, discrimination, social decay) and sees in them an area for the work of the Spirit'.[11] The Child Care Service Program in Central America is run by the Assemblies of God and is the largest evangelical institutional programme of social action in Latin America and one of the largest networks of evangelical educational institutions in the world, providing education for many thousands of children. Pentecostal congregations also provide welfare services to needy families, the sick, the abused and the aged, as well as role models and surrogate parents for deprived children.[12]

In Africa too, pentecostal churches are concerned to provide for the holistic needs of their members. For this reason, some churches form funeral societies, bursary funds for the education of their children, and provide financial assistance for members in financial distress. Some churches have 'welfare committees' responsible for feeding and clothing the poor and the destitute. In South Africa, during 1991, when tin shacks started to appear outside the formal housing areas, several of these churches were involved in providing regular food and clothing for these urban poor. The Zion Christian Church has a nation-wide 'ZCC Burial Assurance Fund' and a 'ZCC Literacy Campaign' with adult education centres scattered throughout the country.[13] As Martin West points out, African pentecostal churches 'meet many of the needs of townspeople which were formerly met by kin groups on a smaller scale in rural areas'. He lists several ways in which the social needs of church members are met in an urban setting: this type of church, as a 'voluntary association', provides its members with a sense of family, friendship (providing support groups in times of insecurity), protection in the form of leadership (particularly charismatic leadership), social control (by emphasising and enforcing certain norms of behaviour), and in practical ways like finding employment, mutual aid in times of personal crisis, and leadership opportunities. The churches thus provide for their members 'new bases for social organisation'.[14] In Latin America, Africa

11. J.M. Bonino, *Faces of Latin American Protestantism* (Grand Rapids: Eerdmans, 1997), pp. 66-67.

12. Petersen, *Not by Might*, pp. 120, 153.

13. Anderson and Otwang, *Tumelo*, p. 61.

14. M. West, *Bishops and Prophets in a Black City* (Cape Town: David Philip, 1975), pp. 196-99.

and elsewhere in the Third World, Pentecostalism is a 'powerful movement of the poor' and as such 'is pregnant with potential for the
transformation of society'.[15]

A Pentecostal Theology of Liberation

Pentecostal scholars in several parts of the world see the roots of Pentecostalism as the basis for their insistence on a pentecostal theology of
liberation. Cheryl Johns points out that the Wesleyan roots—or what
Hollenweger calls the 'catholic roots'—gave the pentecostal movement
'a strong emphasis upon the transforming power of the Holy Spirit for
both personal and social critique', while its roots in black spirituality
gave it 'an emphasis upon the liberating power of the Pentecostal
experience and an emphasis upon the oral-narrative character of the
gospel which involves active participation of everyone'.[16] As shown in
my earlier article in this book, during the struggle for political and
social liberation in South Africa, the 'Relevant Pentecostal Witness'
was formed as a challenge to the 'religious right' within the pentecostal
movement there. Its patron was Frank Chikane, General Secretary of
the South African Council of Churches at the time. Prominent in the
ideology of this organization and reflected in its journal *Azusa*, was a
reminder of the rediscovered 'black roots' of Pentecostalism as a foundation for justice and equality. Black pentecostal scholar Leonard Lovett
notes that 'liberation is always the consequence of the presence of the
Spirit. Authentic liberation can never occur apart from genuine Pentecostal encounter'.[17] My earlier comparative study of concepts of
power within African pentecostal churches, African indigenous religions and Black Power maintained that:

> The power of the Holy Spirit has more than just 'spiritual' significance.
> It also has to do with dignity, authority and power over all types of op-
> pression. God loves and desires the welfare of the whole person; and so
> he sends his Spirit to bestow that divine, liberating ability and strength.[18]

15. Johns, *Pentecostal Formation*, p. 78.
16. Johns, *Pentecostal Formation*, p. 108.
17. V. Synan (ed.), *Aspects of Pentecostal-Charismatic Origins* (Plainfield, NJ: Logos, 1975), p. 140.
18. A. Anderson, *Moya: The Holy Spirit in an African Context* (Pretoria: University of South Africa Press), p. 63.

Returning to the black roots of Pentecostalism in Azusa Street means an acknowledgment of its non-racial character. The pentecostals, with their offer of full participation to all, regardless of race, class or gender, effected what amounted to a democratization of Christianity, a protest against the status quo. Eldin Villafañe is a Hispanic American pentecostal whose book, *The Liberating Spirit: Toward an Hispanic American Social Ethic*, suggests that Hispanic Americans in their situation of political and socio-economic deprivation have in Pentecostalism a 'wholistic spirituality' with a broader social dimension, so that the Spirit is able to empower all areas of life. He acknowledges that pentecostal spirituality has so often been privatized and individualistic, but he asserts that sin is both personal and 'structural/institutional'.[19] The marginalized Hispanic American pentecostals bear many similarities to the first pentecostals at Azusa Street, as indeed they do to other pentecostals in the Third World.[20]

The Essence of the Pentecostal Gospel

Looking at Pentecostalism from this global perspective makes the 'prosperity gospel' and an identification with capitalistic ideology somewhat inconsequential and only found in a fringe minority. It can never be construed as the core of global Pentecostalism—its essence is to be found elsewhere. A fundamental presupposition of pentecostal theology and praxis is the central emphasis on the experience of the working of the Holy Spirit, or what Steven Land calls 'Pentecostal spirituality'.[21] This experience includes 'gifts of the Spirit', especially healing, exorcism, speaking in tongues and prophesying. Pentecostal belief in what was called the 'full' or 'foursquare' gospel not only means that Jesus Christ saves people from sin, but also heals them from sickness and delivers them from the power of Satan in all its various manifestations, not only in private and personal ways. In Pentecostalism, this 'full gospel' is understood to contain good news, 'salvation' for all of life's problems, particularly relevant in Third World societies where disease is rife and access to adequate health care is a luxury. It is in these

19. E. Villafañe, *The Liberating Spirit: Toward an Hispanic American Social Ethic* (Grand Rapids: Eerdmans, 1993), pp. 163, 165, 171.

20. Villafañe, *Liberating Spirit*, p. 89.

21. S.J. Land, *Pentecostal Spirituality: A Passion for the Kingdom* (JPTSup, 1; Sheffield: Sheffield Academic Press, 1993)

societies that the 'here-and-now' emphasis of pentecostal praxis must be evaluated. 'Salvation' is an all-embracing term in these contexts, usually meaning a sense of well-being evidenced in freedom from sickness, poverty and misfortune as well as in deliverance from sin and evil. The majority in the Third World is underprivileged, and state social benefits are lacking, which means *inter alia* that efficient medical facilities are scarce and expensive. Bengt Sundkler, writing about African pentecostal churches in South Africa in the 1940s, said that people receive their healing message as a 'gospel for the poor'.[22] The fact that people believe themselves to be healed means that this understanding of the gospel is a potent remedy for their experience of affliction. Pentecostals relate the gospel directly to their troubles, and the process of understanding the gospel essentially begins in the context of felt needs. The worldview in many of these societies is filled with fearsome and unpredictable occurrences requiring Christian answers. The gospel proclaimed by pentecostals seeks in these contexts to be relevant to life's totality and to proclaim biblical deliverance from the very real fear of evil. Whatever the source—evil, misfortune and affliction are the experience of people everywhere, and pentecostals are endeavouring to provide solutions to these compelling needs.

This understanding of the gospel has to do with salvation from the experience of evil forces ranged against the common people's existence. Because Pentecostalism is such a heterogeneous movement, methods used to receive this deliverance and the perceptions concerning the means of grace may differ, but pentecostals believe that their message reveals an omnipotent and compassionate God who is concerned with all the troubles of humankind. Bishops, pastors, prophets, ministers, evangelists and especially ordinary church members exercise the authority that they believe has been given them by the God of the Bible, reinforced by the power of the Spirit, to announce the good news that there is deliverance from sin, sickness and barrenness, and from every conceivable form of evil, including social oppression, unemployment, poverty and sorcery.

This concept of liberation fundamentally affects the pentecostal understanding of the gospel in most of the Third World. In the context of recent history, indigenous people themselves, without the help of white

---

22. B.G.M. Sundkler, *Bantu Prophets in South Africa* (Oxford: Oxford University Press, 1961), p. 223.

missionaries (who often represented oppressive former colonizing powers), discovered in the gospel their own freedom from bondage, and
that, contrary to previous assumptions, Christianity was not a 'white
person's religion' providing answers to questions that their people were
not asking. Particularly since the comparatively recent translation of the
Bible into vernaculars, people began to discover that the Bible is relevant, that it does fulfil their aspirations and meet their needs, and that
the gospel has much to say about issues that were often not addressed in
western missionary founded churches. Pentecostals were quick to tap
into this new discovery.

There were many variations on this theme of liberation. Principal
leaders of many African pentecostal churches, for example, were seen
as Moses figures, bringing their people out of slavery into the promised
land, a new 'City of Zion'. The Exodus event was seen as a deliverance
from the old life of trouble, sickness, oppression, evil spirits, sorcery
and poverty. Issues of socio-economic or political liberation were usually implied in these religio-cultural protest movements rather than
expressed. The profound holism of Africa does not allow its exclusion,
although the dominant idea is one of religious or spiritual liberation.
The new Israel incarnate in Africa is moving out of Egypt towards the
New Jerusalem, the Zion of God, where all these troubles will be
forgotten. The people of God are the members of this new African
church that has been able to discover its Promised Land for itself. The
concept of Zion, the new Jerusalem, the holy place that is not in some
far off foreign land at some distant time in the past, but is present here
and now, is a prominent theme.

Healing and protection from evil are among the most prominent features of the pentecostal 'full gospel' and are probably the most important part of the liturgy in their evangelism and church recruitment. The
central place given to healing is probably no longer a prominent feature
of western Pentecostalism, but in the Third World the problems of disease and evil affect the whole community and are not simply a private
domain relegated to individual pastoral care. As Harvey Cox observes,
in Africa pentecostals 'provide a setting in which the African conviction that spirituality and healing belong together is dramatically en-
acted.'[23] Indigenous communities were, to a large extent, health-orien-
tated communities and in indigenous religions, rituals for healing and

---

23. H. Cox, *Fire from Heaven: The Rise of Pentecostal Spirituality and the
Reshaping of Religion in the Twenty-first Century* (London: Cassell, 1996), p. 247.

protection are prominent. Pentecostals responded to what they experienced as a void left by a rationalistic western form of Christianity which had unwittingly initiated what was tantamount to the destruction of indigenous spiritual values. Pentecostals declared a message that reclaimed ancient biblical traditions of healing and protection from evil, to demonstrate the practical effects of these traditions, and by so doing to be the heralds of a Christianity with an implicit theology that was really meaningful. Thus pentecostal movements went a long way towards meeting physical, emotional and spiritual needs of people in the Third World, offering solutions to life's problems and ways to cope in a threatening and hostile world.[24]

Pentecostals proclaim a pragmatic gospel and seek to address practical needs like sickness, poverty, unemployment, loneliness, evil spirits and sorcery. In varying degrees, pentecostals in their many and varied forms, and precisely because of their inherent flexibility, attain an authentically indigenous character which enables them to offer answers to some of the fundamental questions asked by indigenous peoples. A sympathetic approach to local life and culture and the retention of certain indigenous religious practices are undoubtedly major reasons for their attraction, especially for those overwhelmed by urbanization with its transition from a personal rural society to an impersonal urban one. At the same time, these pentecostals confront old views by declaring what they are convinced is a more powerful protection against sorcery and a more effective healing from sickness than either the existing churches or the traditional rituals had offered. Healing, guidance, protection from evil, and success and prosperity are some of the practical benefits offered to faithful members of pentecostal churches. All this does not say that pentecostals provide all the right answers, a model to be emulated in all respects, nor to say that they have nothing to learn from other Christians. But we must appreciate the enormous and unparalleled contribution made by indigenous pentecostals entirely on their own to alter the face of world Christianity irrevocably and for the enrichment of the universal church in its ongoing task of proclaiming the gospel of Christ by proclamation and demonstration.

Walter Hollenweger says that evangelism in the New Testament is always dialogical. This type of evangelism is not commonly practised

---

24. Anderson and Otwang, *Tumelo*, p. 32.

in Pentecostalism, however, and all over the world pentecostals are often associated with a more aggressive form of evangelism. From its beginning, Pentecostalism was characterized by an emphasis on evangelistic outreach, and all pentecostal missionary strategy places evangelism as its highest priority. For most pentecostals, evangelism means to go out and reach the 'lost' for Christ in the power of the Holy Spirit. The Azusa Street revival resulted in a category of ordinary pentecostal people called 'missionaries' fanning out to every corner of the globe within a remarkably short space of time. 'Mission' was mainly understood as 'foreign mission' (mostly from 'white' to 'other' peoples), and these missionaries were mostly untrained and inexperienced. Their only qualification was the baptism in the Spirit and a divine call; their motivation was to evangelize the world before the imminent coming of Christ and so, as Hollenweger points out, evangelism was more important than education or 'civilisation'.[25] We can only guess at what incredible mistakes these early pentecostal missionaries must have made, as reports filtering back to the West would be full of optimistic and triumphalistic accounts of how many people were converted, healed and Spirit baptized, seldom mentioning any difficulties encountered or cultural blunders made.

Pentecostal missionaries often had a sense of special calling, of 'divine destiny' that thrust them out in the face of stiff opposition. But in spite of the inevitable cultural and religious indiscretions, it must be acknowledged that these methods were astonishingly successful. Pentecostals claim that the rapid growth of the movement vindicates the apostle Paul's statement that God uses the weak and despised to confound the mighty. Pentecostal churches were missionary by nature and the dichotomy between 'church' and 'mission' that for so long plagued other Christian churches did not exist in Pentecostalism. This 'central missiological thrust' was clearly a 'strong point in Pentecostalism' and central to its existence.[26]

Pentecostal Missiology and Indigenous Churches

In his article, Walter Hollenweger lamented the loss of the missionary vision of Melvin Hodges in pentecostal mission practice in the West.

25. Hollenweger, *Pentecostals*, p. 34.
26. W.A. Saayman, 'Some Reflections on the Development of the Pentecostal Mission Model in South Africa', *Missionalia* 21 (1993), pp. 40-56 (51).

Pentecostal missiologists like Hodges point out that pentecostal missions are quick to raise up financially self-supporting indigenous leaders, and therefore the new churches are indigenized much quicker than older mission churches had been.[27] Hodges' compact but widely influential publication *The Indigenous Church* (1953)[28] not only emphasized creating indigenous churches, but also stressed church planting, a fundamental principle of present pentecostal mission strategy.[29] Through this commitment to indigenization, says Bonino, pentecostals have 'tuned in with the language, concerns and hopes of the people'. But he points out that the fact of present-day globalization means that international missionaries are in danger of carrying the 'transnational' mentality (encouraged in some mission schools) and of remaining 'foreign to a deeper indigenization'. This is dangerous because 'it may subordinate the spontaneous, outgoing, dynamic force of the people of God to the strategies of those who know and can or think and do'. Bonino thinks that Pentecostalism has been 'too limited by some current theological formulations adopted from Anglo-Saxon Evangelical circles' and that 'the spiritual experience and the evangelical praxis of the Pentecostal/ Charismatic Renewal is much larger and richer than those formulations'.[30] Pentecostals in the Third World will do well to heed these warnings.

Hollenweger has rightly identified problems associated with the pentecostal emphasis on 'signs and wonders' and the important role of healing. Pentecostals in the Third World see the practice of healing as good news for the poor and afflicted. The early pentecostals and the mass evangelists to whom Hollenweger has referred expected spectacular miracles to accompany their evangelism. In the Third World especially, healing has been a major attraction for Pentecostalism. In many cultures of the world the religious specialist or 'person of God' has

27. L.G. McClung, 'Spontaneous Strategy of the Spirit: Pentecostal Missionary Practices', in *idem* (ed.), *Azusa Street and Beyond: Pentecostal Missions and Church Growth in the Twentieth Century* (South Plainfield, NJ: Logos, 1986), pp. 71-81 (77).

28. M.L. Hodges, *The Indigenous Church* (Springfield: Gospel Publishing House, 1953).

29. McClung, 'Spontaneous Strategy', p. 78.

30. J.M. Bonino, 'Pentecostal Missions is More than what it Claims', *Pneuma* 16 (1994), pp. 285-88.

power to heal the sick and ward off evil spirits and sorcery. This holistic function, which does not separate the 'physical' from the 'spiritual' (or the 'natural' from the 'supernatural') is restored in Pentecostalism, and indigenous peoples see it as a 'powerful' religion to meet human needs.

We have seen that pentecostal missiology is grounded in its spirituality: a conviction that the Holy Spirit is the motivating power behind all mission activity. This missiology was not always clearly spelt out in the early years of this century, as pentecostal missionaries got on with the job in haste, believing that the time was short and that reflection about the task was not as important as action in evangelism. Their mission theology was a theology 'on the move', and pentecostal scholars have begun to formulate a distinctive pentecostal missiology only recently. The centrality of the Holy Spirit in mission has been a consistent theme in these studies. The pentecostal movement was from its commencement a missionary movement, made possible by the Holy Spirit's empowerment.[31]

The articles by Hollenweger, Lee, and particularly Sepúlveda, discuss the question of 'indigenous' pentecostal churches. Because pentecostals place such strong emphasis on the role of the experience of Spirit baptism in mission, the Holy Spirit is given to every believer without preconditions. One of the results of this was that, as Willem Saayman observes, 'it ensured that a rigid dividing line between "clergy" and "laity" and between men and women did not develop early on in Pentecostal churches', and even more significantly, 'there was little resistance to the ordination of indigenous pastors and evangelists to bear the brunt of the pastoral upbuilding of the congregations and their evangelistic outreach'.[32] This was one of the main reasons for the early and rapid transition from 'foreign' to 'indigenous' church that took place in many pentecostal movements. Leaders tended to come from the lower

---

31. See the following publications by the JPT Supplement Series of Sheffield Academic Press: R. Menzies, *Empowered to Witness: The Spirit in Luke–Acts* (JSPTSup, 6; Sheffield: Sheffield Academic Press, 1994); J. Penney, *The Missionary Emphasis of Lukan Pneumatology* (JPTSup, 12 Sheffield: Sheffield Academic Press, 1997); S. Land, *Pentecostal Spirituality: A Passion for the Kingdom* (JPTSup, 1; Sheffield: Sheffield Academic Press, 1993), who devotes a chapter to 'Pentecostal Spirituality as Missionary Fellowship', p. 122.
32. Saayman, 'Some Reflections', p. 43.

and formally uneducated strata of society, and were trained in an apprentice-type training, where their charismatic leadership abilities were encouraged. Of particular importance was the fact that women were effectively mobilized into service both at home and further afield, and some became founders of significant pentecostal churches. The use of women with charismatic gifts was widespread throughout the pentecostal movement, which accorded well with the prominence of women in many indigenous religious rituals, contrasting again with the prevailing practice of older churches which barred women from entering the ministry or even from taking any part in public worship. The emphasis on women in ministry, however, disappeared in some later pentecostal missions (especially those from North America), and 'the importance of the experience of Spirit-baptism in the lives of female missionaries had to take second place to the general patriarchal structure of church and society'.[33] Hollenweger has shown this to have happened again more recently in the Charismatic movement.

What is often overlooked by western pentecostal missiologists is the fact that thriving pentecostal 'indigenous churches' were established in many parts of the world without the help of any 'foreign missionaries' at all. These churches were founded in innovative mission initiatives unprecedented in the history of mission, motivated by a compelling need to preach and even more significantly, to *experience* a new message of the power of the Holy Spirit. The effectiveness of pentecostal mission in the Third World was based on this unique message, which was both the motivation for the thousands of grassroots emissaries and their source of attraction. All the widely differing pentecostal movements have important common features: they proclaim and celebrate a salvation (or 'healing') that encompasses all of life's experiences and afflictions, and they offer an empowerment which provides a sense of dignity and a coping mechanism for life, and drives their messengers forward into a unique mission. Their mission was to share this all-embracing message with as many people as possible, and to accomplish this, indigenous pentecostal missionaries went far and wide.

In his article, Sepúlveda has shown that in the emergence of Chilean Pentecostalism there was a 'cultural clash' that resulted in a move towards indigenization by early Chilean leaders. This has parallels in other parts of the Third World. The astonishing journeys in 1914 of the

33. Saayman, 'Some Reflections', p. 44.

famous Liberian prophet William Wade Harris throughout the Ivory
Coast to western Ghana, has been described as 'the most remarkable
evangelical campaign Africa has ever witnessed',[34] resulting in tens of
thousands of conversions to Christianity. The Indonesian revival of the
1960s was marked by indigenous missionary teams led by Pak Elias
and others, crossing land and sea to spread their powerful message.
Indigenous pentecostal evangelists in China like Barnabas Zhang travelled the length and breadth of that vast country and even into neigh-
bouring ones. These and many thousands of indigenous preachers emphasized the manifestation of divine power through healing, prophecy,
speaking in tongues and other pentecostal phenomena. The message
proclaimed by these charismatic preachers of receiving the power of the
Holy Spirit to meet human needs was welcome in indigenous societies
where a lack of power was keenly felt on a daily basis. Because western
forms of Christianity were often regarded as superficial and out of
touch with many realities of indigenous life, it was necessary for a new
indigenous Christianity to arise in each context.

The growth of Pentecostalism was not the result of the efforts of a
few charismatic leaders. The proliferation of the movement would not
have taken place without the tireless efforts of a vast number of ordinary women and men, networking across regional and even national
boundaries, proclaiming the same message they had heard others proclaim which had sufficiently altered their lives to make it worth sharing
wherever they went. This mass involvement of the 'laity' in the pentecostal movement was undoubtedly one of the main reasons for its success. There was no need for a theologically articulate clergy, because
cerebral and clerical Christianity had, in the minds of many people, already failed them. What was needed was a demonstration of power by
indigenous people to whom ordinary people could easily relate. This
was the democratization of Christianity, for henceforth the mystery of
the gospel would no longer be reserved for a select privileged and educated few, but would be revealed to whoever was willing to receive it
and pass it on. Unfortunately, the emphasis on self-propagation through
evangelism and church growth has sometimes resulted in pentecostals
being somewhat inward looking and seemingly unconcerned or oblivious to the serious issues of their socio-political contexts, especially
where there were oppressive governments. David Bosch asked whether

34. A. Hastings, *A History of African Christianity 1950–1975* (Cambridge:
Cambridge University Press, 1979), p. 67.

during South Africa's apartheid regime 'the rush into signs and won-ders is, in reality, a flight away from justice for the poor and the op-pressed'.[35]

The style of 'freedom in the Spirit' that characterizes pentecostal liturgy has undoubtedly contributed to the appeal of the movement in many different contexts. This spontaneous liturgy, which Hollenweger has identified as mainly oral and narrative, with an emphasis on a direct experience of God through his Spirit, results in the possibility of ordi-nary people being lifted out of their mundane daily experiences into a new realm of ecstasy, aided by the emphases on speaking in tongues, loud and emotional simultaneous prayer, and joyful singing, clapping, raising hands and dancing in the presence of God. This made pente-costal worship easily assimilated into different cultural contexts, espe-cially where a sense of divine immediacy was taken for granted, and it contrasted sharply with the rationalistic and written liturgies presided over by a clergyman that was the main feature of most other forms of Christianity. Furthermore, this was available for everyone, and the in-volvement of the laity became the most important feature of pentecostal worship, again contrasting with the central role played by the priest or minister in older churches.[36]

Conclusion

This book has only reflected on some of the issues that pentecostals face in the twenty-first century. One thing is for certain: the face of global Christianity and the shape of religion itself throughout the world will never be the same since the pentecostals came on the scene a cen-tury ago. Whatever protests we might make about the lack of 'sophis-tication' in pentecostal praxis or the cultural or political insensitivity of some of the movement's emissaries, we must reckon with this rich diversity of Christian expression with a dynamic message that will surely continue to attract multitudes of people globally well into the next century.

35. D.J. Bosch, 'Church Growth Missiology', *Missionalia* 16 (1988), pp. 13-24 (23).
36. Saayman, 'Some Reflections', p. 47.

INDEX OF AUTHORS

JOURNAL OF PENTECOSTAL THEOLOGY

Supplement Series

1   PENTECOSTAL SPIRITUALITY: A PASSION FOR THE KINGDOM
Steven J. Land
pa £15.95/$21.95
ISBN 1 85075 442 X

2   PENTECOSTAL FORMATION:
A PEDAGOGY AMONG THE OPPRESSED
Cheryl Bridges-Johns
pa £10.95/$13.95
ISBN 1 85075 438 1

3   ON THE CESSATION OF THE CHARISMATA:
THE PROTESTANT POLEMIC ON MIRACLES
Jon Ruthven
pa £15.95/$21.95
ISBN 1 85075 405 5

4   ALL TOGETHER IN ONE PLACE:
THEOLOGICAL PAPERS FROM THE BRIGHTON CONFERENCE
ON WORLD EVANGELIZATION
Harold D. Hunter and Peter D. Hocken (eds.)
pa £15.95/$21.95
ISBN 1 85075 406 3

5   SPIRIT AND RENEWAL:
ESSAYS IN HONOR OF J. RODMAN WILLIAMS
Mark Wilson (ed.)
pa £15.95/$21.95
ISBN 1 85075 471 3

13 THE DEVIL, DISEASE AND DELIVERANCE:
    ORIGINS OF ILLNESS IN NEW TESTAMENT THOUGHT
    John Christopher Thomas
    pa £15.95/$21.95
    ISBN 1 85075 869 7

14 THE SPIRIT, PATHOS AND LIBERATION:
    TOWARD AN HISPANIC PENTECOSTAL THEOLOGY
    Samuel Solivan
    pa £10.95/$13.95
    ISBN 1 85075 942 1

15 PENTECOSTALS AFTER A CENTURY:
    GLOBAL PERSPECTIVES ON A MOVEMENT IN TRANSITION
    Allan H. Anderson and Walter J. Hollenweger
    pa £15.95/$21.95
    ISBN 1 84127 006 7

Lightning Source UK Ltd.
Milton Keynes UK
09 August 2010
158119UK00007B/41/A